GREAT MYTHS
OF PERSONALITY

Series Editors
Scott O. Lilienfeld
Steven Jay Lynn

This superb series of books tackles a host of fascinating myths and misconceptions regarding specific domains of psychology, including child development, aging, marriage, brain science, and mental illness, among many others. Each book not only dispels multiple erroneous but widespread psychological beliefs but provides readers with accurate and up-to-date scientific information to counter them. Written in engaging, upbeat, and user-friendly language, the books in the myths series are replete with scores of intriguing examples drawn from everyday psychology. As a result, readers will emerge from each book entertained and enlightened. These unique volumes will be invaluable additions to the bookshelves of educated laypersons interested in human nature, as well as of students, instructors, researchers, journalists, and mental health professionals of all stripes.

www.wiley.com/go/psychmyths

Published

50 Great Myths of Popular Psychology
Scott O. Lilienfeld, Steven Jay Lynn, John Ruscio, and Barry L. Beyerstein

Great Myths of Aging
Joan T. Erber and Lenore T. Szuchman

Great Myths of the Brain
Christian Jarrett

Great Myths of Child Development
Stephen Hupp and Jeremy D. Jewell

Great Myths of Adolescence
Jeremy D. Jewell, Michael Axelrod, Mitchell J. Prinstein, and Stephen Hupp

Great Myths of Intimate Relationships
Matthew D. Johnson

Great Myths of Education and Learning
Jeffrey D. Holmes

Great Myths of Personality
M. Brent Donnellan and Richard E. Lucas

Forthcoming

Great Myths of Autism
James D. Herbert

50 Great Myths of Popular Psychology, Second Edition
Scott O. Lilienfeld, Steven Jay Lynn, John Ruscio, and Barry L. Beyerstein

GREAT MYTHS OF PERSONALITY

M. Brent Donnellan
Richard E. Lucas

WILEY Blackwell

Registered Office
John Wiley & Sons, Inc., 111 River Street, Hoboken, NJ 07030, USA

Editorial Office
111 River Street, Hoboken, NJ 07030, USA

For details of our global editorial offices, customer services, and more information about Wiley products visit us at www.wiley.com.

Wiley also publishes its books in a variety of electronic formats and by print-on-demand. Some content that appears in standard print versions of this book may not be available in other formats.

Library of Congress Cataloging-in-Publication Data
Names: Donnellan, M. Brent, author. | Lucas, Richard E. (Richard Eric),
    1971– author.
Title: Great myths of personality / M. Brent Donnellan, Richard E. Lucas.
Description: Hoboken, NJ : Wiley-Blackwell, 2021. | Series: Great myths of
    psychology | Includes bibliographical references and index.
Identifiers: LCCN 2020037204 (print) | LCCN 2020037205 (ebook) | ISBN
    9781118521397 (cloth) | ISBN 9781118521359 (paperback) | ISBN
    9781118521441 (adobe pdf) | ISBN 9781118521410 (epub)
Subjects: LCSH: Personality.
Classification: LCC BF698 .D645 2021 (print) | LCC BF698 (ebook) | DDC
    155.2–dc23
LC record available at https://lccn.loc.gov/2020037204
LC ebook record available at https://lccn.loc.gov/2020037205

Cover Design: Wiley
Cover Image: © JakeOlimb/Getty Images

Set in 10/12.5pt Sabon by SPi Global, Pondicherry, India

Printed and bound in Singapore by Markono Print Media Pte Ltd

10 9 8 7 6 5 4 3 2 1

CONTENTS

INTRODUCTION

People are different from one another. Some are cautious, whereas others are brave. Some are energetic and sociable, whereas others are withdrawn and shy. Some have high levels of self-control, whereas others are impulsive and rash. No two people are exactly alike, and this diversity is one of the more interesting aspects of human nature. Appreciating and understanding these differences is at the heart of personality psychology. Although personality psychology is also concerned with the common core of human nature that makes people similar to one another, the subfield is most often identified with individual differences in thoughts, feelings, and behaviors. More specifically, personality psychology seeks to understand at least four broad issues:

1. **How are people different from each other?** Research addressing this question seeks to determine the basic dimensions of personality and levels of individuality. Research in this stream also concerns personality assessment and evaluates different ways to measure personality (e.g., self-report surveys vs. reports from knowledgeable informants vs. behavioral tasks).
2. **Why are people different from each other?** Research addressing this question evaluates genetic and environmental contributions to personality and increasingly seeks to understand how biological factors and life experiences work together to shape personality. Work in this area also evaluates how brain systems, hormones, and specific genes are related to personality.
3. **How and why does personality develop across the life span?** Research addressing this question seeks to chart the course of psychological development from infancy to old age. Research in

Great Myths of Personality, First Edition. M. Brent Donnellan and Richard E. Lucas.
© 2021 John Wiley & Sons, Inc. Published 2021 by John Wiley & Sons, Inc.

this strand of personality psychology addresses classic questions related to stability and change in personality and what processes account for stability and change.

4. **Do individual differences matter for consequential life outcome (such as health, wealth, and mortality)?** Research addressing this question is ultimately about the importance of personality for everyday life, such as relationship functioning, well-being, physical health, and work-related outcomes. It would be hard to imagine how research on the other three questions would matter if personality attributes themselves did not predict real-world outcomes. Personality would turn out to be a pretty esoteric and irrelevant topic if it did not relate to basic functioning in important life domains.

This book is ultimately about the scientific research that evaluates these kinds of questions by addressing some of the common myths that surround personality. Our global objective is to help you better understand common myths about personality and the actual evidence supporting (or refuting) the myth. However, we also have a couple deeper objectives.

First, we want to help you acquire the skills needed to be a critical consumer of psychological research. Specifically, we want you to understand the process of research and learn to be skeptical about overstated claims you might come across in everyday life, especially with respect to how social science research is conducted. We hope that you routinely ask questions about the quality and robustness of research evidence whenever psychological research is presented in everyday conversation, textbooks, and popular media. Our maxim is that you should not believe everything you read! Curious skepticism is a perfectly acceptable stance to take to psychological research. It is fine to be intrigued by research findings, but there is no reason to ever believe that a single study is definitive. For example, no one should take a hot shower to combat loneliness, to take an example from some of our research raising concerns about this association (see Donnellan, Lucas, & Cesario, 2015). To quote a famous rap lyric from the 1980s, don't believe the hype. And hype can be found in popular press articles as well as journal articles and textbooks.

Second and most importantly, we hope to illustrate that personality psychology is useful for everyday life by helping you appreciate the complexity of psychology and psychological research. We hope you learn new ways to think about enduring questions and perhaps find at least a few reasons to dig deeper and read more about the research investigating the myths we describe in this book. This will further develop your critical thinking skills and let you learn more about psychology. We will have done our job well if we motivate you to read the articles we cite so you can have better informed opinions about the myths we describe. In some cases, you might even disagree with our interpretations. This strikes us as exciting. After all, we just told you that we think skepticism is a virtue. Thus, in the end, we hope this book serves as a travel guide and introduction to the world of contemporary personality psychology. Welcome.

You will soon find that personality psychology investigates many of the basic questions that have captured human attention for centuries. This makes personality research accessible to people in ways that usually do not apply to research into chemistry or physics. Everyone is an armchair personality psychologist! Indeed, most of us interact with others on a daily basis, and we have probably thought about own personalities for at least some portion of our lives. Some of us have probably spent way too much time thinking about personality. We suspect that many of you have thought about many of these myths and the broad answers to the four opening topics at some point in your life. In contrast, few of us smash atoms or work in a chemical laboratory. Thus, the basics of personality psychology are much more familiar to people than, say, the basics of chemistry or particle physics.

In some ways, familiarity with personality is an asset when it comes to learning about research in this field. But it can get in the way, so we ask that you try to keep an open and critical mind. This is important because you might already have strong opinions about one or more of the myths we discuss. These opinions might be examined or unexamined, reasonable or not. Indeed, simple observations about the world without careful scientific investigations can often lead people astray: People used to believe that the sun rotated around the Earth, after all. Ideas like this seemed reasonable enough at the time because they seemed to match with simple observations about how the universe worked, but they are simply wrong. Keep this mantra in mind as you read our book—it is possible to be wrong, so it is a good idea to test your insights with data. This approach is at the heart of the scientific method.

Indeed, this book is grounded in the science of personality psychology. Entire books, college courses, and even academic careers have been devoted to understanding what it means to take a scientific approach to a specific topic. We cannot do the topic justice in a few short paragraphs. But we can try to emphasize the importance of *empiricism*. You have probably developed your own insights about the topic of personality by reflecting on past experiences, by thinking about people you have known, or perhaps by learning from books or articles. These are all potentially useful ways of acquiring knowledge, but personality psychologists conduct systematic investigations and collect verifiable data on these topics. This means that personality research is grounded in empirical findings. Testing ideas with data allows personality psychologists to draw conclusions about whether our beliefs about how personality works are supported by evidence or not. As personality scientists, we are open to the possibility that data will challenge our assumptions. We know we can be wrong, and we care about evidence.

The focus on empiricism is why researchers appear to be obsessed with measurement, research design, and statistics. We promise to keep the statistics simple and grounded in the correlation coefficient (a concept we explain later), but we cannot promise to avoid all technical topics related to measurement (topics such as *reliability* and *validity*). This preoccupation with research methods is critical because it pertains to quality of the evidence generated by a given study. We want you to learn how to evaluate the quality of the evidence so it can be appropriately weighted when it comes time to drawing conclusions about research.

Uncertainty is always present, but researchers do their best to quantify and ideally minimize uncertainty when drawing conclusions. In fact, you might be surprised about how much uncertainty actually exists in personality psychology when it comes to the myths we discuss. This can cause alarm in some people, and it might even strike some readers as demoralizing. But this type of uncertainty is a feature, not a bug, of science, and most scientists actually find this uncertainty exciting. Our strategy is to give you a sense of the evidence against each myth so you are better able to judge the evidence for yourself. This could lead you to accept or reject a myth. But this process might also motivate you to reserve judgment on a myth until more data are available. This is a perfectly acceptable reaction and even rational—it is often much better to admit you don't know something rather than blindly accepting a wrong idea. Uncertainty is not necessarily a bad thing. You don't always have to make up your mind about something. Sometimes you need to wait until more information is available.

We also want to add that we sometimes tackle myths that are present in academic psychology rather than popular thinking. Some of the ideas we interrogate might be present in textbooks for other classes. Hopefully this book helps make you a critical consumer of other findings and ideas that exist within psychology. We think this is a good thing. Again, sometimes textbooks are overstated and outdated. The goal is to help you become a more critical consumer of all research.

Given that this book is ultimately about the science of personality psychology, we need to touch on some issues in statistics and research methodology before discussing specific myths. This material is not intended as a substitute for one of those long chapters on research methods that can be found near the early parts of any of the outstanding personality textbooks on the market. Our point here is to explain the set of tools that personality researchers use to research the myths we describe.

Research methods 101

Personality psychologists use systematic methods to address research questions. The objective is to develop a procedure that other scientists can follow to answer the same question. In the ideal case, outside researchers would follow that script and come to the same conclusions (the process of replication). Personality psychologists (and other scientists) often distinguish between experimental and correlational procedures or methods. *Experimental methods* involve exposing participants (typically humans in psychology, but not always) to precise manipulations and then observing the impact of those manipulations on specific variables. The prototypical example of an experiment is a drug trial in which participants either receive a pill with the active ingredient (the experimental condition) or a sugar pill (the control condition or placebo condition) to evaluate the effectiveness of the drug on a medical condition. The critical element of an experiment is the process of randomly assigning participants to experimental conditions. Participants in our drug trial example should either receive the drug pill or placebo based on a coin flip. This ensures there is no connection between background characteristics and the conditions of the experiment. Who you are should not influence whether you receive the active pill or the sugar pill. Imagine what would happen if researchers only gave the active drugs to sick participants. This procedure would seriously cloud (or, as scientists might say, *confound*) the interpretation of any observed difference between the experimental and control conditions. If only sick people got the drug and only healthy people got the sugar pill, what could we conclude when researchers observed differences between the two groups? It would be impossible to determine whether any differences in symptoms that emerged were due to the drug or to the preexisting differences in health between those who got the drug and those who did not.

Experiments are the most basic tool for making causal inferences in the social sciences. The ability to use random assignment makes it much more straightforward to attribute some sort of causal agency to the experimental condition or treatment. The problem is that experiments are often impractical, unethical, or both when it comes to personality research. It would be very difficult and morally problematic to randomly assign individuals to the experience of childhood trauma or to a control "happy childhood" condition to determine whether early traumas impact adult personality outcomes. Experiments can also feel quite artificial because the types of things that psychologists can easily manipulate (especially in the lab) may not map well on to real-world experiences and events. Finally, when it comes to personality psychology, some of the manipulations that personality researchers might want to do can be extremely difficult, if not impossible, to carry out. Remember, personality traits are relatively stable even over long periods of time; researchers might want to study whether high levels of extraversion cause some outcomes like happiness, but how could they manipulate the stable personality trait of extraversion itself?

These and other factors often motivate personality researchers to use *correlational methods*. Here the object is to quantify the strength of the association between naturally occurring variation in two variables. For instance, researchers can correlate extraversion scores with scores on a measure of happiness. A positive correlation would indicate that high levels of extraversion tend to go along with high levels of happiness. Zero correlation would suggest there is no linear association. A negative correlation would suggest low levels of extraversion tend to occur with higher levels of happiness.

The limitations of correlational designs are legion, and most people have heard the phrase (or some variant) that *correlation does not prove causation*. Just knowing that extraversion is positively associated with happiness does not allow researchers to determine whether extraversion actually causes happiness. Happiness could cause extraversion, or a third variable could cause both. For example, physical attractiveness might cause both happiness and the tendency to be outgoing. This could explain a positive correlation between happiness and extraversion. This is an instance of the classic "third variable" problem with correlational findings.

The range of potential third variable possibilities motivates the use of more sophisticated correlational approaches, including those that examine many different variables at once (such analyses are referred to as "multivariate" approaches). The idea behind these approaches is that one can take the statistical associations of other variable into consideration when evaluating correlations (hence the name multivariate for multiple variables). For instance, researchers could statistically predict happiness from both attractiveness and extraversion at the same time. If extraversion is still related to happiness even after accounting for the fact that attractive people might be more extraverted than average and happier than average, then it might help to rule out the possibility that the correlation between extraversion and happiness is due simply to attractiveness. The trick to using multivariate analyses successfully is to come up with measures of all possible confounders to include in the statistical analyses. This is no easy task.

Indeed, the biggest limitation of multivariate analysis of correlational designs is that it is nearly impossible to imagine all possible third variables, let alone take good measurements of all of these factors. Therefore, the best that can be done is to think of a number of plausible (or reasonable) additional variables that might explain an association and then attempt to measure those variables in a given study. The task for critics and skeptics is to evaluate what was left out of the multivariate model. Judgment calls are critical at this stage.

Regardless of the statistical mechanics, the basic goal of these multivariate approaches is to help with causal inferences. Although correlation does not prove causation, causal relationships between two variables often produce correlations between two variables (or at least some statistical connection). Accordingly, researchers who do their best to design a good study and fail to find any sort of statistical connection between their variables of interest might start to change their minds about the possibility of a causal connection between two variables. For example, if researchers consistently find that extraversion is statistically unrelated to happiness, they might rethink the plausibility of a causal connection between the two.

At this point in the book, it is important to be honest about a critical issue: Causal inference in personality research is very challenging (see Shadish, Cook, & Campbell, 2002; West & Thoemmes, 2010). This is partly due to the fact that experiments are difficult in personality research, but the difficulties extend beyond this simple issue. Even fields that rely on experiments may have trouble drawing strong causal conclusions if the experiments that researchers in these fields conduct lack fidelity to the real world. Causal inference in the broadest and most important sense involves generalizations from research to the real world. The controlled aspects of experiments can make real-world generalizability tricky. The artificial conditions of many experiments raise questions about whether conditions in the lab have anything to do with the real world.

In short, no design is perfect when it comes to causal inference. The solution is to use multiple methods and hope that they all point to similar conclusions. This is known as the strategy of finding converging lines of evidence. It is the one that we endorse when thinking about personality research findings. Don't trust a claim based on a single piece of evidence. Instead look for claims that are based on multiple pieces of evidence that all support the same conclusion.

This background should give you the basic tools to understand the research we will discuss for the remainder of this book. Remember to keep an open mind and even try to have fun. We have arranged the different myths in an order that we think makes sense, but we tried to write each chapter after this introduction and Chapters 1 and 2 to mostly stand on their own. So feel free to jump around and pick the myths you find most interesting. The next section describes the organization of this book to help guide your reading. The last section provides a glossary of key terms that will appear again and again in the chapters.

Organization of chapters

Foundational material

Chapters 1 and 2 cover foundational issues in personality research. Chapter 1 describes the myth that personality traits are unimportant factors when considering behavior. This chapter also discusses the person–situation debate and addresses the possibility that personality itself is a myth. Chapter 2 continues the themes in Chapter 1 by specifically quantifying the prediction of behavior from personality attributes. It explains effect sizes in detail so the material on correlations discussed here in the introduction is also emphasized in Chapter 2. We return to many of the themes in Chapters 1 and 2 later, so they are probably useful to read as a foundation for the other material in the book.

Biological aspects of personality

Chapters 3 and 4 delve into personality myths related to biological considerations covering genes and evolutionary processes. We introduce some methods used to study genetic influences in Chapter 3 and then discuss big-picture issues with evolutionary approaches to personality in Chapter 4.

Personality assessment

Chapters 5–11 are broadly about myths related to personality assessment. Chapter 5 describes debates about types versus dimensions and is relevant for considering a famous personality measure described in Chapter 8—the Myers–Briggs Type Indicator. Chapter 6 discusses the difficulties in measuring personality but makes an argument that it is possible to measure attributes if done with appropriate expectations and empirical rigor. Chapters 7, 9, and 10 describe specific issues with personality assessment in terms of faking, using projective techniques, or unstructured interviews. We attempt to make a broad point about human judgments in Chapter 10. Chapter 11 covers basic issues in psychometric research to understand myths about the utility of personality quizzes found in magazines and on Internet sites.

Personality development

Chapters 12–17 detail myths related to personality development. Chapters 12 and 13 discuss whether traits are lacking in any consistency over time or completely set in stone by age 30. Some of the themes discussed in Chapter 1 reappear in Chapter 12. Chapter 14 evaluates whether life events impact personality trait development. Chapter 15 covers myths about adolescence. Chapters 16 and 17 describe myths related to family dynamics, including birth order and parenting. The material in Chapter 17 has parallels to the discussion about genetic influences covered in Chapter 3.

Well-being/happiness

Chapters 18–21 describe myths related to happiness and these chapters cover issues related to stability and change in happiness as well as the impact of life events on happiness. The material about life events and happiness echoes themes in Chapter 14 and even Chapter 3 regarding genetic influences on personality. Chapter 21 evaluates a myth about well-being in terms of the ideal ratio of positivity to negativity in psychology. This chapter provides some useful lessons about the importance of skepticism when consuming popular psychology books.

Applications of personality

Chapters 22–28 cover a range of issues in personality psychology that do not fit neatly into the five other sections. Chapters 22 and 23 describe myths related to personality similarity and relationships. Chapter 24 covers a myth about self-esteem and narcissism. Chapters 25 and 26 details myths related to national stereotypes and cross-cultural aspects of personality. Chapter 27 evaluates a myth related to sex difference. Last, Chapter 28 describes personality disorders and challenges the myth that personality disorders are untreatable.

Basic vocabulary

Agreeableness. One of the Big Five personality trait domains. Captures attributes such as cooperative and kind.

Big Three. A model of the structure of personality traits that consists of three broad domains of human individuality: negative emotionality or negative affectivity (susceptibility to distressing emotions and adversarial interpersonal interactions; see also Neuroticism), positive emotionality or positive affectivity (susceptibility to positive emotions and social potency; see also Extraversion), and constraint or low disinhibition (self-control and inhibition; see also Conscientiousness). Negative emotionality is similar to neuroticism, positive emotionality is similar to extraversion, and constraint is similar to conscientiousness in the Big Five trait model.

Big Five. A model of the structure of personality traits that consists of five broad domains: extraversion, agreeableness, conscientiousness, neuroticism (or low emotional stability), and openness.

Characteristic adaptations. Elements of personality that are narrower than dispositional traits such as attitudes, skills, motivations, and attachment styles. Researchers often think that characteristic adaptations are influenced by dispositional traits and environmental circumstances. Although characteristic adaptations are important elements of personality, much of this book focuses on traits.

Conscientiousness. One of the Big Five personality trait domains. Captures attributes such as responsible, dependable, and orderly.

Correlation coefficient. A statistic that ranges from –1 to 1 and summarizes the strength of the linear association between two variables. A zero correlation indicates no linear association. A positive correlation coefficient indicates that higher scores on one variable are associated with higher scores on another variable (e.g., conscientiousness and grade point average). A negative correlation coefficient indicates that higher scores on one variable are associated with lower scores on another variable (e.g., test anxiety and test performance). Correlation coefficients are statistical summaries of association and do not (by themselves) establish cause-and-effect relations.

Extraversion. One of the Big Five personality trait domains. Captures attributes such as talkative, energetic, and enthusiastic.

Neuroticism. One of the Big Five personality trait domains. Captures attributes such as being easily upset, anxious, and nervous.

Openness. One of the Big Five personality trait domains. Captures attributes such as curious and intellectual.

Subjective well-being. Feelings of personal happiness and satisfaction with life.

Traits. Relatively stable patterns of thinking, feeling, and acting that characterize the individual. Also called dispositional traits.

References

Donnellan, M. B., Lucas, R. E., & Cesario, J. (2015). On the association between loneliness and bathing habits: Nine replications of Bargh and Shalev (2012) study 1. *Emotion*, *15*(1), 109–119.

Shadish, W. R., Cook, T. D., & Campbell, D. T. (2002). *Experimental and quasi-experimental designs for generalized causal inference*. Boston, MA: Houghton Mifflin.

West, S. G., & Thoemmes, F. (2010). Campbell's and Rubin's perspectives on causal inference. *Psychological Methods*, *15*, 18–37.

1 SITUATIONAL FACTORS OVERWHELM PERSONALITY WHEN PREDICTING BEHAVIOR

We start this book off with the biggest myth in all of personality psychology—the idea that situational forces overwhelm the effects of personality traits when it comes to explaining people's behavior. People who believe this idea argue that features of the situation and environment play a stronger role in determining behavior than the characteristics of the person. Taken to the extreme, proponents of this idea might even argue that personality does not exist at all, and that our perception that people have stable personalities is an illusion. This myth was so powerful and was so widely accepted that it almost destroyed the field of personality psychology as an academic discipline starting in the 1970s. Thus, this is a critical myth to address. If personality itself is a myth, then there isn't much point to the rest of the book. In addition, in addressing this myth, we set the stage for many other myths that we cover in this book. Questions about the stability of personality over the life span, for instance, necessarily build on issues regarding stability from one moment to the next, one day to the next, and one month to the next. Therefore, we will try to introduce some basic ideas about what personality is and what we should expect from people's personalities.

Great Myths of Personality, First Edition. M. Brent Donnellan and Richard E. Lucas.
© 2021 John Wiley & Sons, Inc. Published 2021 by John Wiley & Sons, Inc.

Defining personality

So what is personality? As we noted in the introduction, personality focuses on the ways that people differ from one another. One widely cited definition was proposed by Gordon Allport (see 1937, 1961). Allport was a famous personality psychologist who wrote one of the first major texts on the topic, and he is often regarded as founding father of the field. According to Allport (1961, p. 28), "Personality is the dynamic organization within the individual of those psychophysical systems that determine [the person's] characteristic behavior and thought." If we break this definition down into its component parts, we can identify a few key features that will be important for our discussion about personality in this book.

Most importantly, personality is "within the individual." It is something that the person carries around from situation to situation. Thus, this implies that there will be at least some form of stability over time and across situations. Note that we do not yet explain precisely what form of stability we expect to see—this will become important as we discuss the responses to the myth addressed in this chapter. Furthermore, these features that are within the individual determine that person's "characteristic behavior and thought." In an earlier version, Allport (1937, p. 48) wrote that personality determines a person's "unique adjustments to [his or her] environment." In other words, depending on their personalities, people will react differently to the same situation. This part of the definition also implies that all behaviors reflect the interaction between the person and his or her environment. Personality does not exert its effects in a vacuum. Finally, Allport notes that personality reflects a "dynamic organization" of features within the individual. This means that the different characteristics that people have may work together in a unique manner to create their reactions to the world. In other words, one personality characteristic may have a different influence on behavior depending on the other personality characteristics that the person has. Consider a person who is both anxious and highly self-controlled. How might that person react to news that he or she is at higher risk for heart disease compared to someone who is anxious but quite low in self-control?

Allport's definition suggests that knowing something about a person's personality will allow us to predict (with some degree of uncertainty) how that person will respond to a specific situation in the future. As you can imagine, this is extremely useful information. At the most basic level, if personality exists and has a reasonably important influence on behavior, then we can expect at least some consistency when we encounter the same person in the same situation on two occasions. When you choose a person who has been kind and considerate to you in the past to be your roommate or even your spouse, you are doing so precisely because you believe this person has some stable personality characteristics that will cause them to act similarly in the future. In short, anytime you choose to interact with someone based on your expectations of how they will behave in the future, you are implicitly endorsing the idea that personalities exist and affect behavior.

As a science of human behavior, personality psychology goes even further than the ideas reflected in this belief. Personality psychologists believe that if they can begin to understand the "dynamic organization" of personality characteristics within people, they can not only expect stability across similar situations, they can also predict new behaviors in new situations based on the understanding of that person's personality characteristics (along with an understanding of the features of the new situation). This expectation explains why personality psychologists often examine the connections between specific personality traits (like conscientiousness) and theoretically relevant and practically important real-world outcomes like success in school or work (Ozer & Benet-Martinez, 2006; Roberts, Kuncel, Shiner, Caspi, & Goldberg, 2007; Wilmot & Ones, 2019). If personality exists and has a reasonably powerful effect on behavior, then you can see why researchers might want to document the strength of any connections in a systematic fashion.

Personality and assessment

However, in the late 1960s, something happened that led people to call into question the most basic tenets of personality psychology. Specifically, Walter Mischel published an influential book called *Personality and Assessment* (Mischel, 1968). In this book, Mischel laid out a set of critiques about the state of personality research and theory at the time. It is important to understand the nature of these critiques, along with the ways that these critiques were interpreted, to understand the myth about the power and primacy of situational factors we cover here. This is also a place where some of our discussion of myths touches upon how personality research is presented in other parts of psychology.

Mischel (1968) was highly critical of "broad" personality traits, especially those that were "decontextualized" or not linked to a specific situation. When researchers talk about broad traits, they usually refer to abstract ideas that capture individual differences in a range of specific attributes that are thought to reflect a general underlying tendency.

For instance, extraversion is a broad trait that reflects not just whether you enjoy parties (a narrow tendency) but also whether you are highly active, whether you tend to experience positive emotions, whether you enjoy exciting activities, and whether you are assertive with others. Although not every person who is assertive also enjoys parties, these characteristics tend to go together to form the broad trait of extraversion. Furthermore, decontextualized traits are those that are thought to lead to the same or very similar behaviors across a wide range of contexts. The fact that people who are extraverted might be sociable at parties, at work, in the classroom, and even with a bunch of strangers means that their extraverted behavior does not depend all that much on the specific context—it is decontextualized. It is these broad, decontextualized traits that Mischel targeted with his critique (though some people took his ideas even further and argued that we should be skeptical of the idea of stable personality characteristics as a whole). Other broad traits include the Big Five attributes described in the introduction and other attributes such as aggressiveness, self-control, and shyness.

Mischel acknowledged that when people were asked to describe their personality across different situations or on different occasions, their responses were quite stable. In other words, people believed that decontextualized and cross-situationally stable personality traits existed. However, according to the research that Mischel reviewed, when psychologists actually looked at the specific behaviors that people exhibited, this behavior was not especially stable either across different situations or even in the same situation at different times. This discrepancy between what people believe about the consistency of their behavior and what they actually do across situations was an important part of this critique because it suggested that people fool themselves about how consistent they are. People might not actually know themselves at all.

What was the evidence that Mischel identified to buttress his claims about personality traits? One of the most famous studies that Mischel reviewed was conducted by Hartshorne and May (1928). In this study, researchers tested the honesty of a group of children[1] using a variety of different behavioral tests. If honesty is conceptualized as a broad trait, then it should be reflected in a range of specific behaviors. After all, these specific behaviors are thought to reflect a general tendency to be

---

[1] In retrospect, it might have been something of a mistake to focus on children as opposed to adults given that researchers have learned that personality in children is more of a work in progress than personality in adults. The generalizations of this classic study might say more about personality in children than personality in adolescents or adults per se.

truthful, forthcoming, and morally upstanding. For example, the children in these studies were presented with opportunities to cheat on tests, but the precise behavior that was required to cheat (like copying answers from an answer sheet vs. copying from a friend) differed. Hartshorne and May found that these dishonest behaviors were not especially stable from one situation to the next; those children who cheated in one situation were not necessarily those who cheated in a different situation. In fact, the correlations between any two behaviors were often extremely low, sometimes close to zero (meaning that you could not predict how one child would behave from his or her behavior in a different type of cheating opportunity). This and other evidence led Mischel to conclude that despite people's perception that broad traits like "honesty" exist, specific honest acts are not especially stable from one situation to the next. Instead, because behavior varied—even across subtly different situations—situations must have more power than something like a broad, decontextualized personality trait. In stark terms: There isn't much utility in thinking there is a construct like "honesty" that can be used to predict behavior.

Mischel even went so far as to suggest a maximum size for the cross-situational correlation between the same behavior in two different situations. (Note: Mischel did not conduct a systematic review, nor did he use modern meta-analytic techniques to generate a figure based on the results of many studies. Thus, this number should be interpreted cautiously). He suggested that cross-situational consistency coefficients rarely exceeded .30. This number (or "effect size") was interpreted as being very small. The reason for this evaluation has to do with a somewhat technical point about statistics. If this sort of thing tends to make your eyes glaze over, feel free to skip this next paragraph.

The statistical reason that .30 was considered tiny was that if you take the square of a correlation (i.e., you multiply the size of the correlation by itself), you get the amount of variability in an outcome that can be explained by that predictor (at least according to the conventional way that many psychologists treat correlations; but see Funder & Ozer, 2019). In this case, a correlation of .30 would mean that only 9% of the variance ($.30 \times .30 = .09$ or 9%) in a single behavior could be explained by a person's behavior on a previous occasion. Simplistically, researchers assumed that the remaining 91% of the variance could be explained by situational factors, though this belief was never tested explicitly. In any case, this number of .30 was labeled the "personality coefficient," a derogatory label that, intentionally or not, served to diminish the importance of personality as a predictor of behavior.

Mischel (1968) was careful to note that his critique was not an attack on personality as a whole, only on the idea of broad, decontextualized traits described above. Indeed, until the time of his death in 2018, Mischel identified as a personality psychologist, and his primary goal in writing *Personality and Assessment* was to convince other personality psychologists that to understand behavior, researchers must focus on narrower psychological units. Specifically, he argued, researchers should focus on narrow cognitive and affective units (quite specific ways of thinking and feeling) that interact with specific features of situations to drive behavior (Mischel & Shoda, 1995). For instance, some of the children in the Hartshorne and May study described earlier may have had a fear of authority or perhaps even a very specific fear of elementary school teachers. This specific fear might have prevented them from cheating on an honesty test whenever that authority figure was around (which would lead to temporal stability in the exact same situation), but it might not have affected them when they were given a different opportunity to cheat while alone or in the presence of other adults. Thus, the child might exhibit honest behavior in one situation and dishonest behavior in other situations, depending on whether this narrow cognitive/affective unit was activated. The child is not globally fearful but rather only fearful of a specific teacher.

Note that Mischel's proposed alternatives to traits did not challenge the existence of personality, the strength of personality effects, or even the stability of personality characteristics over time. Instead, it was a challenge to a specific way of doing personality research and to the lay belief that broad, decontextualized dispositions are an actual feature of human nature. However, some psychologists latched on to the idea that the belief in strong, stable, and cross-situationally consistent patterns of behavior (broad or narrow) was an illusion. This seemed to be taking the critique of personality traits much further than Mischel had proposed. For instance, Nisbett and Ross (1980) argued that "personality theorists' (and the layperson's) conviction that there are strong cross-situational consistencies in behavior may be seen as merely another instance of theory-driven covariation assessments operating in the face of contrary evidence" (p. 112). In other words, not only do lay people mistakenly believe that they have cross-situationally consistent personality traits but also that personality psychologists themselves are fooled by their own intuitions and flawed judgments. Many academic psychologists bought into Nisbett and Ross's ideas and started turning away from personality psychology as a legitimate field of research. Here is an instance of a myth about personality traits that may exist in other areas of psychology and perhaps even in textbooks for those courses.

As a result of the Nisbett and Ross critique and similar others, interest in personality research waned in the 1970s (Swann & Seyle, 2005). Many psychology departments disbanded their personality psychology programs, and research increasingly focused on social determinants of behavior, rather than internal, personality-based determinants. One interesting aspect of recent history is the fact that some of the classic studies purporting to demonstrate the overwhelming power of the situation, such as the Stanford prison experiment, are being reevaluated in light of concerns about experimenter demand effects and selection effects (e.g., Bartels, 2019; Carnahan & McFarland, 2007; Le Texier, 2019). Fortunately, personality research did not die completely during this period, and there has been a resurgence of interest in recent years (again, see Swann & Seyle, 2005). However, in the years following the publication of Mischel's (1968) book, skepticism about the utility of personality psychology increased, and research on the topic declined.

Responding to *personality and assessment*

Was this reaction in academic psychology justified? Did Mischel (1968) identify a fundamental truth that broad personality traits were limited in their predictive ability, at least when compared to the overwhelming power of the situation? Well, given that we have identified this as the most important myth of our book, it is probably clear that we believe that the answer to these questions is "No."

First, even if we accept that the personality coefficient is really .30, one could make the argument that this is really not that small at all (see also Funder & Ozer, 2019). Indeed, the very idea that it is small comes from conventions for interpreting correlations that are just that—conventions. Some very small correlations can have extremely large practical importance; and in fact, some large correlations can have almost no practical importance. Thus, falling back on the idea that the effect of personality is small simply because the average correlation has traditionally been described as "small" is not especially convincing. As just one example, Roberts et al. (2007) reviewed the literature on the power of personality traits to predict future outcomes such as mortality, divorce, and occupational attainment. Rather than just relying on their own impressions about which effect sizes are large and which are small, the authors explicitly compared effect sizes for personality to those effect sizes from other areas of research that are known to be important for these outcomes, such as socioeconomic status and intelligence. In a result that would probably be quite surprising to critics from the 1970s, personality traits predicted many important life outcomes as well as these more widely studied characteristics. Although the sizes of these effects were actually weaker than the personality coefficient that Mischel identified, Roberts et al. clarified how these small effects can translate into important differences between people who are high or low on a specific trait.

Second, as we noted when we introduced the personality coefficient, it was often assumed that if a single personality trait correlates .30 with a behavior in a single situation (which means that only 9% of the variance in the behavior can be accounted for by differences in that trait), then 91% of the variance in the behavior must be due to features of the situation. However, this argument is flawed for a number of reasons. First, there is no reason to believe that any single behavior should be caused by just a single personality trait. Consider whether you go to parties. Should researchers be able to predict whether you go to a party this Friday night based solely on your level of extraversion? What if you had a big assignment due on Monday, and you were worried about your ability to complete it on time? Shouldn't your levels of conscientiousness and perhaps neuroticism influence whether you choose to go to the party or to stay at home and work? For just about any behavior that researchers or non-scientists might wish to predict or explain, there are plausible explanations for why multiple traits might be relevant. And if more than one trait influences the behavior, then the size of the correlation between any one trait and that behavior will be reduced, often considerably (Ahadi & Diener, 1989). Therefore, relatively small correlations between any single trait and any single behavior may simply reflect the fact that behaviors are determined by many different personality traits operating simultaneously (and in concert with features of the situation that might make certain of these traits more relevant than others).

In addition to this warning about the expectations for individual correlations, there is also empirical evidence that the remaining 91% of the variance in behavior is not clearly linked to specific situational factors. When the type of review that Mischel conducted is repeated for effects from social psychology (a field that traditionally focuses on situational influences), the effect sizes are no greater than those from personality psychology (Funder & Ozer, 1983; Richard, Bond, & Stokes-Zoota, 2003). Indeed, the average correlation identified across all of social psychology was .21—quite a bit smaller than the personality coefficient identified by Mischel. Does this mean that human behavior is completely random? No, it means that behavior is complex and multiply determined and that researchers need to adjust their expectations regarding effect sizes for single predictors. Remember, the idea that a correlation of .20 or .30 is small is based on arbitrary conventions; researchers need to go beyond these simple conventions to determine whether an effect of this size has practical significance within a particular context.

It is also clear that equating the "power of personality" with the ability of personality traits (or previous instances of behavior) to predict any single behavior at a single point in time is problematic. Think about how well a baseball player's season batting average predicts whether that player will get a hit on a specific pitch or even a single at-bat. It is often quite hard to tell good baseball batters from poor batters based on observing a few innings of baseball (see Abelson, 1985). Fans of the sport need to observe multiple at-bats to be able to tell good hitters from poor hitters. Likewise, personality emerges through patterns of behavior that people exhibit over time. In other words, people may deviate from expectations on any given occasion yet still exhibit their personality traits through aggregate behaviors observed over multiple occasions. Let's take the example of the prototypical extravert again. This person may love going to parties, but if he or she is also highly conscientious, he or she may decide to stay home one Friday night when that important paper is due (the looming deadline of the assignment is acting as a stronger situational factor than the pull of a raucous night out). The fact that this may happen reduces the researcher's ability to predict whether this person goes to a party on any night, while he or she may still go to more parties over the course of a semester than does the typical introvert. Examples such as this show that perceptions of personality may be based on behavior in the aggregate, and that people (including researchers) can only see the effects of personality through this type of aggregation (Epstein, 1979).

As a final caveat, we must acknowledge that despite our defense of the strength of personality effects, it is still possible that people place too much emphasis on their own first impressions when trying to predict how an acquaintance will behave in the future. Personality may play a critical role in determining behavior, yet people might still overestimate the effect that stable personality traits have on behavior when trying to predict how someone will act in a new situation. Questions about the extent to which people's beliefs about personality map on to the actual effects of personality have not been settled (Malle, 2006; Sabini, Siepmann, & Stein, 2001). However, to say that people overestimate the importance of personality is a far cry from arguing that personality does not exist.

Indeed, even if people's intuitions about these matters are not entirely correct, this does not mean that personality plays only a weak role in behaviors or that situational effects swamp personality effects. In the late 1960s and early 1970s, based partly on a problematic understanding of effect sizes and their own unexamined beliefs about the power of the situation, social psychologists seized upon the idea that personality was a much weaker predictor of behavior than they expected and seemed to think this meant that situational factors were more powerful. After many decades of research examining these claims, it is now clear that this truly is a myth. To the extent that such comparisons can be quantified, personality factors and situational factors tend to come out as being on equal footing. In addition, personality characteristics are stable over time and can statistically predict consequential behaviors (see the next chapter). Thus, the intuitions that guide most people's choices of relationship and work partners—intuitions that suggest that the person who was nice and helpful in the past will continue to be so in the future—are supported by solid empirical research.

References

Abelson, R. P. (1985). A variance explanation paradox: When a little is a lot. *Psychological Bulletin, 97*(1), 129–133.

Ahadi, S., & Diener, E. (1989). Multiple determinants and effect size. *Journal of Personality and Social Psychology, 56*(3), 398–406.

Allport, G. W. (1937). *Personality: A psychological interpretation.* New York, NY: Holt.

Allport, G. W. (1961). *Pattern and growth in personality.* New York, NY: Holt.

Bartels, J. (2019). Revisiting the Stanford prison experiment, again: Examining demand characteristics in the guard orientation. *The Journal of Social Psychology, 159*(6), 1–11.

Carnahan, T., & McFarland, S. (2007). Revisiting the Stanford prison experiment: Could participant self-selection have led to the cruelty? *Personality and Social Psychology Bulletin, 33*, 603–614.

Epstein, S. (1979). The stability of behavior: I. On predicting most of the people much of the time. *Journal of Personality and Social Psychology, 37*(7), 1097.

Funder, D. C., & Ozer, D. J. (1983). Behavior as a function of the situation. *Journal of Personality and Social Psychology, 44*(1), 107–112.

Funder, D. C., & Ozer, D. J. (2019). Evaluating effect size in psychological research: Sense and nonsense. *Advances in Methods and Practices in Psychological Science, 2*(2), 156–168.

Hartshorne, H., & May, M. A. (1928). *Studies in the nature of character, Vol. 1: Studies in deceit.* New York, NY: Macmillan.

Le Texier, T. (2019). Debunking the Stanford prison experiment. *The American Psychologist, 74*(7), 823–839.

Malle, B. F. (2006). The actor-observer asymmetry in attribution: A (surprising) meta-analysis. *Psychological Bulletin, 132*(6), 895.

Mischel, W. (1968). *Personality and assessment.* New York, NY: Wiley.

Mischel, W., & Shoda, Y. (1995). A cognitive-affective system theory of personality: Reconceptualizing situations, dispositions, dynamics, and invariance in personality structure. *Psychological Review, 102*(2), 246–268.

Nisbett, R. E., & Ross, L. D. (1980). *Human inference: Strategies and shortcomings of social judgment.* New York, NY: Prentice-Hall.

Ozer, D. J., & Benet-Martinez, V. (2006). Personality and the prediction of consequential outcomes. *Annual Review of Psychology, 57,* 401–421.

Richard, F., Bond, C. F., & Stokes-Zoota, J. J. (2003). One hundred years of social psychology quantitatively described. *Review of General Psychology, 7*(4), 331–363.

Roberts, B., Kuncel, N., Shiner, R., Caspi, A., & Goldberg, L. (2007). The power of personality: The comparative validity of personality traits, socioeconomic status, and cognitive ability for predicting important life outcomes. *Perspectives on Psychological Science, 2*(4), 313–345.

Sabini, J., Siepmann, M., & Stein, J. (2001). The really fundamental attribution error in social psychological research. *Psychological Inquiry, 12*(1), 1–15.

Swann, W. B., & Seyle, C. (2005). Personality psychology's comeback and its emerging symbiosis with social psychology. *Personality and Social Psychology Bulletin, 31*(2), 155–165.

Wilmot, M. P., & Ones, D. S. (2019). A century of research on conscientiousness at work. *Proceedings of the National Academy of Sciences, 116*(46), 23004–23010.

2 PERSONALITY MEASURES DO NOT PREDICT CONSEQUENTIAL OUTCOMES (LIKE HEALTH, WEALTH, AND DIVORCE) WELL ENOUGH TO BE USEFUL

This second myth is directly tied to the person–situation debate described in the previous chapter. So now would be a good time to quote the entire passage about the personality coefficient from *Personality and Assessment* because it illustrates the underlying idea of this myth in detail:

> Indeed, the "personality coefficient" might be coined to describe the correlation between .20 and .30 which is found persistently when virtually any personality dimension inferred from a questionnaire is related to almost any conceivable external criterion involving responses sampled in a different medium—that is, not by another questionnaire. Generally such correlations are too low to have value for most individual assessment purposes beyond gross screening decisions.

(Mischel, 1968, p. 78)

Great Myths of Personality, First Edition. M. Brent Donnellan and Richard E. Lucas.
© 2021 John Wiley & Sons, Inc. Published 2021 by John Wiley & Sons, Inc.

This passage has been parsed, interpreted, and reinterpreted in multiple ways over the years in academic psychology. It would be a stretch to say that it has fueled fistfights, but only by a little. Indeed, we have seen debates about the size of personality coefficients and correlations devolve into shouting matches!

As we previously noted, one popular interpretation of Mischel's 1968 book was that traits are inconsequential (see, e.g., Funder, 1991, 2009; Ozer & Benet-Martínez, 2006; Roberts, 2009; Roberts, Kuncel, Shiner, Caspi, & Goldberg, 2007). This leads directly to the myth that traits are useless for predicting outcomes that people (psychologists or otherwise) care about. The goal in this chapter is to define the key terms in this myth and then to consider the overall evidence about the predictive power of personality measures.

Defining the terms

The first task in unpacking this myth is to define consequential outcomes. What makes something consequential? Who gets to decide whether something is consequential or not? We recognize that different readers may hold different opinions about this issue, and we draw on insights by Daniel Ozer and Veronica Benet-Martínez (2006), who proposed that consequential outcomes are those that matter for people in their own lives. Specifically, they argued that consequential outcomes are things like physical and mental health, relationship outcomes, career success, and criminality. For some of these outcomes, there is empirical evidence that nonscientists value them; for example, Karney and Bradbury (2005) reported that more than 90% of people across diverse socioeconomic groups endorse the idea that a happy marriage is one of the most important things in life. For other outcomes, psychologists assume that the outcomes matter because people seem to invest considerable time and energy to obtain them. We suspect there is more consensus about what counts as a consequential life outcome than there would be about other topics investigated by psychologists, though we acknowledge that this idea has not been tested explicitly.

One thing to remember about consequential life outcomes (something that was discussed in Chapter 1) is that broad and important outcome variables are likely influenced by a wide range of factors. This means it is unlikely that any single factor will account for all of the variation in that kind of variable. Let's return to the baseball example from Chapter 1 to illustrate (both authors have at least a passing interest in the sport, so please bear with us!). Think about something like the number of wins a baseball team accumulates over the course of a season. The number of potential contributors to this outcome variable is large and interconnected. Indeed, the complex interrelations among the various factors that lead to success are part of the reason baseball is fascinating to at least some people. The factors that might play a role include the quality of the offense, the quality of the pitching rotation, the quality of the defense, and the quality of the competition. Somewhere in all of this are factors like injuries, payroll, and the attributes of the manager (maybe even the personality of the manager!). Given this, it would be hard to imagine that any one factor—say, the average performance of the pitchers—explained all of a team's success. Even with a stellar pitching staff, the quality of the offense matters. Teams that cannot score many runs often lose baseball games no matter how well their pitchers perform. Life outcomes like mortality, wealth, and happy relationships are probably like baseball wins over the course of a season in the sense of being a product of many factors. There is likely to be no single critical element that explains all differences in life outcomes.

The next task in unpacking this myth is to define what it means for a predictor to be useful. Sometimes a correlation between predictor and outcome can be so low that knowing something about the predictor has no practical value in helping us understand the outcome. In thinking about these issues, it is useful to make a distinction between *absolute* usefulness and *relative* usefulness. Absolute usefulness entails an overall, bottom-line judgment about how much a given predictor matters for the prediction equation (i.e., is the correlation .03 or .30 or .60). Relative usefulness, on the other hand, is inherently comparative: To assess relative usefulness, we could compare correlations for personality predictors of consequential outcomes to correlations for other factors that many people agree matter.

It turns out to be quite difficult to define absolute usefulness because different people have different standards. Drawing on the metric of correlations, for example, some people might consider a variable consequential only if the correlations between predictor and outcome are stronger than some specific threshold like a correlation of .50. The problem is that any threshold is somewhat arbitrary, and different people will likely select different thresholds. Think about baseball again. How many home runs must one hit to be a superstar? Is 30 home runs a year acceptable? What about 40; is that good enough? Given the complexities involved in determining these absolute criteria, many personality psychologists believe that it will be easier to make judgments about the usefulness of personality measures with respect to other benchmarks.

One benchmark for making relative judgments about the predictive power of personality measures could be the size of the correlation between tests of academic aptitude and grades. Millions of students take the SAT each year in hopes of gaining admission to the college or university of their choice. The basis for selection on SAT scores is the idea that higher scores predict better achievement in college. A common finding is that the correlation between SAT scores and first-year grades is about .35 (Kuncel, Ones, & Sackett, 2010).[1] Similarly, IQ tests and grades tend to be correlated around .25 (Poropat, 2009). These correlations—correlations that tap real-world associations that nonscientists might be relatively familiar with—thus provide a useful benchmark against which we can compare the associations with personality.

Another benchmark could be measures of socioeconomic status (SES). SES is usually a composite of variables like income, education, and occupational prestige. This collection of variables is designed to capture power, prestige, and economic standing. Scientists and nonscientists alike seem to believe that SES is an important factor in predicting consequential life outcomes (see Roberts et al., 2007). Thus, correlations between SES and consequential outcomes provide a natural comparison for researchers who wish to evaluate the importance of personality traits as predictors of these same outcomes.

It turns out that measures of things like scholastic aptitude and SES predict broad consequential outcomes with correlations somewhere in the .10–.40 range. This can provide a reasonable comparison standard that can be used to decide whether personality traits have anything to offer when predicting, and even explaining, individual differences in consequential outcomes. Indeed, even as personality psychologists who believe in the importance of personality traits, we think it would actually be quite shocking if we were to find that personality trait measures consistently outperformed these other kinds of variables as predictors of important life outcomes.

Considering the evidence

Now that we have considered how we might think about predictors of consequential life outcomes, we can address the evidence for the predictive power (or lack thereof) of personality attributes. Fortunately, our

---

[1] There is a large literature on this topic, and there are sophisticated ways to adjust these kinds of correlations for the fact that the lowest scoring students on the SAT do not typically attend college, thereby restricting the range of the predictor variable. Adjustments can also be made to account for the fact that students with higher SAT scores might actually select into more difficult courses. These adjustments usually result in an increase in the correlation between SAT and grades. Likewise, there is research looking at how SAT scores predict grades adjusting for SES (see Sackett, Kuncel, Arneson, Cooper, & Waters, 2009).

task is made easier by the existence of a number of meta-analyses of relevant literatures. Meta-analysis is a statistical technique for summarizing entire research literatures.

Now it might be good to take a brief side tour and say something about meta-analysis. To do this, we can compare a meta-analysis to a traditional narrative literature review. The first step in both types of reviews is to identify and collect available research literature on a topic. In a traditional literature review, the researchers' goal is to decide in a very general (and frequently subjective) way what a set of studies on a given topic has to say. In a traditional review, researchers develop qualitative impressions about the state of the literature: Is the evidence for an association strong or weak? Is the evidence mixed or consistent? What factors seem to matter in terms of amplifying or diminishing the association? The judgments in this kind of review are based on the informed expert opinion of the reviewer. Informed expert opinion is important, but problems occurs when different expert disagree. Such disputes can be hard to adjudicate. And these sorts of judgments are not quantitative in nature but rather impressionistic and even subjective. This fact adds further ambiguity to traditional narrative reviews.

A meta-analysis approaches the task of summarizing the literature in a quantitative fashion by computing an effect size (a correlation is one type of effect size) for each study and then combining the different effect sizes to obtain an estimate of the overall effect size by pooling information across studies. For example, researchers might want to summarize the literature about how well conscientiousness predicts performance at work. Thus, researchers would compute a correlation between conscientiousness and work performance from each study and then arrange all of those values in a computer spreadsheet. They would also record the sample size and other study characteristics that could be important (things like the type of measure of conscientiousness, the design of the study as either cross-sectional or longitudinal, the age of the participants, etc.). But the basic idea is to first collect all of the available effect sizes from studies on the topic.

Once the effect sizes have been collated, the researcher can use statistical models to compute the overall effect size estimate. Although complex models are often involved, an easy way to think about the overall effect size estimate is that it is an average. In more technical terms, it is the average of all of the individual correlations with higher weights given to larger studies relative to smaller studies. The logic here is that larger studies are more accurate and thus, if researchers want the best overall estimate, larger studies should be given more influence in the analysis.

The logic is just like the results of a political poll—a poll of 100 people is not as accurate for judging the preferences of the electorate as a pool of 1,000 people (assuming that the two polls are equal in every other way). Likewise, a sound meta-analytic approach typically gives more weight to the larger studies.

Beyond getting estimates of the overall relation between one specific trait and some consequential outcome, researchers can also see how much variation exists across studies and quantify that in statistical terms. Assuming there is nonrandom variation, researchers can also investigate what study characteristics might influence the size of the overall effect. For example, researchers can test whether cross-sectional studies suggest a stronger relation than longitudinal studies or whether the Acme™ personality measure provides stronger correlations than does the measure from Assessments R Us™. All of this can be done once researchers comb through the literature to identify all of the studies on a given topic.[2]

As we noted, a number of meta-analyses have summarized how personality attributes are related to consequential life outcomes. These include meta-analyses on the personality predictors of achievement (Poropat, 2009), health (Bogg & Roberts, 2004), job performance (Barrick & Mount, 1991), job satisfaction (Judge, Heller, & Mount, 2002), leadership (Bono & Judge, 2004), marital quality (Karney & Bradbury, 1995), and well-being (Heller, Watson, & Ilies, 2004; Steel, Schmidt, & Shultz, 2008). Readers interested in a specific area could use resources like Google Scholar (https://scholar.google.com) to search their topic of choice. Simply adding the search term "meta-analysis" to terms representing the outcome of interest can reveal whether a quantitative review is available (pick the most recent one as a starting point if multiple meta-analyses turn up). We only provide some illustrative results here, drawing on the previously cited meta-analyses and a comprehensive overview by Roberts et al. (2007). The Roberts et al. (2007) review was limited to prospective studies (i.e., studies that measured personality before the important life outcome) to improve causal inferences. As you will see, the results from these meta-analyses undermine the claim that that personality is inconsequential.

As Table 1 shows, this smattering of meta-analytic evidence supports the claim that personality traits are related to consequential outcomes.

---

[2] You might be wondering if it is ever possible to find all of the studies on a particular topic. You would be right to be skeptical. A big worry is whether researchers doing meta-analysis can find most of the studies on a topic and whether they can assume that they just missed some studies for random reasons. Many books and articles have been written to address these complex issues; we are describing the idealized situation so you can get the general idea.

Table 1 Effect sizes in the correlational metric for variables associated with important life outcomes

Outcome	Personality predictor	Correlation	Source
Academic performance	Conscientiousness	.19	Poropat (2009, p. 328)
Drug use	Conscientiousness	−.29	Bogg and Roberts (2004, p. 908)
Excessive alcohol use	Conscientiousness	−.25	Bogg and Roberts (2004, p. 908)
Job satisfaction	Neuroticism	−.24	Judge et al. (2002, p. 533)
	Conscientiousness	.20	
	Extraversion	.19	
Mortality	Conscientiousness	−.09	Roberts et al. (2007, p. 322)
Marital satisfaction	Neuroticism	−.26	Heller et al. (2004, p. 589)
	Agreeableness	.24	Heller et al. (2004, p. 589)
Violence	Conscientiousness	−.25	Bogg and Roberts (2004, p. 908)

This evidence is therefore a strong challenge to the myth that personality is inconsequential. It is important to acknowledge that the specific size of effects that are typically found in these meta-analyses do not refute the absolute size of Mischel's "personality coefficient." Indeed, all of these meta-analytic averages are below the .30 cutoff that Mischel identified in his famous book.

A major advance in the personality literature in the time since Mischel wrote his book and launched concerns about personality traits is the availability of relevant comparison standards against which personality correlations can be compared. The debate can shift from discussions about absolute to relative predictive power. Researchers now know that most effects in social and personality psychology fall in a very similar range to these meta-analytic estimates (Hemphill, 2003; Richard, Bond, & Stokes-Zoota, 2003). Researchers also know that other widely studied, intuitively important predictors such as IQ and SES predict consequential outcomes with correlations that are quite similar. Thus, we believe and teach our students that personality effects are probably as important as many other factors researchers can identify. Accordingly, we believe there is no reason to dismiss personality correlations as inconsequential in comparison to other variables. Moreover, we believe it is simply a myth that any single psychological variable can have huge correlations with multiply determined consequential outcomes. Consequential outcomes are produced by many things. Behavior is not simple, but single personality traits taken in isolation (i.e., by themselves) probably predict behavior as well as many other single variables researchers have identified.

References

Barrick, M. R., & Mount, M. K. (1991). The Big Five personality dimensions and job performance: A meta-analysis. *Personnel Psychology, 44*(1), 1–26.

Bogg, T., & Roberts, B. W. (2004). Conscientiousness and health-related behaviors: A meta-analysis of the leading behavioral contributors to mortality. *Psychological Bulletin, 130*(6), 887–919.

Bono, J. E., & Judge, T. A. (2004). Personality and transformational and transactional leadership: A meta-analysis. *Journal of Applied Psychology, 89*(5), 901–910.

Funder, D. C. (1991). Global traits: A neo-Allportian approach to personality. *Psychological Science, 2,* 31–39.

Funder, D. C. (2009). Persons, behaviors, and situations: An agenda for personality psychology in the postwar era. *Journal of Research in Personality, 43,* 120–126.

Heller, D., Watson, D., & Ilies, R. (2004). The role of person versus situation in life satisfaction: A critical examination. *Psychological Bulletin, 130*(4), 574–600.

Hemphill, J. F. (2003). Interpreting the magnitudes of correlation coefficients. *American Psychologist, 58,* 78–79.

Judge, T. A., Heller, D., & Mount, M. K. (2002). Five-factor model of personality and job satisfaction: A meta-analysis. *Journal of Applied Psychology, 87*(3), 530–541.

Karney, B. R., & Bradbury, T. N. (1995). The longitudinal course of marital quality and stability: A review of theory, methods, and research. *Psychological Bulletin, 118*(1), 3–34.

Karney, B. R., & Bradbury, T. N. (2005). Contextual influences on marriage implications for policy and intervention. *Current Directions in Psychological Science, 14,* 171–174.

Kuncel, N. R., Ones, D. S., & Sackett, P. (2010). Individual differences as predictors of work, educational, and broad life outcomes. *Personality and Individual Differences, 49,* 331–336.

Mischel, W. (1968). *Personality and assessment.* New York, NY: Wiley.

Ozer, D. J., & Benet-Martínez, V. (2006). Personality and the prediction of consequential outcomes. *Annual Review of Psychology, 57,* 401–421.

Poropat, A. E. (2009). A meta-analysis of the five-factor model of personality and academic performance. *Psychological Bulletin, 135,* 322–338.

Richard, F. D., Bond, C. F., Jr., & Stokes-Zoota, J. J. (2003). One hundred years of social psychology quantitatively described. *Review of General Psychology, 7*(4), 331–363.

Roberts, B. W. (2009). Back to the future: *Personality and Assessment* and personality development. *Journal of Research in Personality, 43,* 137–145.

Roberts, B. W., Kuncel, N., Shiner, R., Caspi, A., & Goldberg, L. R. (2007). The power of personality: The comparative validity of personality traits, socio-economic status, and cognitive ability for predicting important life outcomes. *Perspectives on Psychological Science, 2,* 313–345.

Sackett, P. R., Kuncel, N. R., Arneson, J. J., Cooper, S. R., & Waters, S. D. (2009). Does socio-economic status explain the relationship between admissions tests and post-secondary academic performance? *Psychological Bulletin, 135,* 1–22.

Steel, P., Schmidt, J., & Shultz, J. (2008). Refining the relationship between personality and subjective well-being. *Psychological Bulletin, 134*(1), 138–161.

3 THERE IS A SINGLE GENE FOR A SINGLE PERSONALITY TRAIT

The complex processes by which genes influence human characteristics such as personality traits are one of the most fascinating topics in all of psychology. Unfortunately, the precise mechanisms that underlie genetic effects are so difficult to grasp that some degree of oversimplification is inevitable. One form of oversimplification comes in the form of the belief that complex personality traits can be traced back to the influence of a single gene.

Although the pace of stories about how scientists have discovered a gene for a particular personality trait seems to have slowed in recent years, it is still possible to read about a new study showing a link between genes and personality differences. This often leads to inflated claims that scientists have found "the gene" for a given trait. Imagine learning that people with one form of a gene are high in sensation seeking, and those with other forms are low in sensation seeking. Such news stories might prompt regular people to pay hard-earned money to learn about their genotypes. After all, it would be fascinating to learn about your own personality by shipping off a container of spit to a company that extracts deoxyribonucleic acid (DNA) from saliva. DNA, as you probably know from high school biology, is the twisty (and tiny) substance shaped like a double helix that contains the genetic profile for each individual. Scientists are learning more and more about how DNA influences physical and psychological variables. Researchers in psychology who are interested in how DNA and genetic material are related to thoughts, feelings, and behaviors are called behavioral geneticists.

Great Myths of Personality, First Edition. M. Brent Donnellan and Richard E. Lucas.
© 2021 John Wiley & Sons, Inc. Published 2021 by John Wiley & Sons, Inc.

Here is an important piece of advice—as of right now, you will learn more about your personality from completing a self-report of a well-validated trait measure than by having a complete and detailed readout of your DNA. Put simply, although genes are highly relevant for personality, it is a myth that a single gene, or even a small set of genes, is responsible for any single personality trait. The best evidence suggests that an exceptionally large number of different genes are collectively responsible for the overall genetic contribution to personality variation, with each gene having a tiny overall effect (Chabris, Lee, Cesarini, Benjamin, & Laibson, 2015). People are different from one another, in part, because they have different configurations of DNA in the aggregate. Most single genes explain very little about personality variation. The myth we address here is about the power of single genes.

How personality psychologists use twins to study genetic influences

Before addressing this myth specifically, it is important to take a detour into a discussion of what we do know about heritability or the degree of variation in a trait in a population that is related to genetic differences. Psychologists have long been aware that genetic differences between people help explain variation in personality traits. The evidence for this conclusion typically came from twin studies. Twin studies take advantage of experiments of nature whereby genetic clones exist in the form of identical or monozygotic (MZ) twins. Identical twins come from the same fertilized egg and have 100% similar DNA. These kinds of twins are different from fraternal or dizygotic (DZ) twins, who are simply "regular" siblings who grow from two separate fertilized eggs and thus share, on average, 50% of their DNA.

Researchers can use these simple facts about the differences in genetic relatedness between identical and fraternal twins to make inferences about the source of variation in observable human characteristics. For instance, one simple approach is to test how similar identical twins are to one another, especially in cases where the two twins were reared apart since early childhood or even birth. Although these types of twin pairs are fairly rare (Bouchard, Lykken, McGue, Segal, & Tellegen, 1990), some studies have identified enough of them to begin to understand genetic contributions to personality (Tellegen et al., 1988). Specifically, once twins are identified, similarity between the twins can be tested with simple correlation coefficients. As with any correlation, a value near zero indicates that scores from one twin are not related to those from the other twin, and a positive coefficient that approaches 1.0 indicates a high degree of similarity. As just one example of what studies like this typically find, Tellegen et al. (1988) estimated that the similarity correlation for constraint (a Big Three trait that captures self-control akin to Big Five conscientiousness) was .57 for identical twins reared apart. This remarkable result suggested even those identical twins who grew up in different homes tend to be far more similar than any two strangers picked at random when it comes to constraint (assuming that the correlation between random pairs of people is zero).

The next step is to interpret similarity correlations to make inferences about the origins of personality differences. The case of identical twins reared apart is fairly straightforward: The obvious common factor between these twins, and, really, the only factor that can explain their similarity, is the fact that they share 100% of their genes. Remember, these twins grew up in different households with different families. Therefore, environmental factors like shared parenting across siblings in the same family cannot explain the similarity that these twins exhibit. The twins had different parents growing up. In short, a correlation between identical twins reared apart is usually taken as clear evidence that genetic factors are implicated in a trait. The fact that identical twins reared apart are not perfectly similar also indicates a role for environment factors; personality is not entirely genetic.

Although identical twins who were reared apart allow for strong conclusions about the impact of genes on attributes like personality traits, alternative approaches to understanding heritability do exist. In fact, alternative designs that focus on the more common case where twins are raised together in the same household provide the vast majority of what is known about the heritability of human personality traits. In these studies, researchers look at twin similarity correlations separately for identical and fraternal twins and then compare the two. Remember, identical twins are twice as similar (genetically speaking) than fraternal twins. If observable characteristics were due entirely to genes, then identical twins should be twice as similar as fraternal twins in these characteristics. Therefore, comparing the similarity of these two types of twins allows researchers to infer something about how heritable a specific personality trait is. Specifically, a ballpark estimate of the so-called heritability coefficient can be obtained by doubling the difference between the similarity correlations for identical and fraternal twins. That is, heritability (abbreviated as h^2) = 2 × (Identical-Twin Similarity Coefficient minus the Fraternal-Twin Similarity Coefficient).

Importantly, twin studies also help clarify the ways that certain environmental factors contribute to personality. If it is the shared rearing environment that causes twins to be similar, then growing up in the same environment should cause identical and fraternal twin pairs to be equally similar to one another. If they are equally similar, despite the fact that identical twins are twice as genetically similar as fraternal twins, this suggests there is something about the common rearing environment that promotes personality similarity. Furthermore, if a researcher has samples of both twins reared together and twins reared apart, it is possible to estimate the role of the environment even more precisely. If the environmental factors that twins share affect their personality, then those twins who are reared together should be more similar than those reared apart (regardless of whether they are identical or fraternal twins).

An example might help make this even more concrete. In the Tellegen et al. (1988) study we previously mentioned, the researchers also collected data from identical and fraternal twins who were reared together. The similarity coefficient for the personality trait of constraint was .58 for identical twins reared together versus .25 for fraternal twins reared together. The difference between .58 and .25 is .33. Doubling that difference yields an estimate for heritability (h^2) of .66. The heritability coefficient is interpreted as the proportion of variance in a population for a given trait (constraint in this case) that can be attributed to genetic differences between people.

As it turns out, the heritability estimates for a range of personality traits taken across a number of studies turn out to be in the ballpark of .40 to .60 (Bouchard & Loehlin, 2001; Krueger & Johnson, 2008; see South & Krueger, 2008, for a review). If you had to place a bet on the results of a twin study of personality, putting money on a heritability coefficient of .50 would be a good way to avoid losing big More broadly, twin studies almost always produce heritability estimates that are above zero. At the most basic level, this means that genetic differences between people help to explain why there is variation in a given attribute. This finding is so robust that it has even been enshrined as the first law of behavior genetics by Eric Turkheimer (2000): "All human behavioral traits are heritable." Personality traits definitely fall under this first law.

Specific genes and personality traits

Now that you have a basic understanding of the types of evidence that have been used to show broad genetic effects on personality, we can return to the topic that is the main focus of this chapter: whether personality trait differences result from large effects of single genes. Studies linking specific genetic variants and personality traits started to appear in the mid-1990s. A few high-profile papers purported to show that specific variants of individual genes were associated with individual differences in specific personality traits. Two of the initial traits linked to specific genes were novelty seeking (Ebstein et al., 1996) and anxiety (Lesch et al., 1996). These studies generated considerable initial excitement because they seemed to offer a solution to a longstanding issue in personality research.

Specifically, although the large and robust body of research reviewed at the beginning of this chapter clearly showed that genes matter for personality, one missing piece to this puzzle concerned precisely how genes were linked to specific personality traits. Put differently, the specific details about the mechanisms that linked genetic factors to personality traits were elusive. Thus, initial research that seemed to match specific genes with different personality traits was exciting because it seemed to fill a gap in knowledge about the ways we get from genes to the individual differences that we observe in ourselves and others.

Unfortunately, subsequent studies did not always reproduce the original results of the promising initial studies, or at the very least, they provided effect size estimates for the impact of these individual genes that were much smaller than the original studies (e.g., Munafò et al., 2003; Munafò & Flint, 2004; Munafò, Yalcin, Willis-Owen, & Flint, 2008). With additional study, the evidence that a single genetic variant represented the gene for a given personality trait like sensation seeking or extraversion became murkier.[1] The initial excitement wore off for studies that purported to find evidence for strong effects of single genes (see also Chabris et al., 2015).

The current thinking is that variation in a large number of genes each contributes a tiny bit to the overall variation in things like personality attributes and even many diseases (Manolio et al., 2009). This appears to the case for physical attributes such as height (Visscher, McEvoy, & Yang, 2010), and so it certainly seems likely that this principle would also apply to variables as complex (and multiply determined) as personality. Just as there is no single gene that determines whether someone is tall versus short, it would seem unlikely that complex attributes like personality

---

[1] A pattern whereby the evidence in favor of an initial finding that weakens over time is actually common in the typical cycle of research. Thus, healthy skepticism is a perfectly normal reaction to the results of any single study. It is often prudent to reserve judgment until a large number of studies have been conducted to wait to see if results are duplicated again and again.

traits could be traced to the influence of a single gene. The genetic architecture of so-called complex traits involves a large number of genes that each exerts rather tiny (even infinitesimally tiny, to use a rather technical term) effects on their own. Given these considerations, the idea that there is a single gene for personality traits or almost any psychological attribute is myth. A recent study showed this kind of complicated pattern of results for the association between DNA and same-sex sexual behavior (Ganna et al., 2019). Genetic factors are relevant, but no one can identify a specific gene that has an especially powerful association with same-sex behavior.

In sum, the genetics of personality are complicated. Personality traits are likely to be a quintessential example of a *polygenic attribute*, an attribute that involves multiple genes (Plomin, Owen, & McGuffin, 1994). It is extremely unlikely (and empirical evidence confirms this view) that a single gene exists that exclusively determines whether a person has either high or low levels of a broad personality trait like sensation seeking, novelty seeking or any of the Big Three and Big Five dimensions. Thinking about personality in the same way that one might think about the genetics of eye color—an attribute that can be dramatically affected by a single gene—is not terribly useful. Indeed, Chabris et al. (2015) coined the idea of the fourth law of behavior genetics: "A typical human behavioral trait is associated with very many genetic variants, each of which accounts for a very small percentage of the behavioral variability" (p. 305). So it is a myth to assert that there is a single gene for a single personality trait. In rejecting this myth, however, it is important not to ignore the basic fact that genetic factors play an important role in understanding why people are different from one another in personality traits.

References

Bouchard, T. J., Jr., & Loehlin, J. C. (2001). Genes, evolution, and personality. *Behavior Genetics*, 31(3), 243–273.

Bouchard, T. J., Lykken, D. T., McGue, M., Segal, N. L., & Tellegen, A. (1990). Sources of human psychological differences: The Minnesota study of twins reared apart. *Science*, 250(4978), 223–228.

Chabris, C. F., Lee, J. J., Cesarini, D., Benjamin, D. J., & Laibson, D. I. (2015). The fourth law of behavior genetics. *Current Directions in Psychological Science*, 24(4), 304–312.

Ebstein, R. P., Novick, O., Umansky, R., Priel, B., Osher, Y., Blaine, D., … Belmaker, R. H. (1996). Dopamine D4 receptor (D4DR) exon III polymorphism associated with the human personality trait of novelty seeking. *Nature Genetics, 12*(1), 78–80.

Ganna, A., Verweij, K. J., Nivard, M. G., Maier, R., Wedow, R., Busch, A. S., ... Lundström, S. (2019). Large-scale GWAS reveals insights into the genetic architecture of same-sex sexual behavior. *Science, 365*(6456), eaat7693.

Krueger, R. F., & Johnson, W. (2008). Behavioral genetics and personality: A new look at the integration of nature and nurture. In L. A. Pervin, O. P. John, & R. W. Robins (Eds.), *Handbook of personality: Theory and research* (3rd ed., pp. 287–310). New York, NY: Guilford Press.

Lesch, K. P., Bengel, D., Heils, A., Sabol, S. Z., Greenberg, B. D., Petri, S., ... Murphy, D. L. (1996). Association of anxiety-related traits with a polymorphism in the serotonin transporter gene regulatory region. *Science, 274*(5292), 1527–1531.

Manolio, T. A., Collins, F. S., Cox, N. J., Goldstein, D. B., Hindorff, L. A., Hunter, D. J., ... Visscher, P. M. (2009). Finding the missing heritability of complex diseases. *Nature, 461*(7265), 747–753.

Munafò, M. R., Clark, T. G., Moore, L. R., Payne, E., Walton, R., & Flint, J. (2003). Genetic polymorphisms and personality in healthy adults: A systematic review and meta-analysis. *Molecular Psychiatry, 8*(5), 471–484.

Munafò, M. R., & Flint, J. (2004). Meta-analysis of genetic association studies. *Trends in Genetics, 20*(9), 439–444.

Munafò, M. R., Yalcin, B., Willis-Owen, S. A., & Flint, J. (2008). Association of the dopamine D4 receptor (*DRD4*) gene and approach-related personality traits: Meta-analysis and new data. *Biological Psychiatry, 63*(2), 197–206.

Plomin, R., Owen, M. J., & McGuffin, P. (1994). The genetic basis of complex human behaviors. *Science, 264*(5166), 1733–1739.

South, S. C., & Krueger, R. F. (2008). An interactionist perspective on genetic and environmental contributions to personality. *Social and Personality Psychology Compass, 2*(2), 929–948.

Tellegen, A., Lykken, D. T., Bouchard, T. J., Wilcox, K. J., Segal, N. L., & Rich, S. (1988). Personality similarity in twins reared apart and together. *Journal of Personality and Social Psychology, 54*(6), 1031–1039.

Turkheimer, E. (2000). Three laws of behavior genetics and what they mean. *Current Directions in Psychological Science, 9*(5), 160–164.

Visscher, P. M., McEvoy, B., & Yang, J. (2010). From Galton to GWAS: Quantitative genetics of human height. *Genetics Research, 92*(5–6), 371–379.

4 EVOLUTIONARY PERSPECTIVES ARE NOT RELEVANT FOR PERSONALITY

Variation is a feature of natural populations and every population produces more progeny than its environment can manage. The consequence of this overproduction is that those individuals with the best genetic fitness for the environment will produce offspring that can more successfully compete in that environment. Thus the subsequent generation will have a higher representation of these offspring and the population will have evolved.

(Charles Darwin from *On the Origin of Species*)

Most *heritable* personality differences are *not* the expression of different adaptive strategies. They are either mutationally driven genetic noise, or else an incidental by-product of an adaptation that has nothing to do with personality per se.

(Tooby & Cosmides, 1990, p. 19)

Consequently, some of the key founders of evolutionary psychology have argued that heritable individual differences are best viewed as "noise" and are thus irrelevant to the basic functioning of the psychological machinery, much like differences in the colors of the wires of a car engine do not affect its basic functioning.

(Buss, 2009, p. 360)

Great Myths of Personality, First Edition. M. Brent Donnellan and Richard E. Lucas.
© 2021 John Wiley & Sons, Inc. Published 2021 by John Wiley & Sons, Inc.

Many of the myths discussed in this book focus on characteristics that differ from one person to the next; as we discussed in the introduction, personality psychology, almost by definition, concerns the factors that differ across individuals. Yet at the same time, at least some parts of personality psychology focus on human commonalities. Some types of thoughts, feelings, and behaviors likely reflect something fundamental about "human nature" that might be consistent across the species. These components of human nature have been shaped by natural selection in ways that create species-typical characteristics. According to this idea, some patterns of thoughts, feelings, and behaviors exist because they helped our ancestors survive and reproduce. Psychologists who consider these issues are called evolutionary psychologists. Traditionally, evolutionary psychology has not been much concerned with individual differences; but that is beginning to change.

The broad goal of evolutionary psychology is to explain the ways that human thinking, feeling, and behaving have been shaped by the processes of natural selection (e.g., Buss, 1991). Taking an evolutionary approach to personality means trying to explain how personality differences could be understood using the logic of natural selection. Historically (or at least as far back as the early 1990s), some evolutionary psychologists expressed skepticism about using natural selection to understand differences in personality attributes like the Big Five trait domains. Although it seems fairly innocuous, calling something "noise" in academic circles (as indicated by the last quotation in the opening) is generally seen as dismissive—it is often a roundabout way of saying that something is unimportant. After all, most people care about signal (the important stuff) rather than noise (the static that masks the signal). More recent work, however, has used principles from evolutionary psychology to better understand variation in personality. The objective of this chapter is to illustrate how such advances are changing how personality attributes are understood from evolutionary perspectives (e.g., Buss & Hawley, 2011; Nettle, 2006).

Accordingly, the goal of this chapter is to illustrate why it is a myth to assume that evolutionary psychology is not relevant to personality psychology. This chapter departs from other chapters by focusing on the broad field of personality psychology rather than on specific findings related to personality. This chapter is also an example of a place where we tackle a myth that might be more prevalent in academic psychology rather than everyday thinking. Recall that one of our goals for this book is to help make you a better consumer of the personality research presented in both textbooks and popular media articles. So we think it makes sense to consider whether evolutionary perspectives have much to offer to personality psychology. Moreover, the general perspective of evolutionary psychology can open the door to provocative questions about human behavior. It also generates some degree of controversy, so it is worth learning a bit about the perspective to be able to navigate any controversy.

Evolutionary psychology 101

Before illustrating how evolutionary perspectives are relevant to personality psychology, it is useful to provide a quick background on evolution by natural selection. Fortunately, the idea is simple and can be quickly summarized with four basic points (drawing on Darwin, 1871).

1. Certain kinds of attributes and patterns of behavior facilitate survival and reproduction.
2. Organisms differ in these attributes, and some of these differences are passed from parents to offspring via genes (these are called heritable attributes).[1]
3. Environmental factors limit survival and reproduction. Not all organisms are able to survive for long enough periods of time to reproduce. Not all offspring survive.
4. Organisms that lack attributes that promote survival and reproductive success die off quickly. Organisms that have heritable attributes that facilitate survival and reproduction pass them to their offspring. As a result, heritable attributes that facilitate survival and reproduction increase in populations over successive generations. It is important to remember that populations evolve, whereas individuals do not.

When thinking about evolution and evolutionary theory, you might first think about physical adaptations that help survival and reproduction. Indeed, evolutionary biologists typically study such characteristics; for instance, they might focus on differences in the eye shape between species that are predators versus those that are prey (e.g., Banks, Sprague, Schmoll, Parnell, & Love, 2015). Evolutionary psychologists, on the other hand, tend to focus on heritable psychological adaptations that facilitate reproduction and survival. Rather than studying physical differences between species, evolutionary psychologists might study patterns of

---

[1] Please note that heritable has a different meaning in personality psychology than the concept of heritability that was discussed in Chapter 3.

thoughts, feelings, and behaviors that help people avoid diseases, attract mates, successfully raise their offspring, and protect themselves from harm (see Neuberg, Kenrick, & Schaller, 2010).

Evolutionary approaches to personality psychology generally attempt to understand how personality variability could be viewed as an adaptation or may result from specific adaptations to ancestral challenges. Thus, an objective of evolutionary psychology as applied to personality psychology is to determine whether it makes theoretical sense to try to explain why individual differences exist in the context of these adaptations. This is often accomplished by thinking about the consequences of personality variation for survival and reproduction. A key insight of this kind of analysis is that the consequences of trait variation for things that "matter" for evolution (i.e., survival and reproductive success) depend on features of the environment.

Evolutionary psychology and the existence of personality variation

One evolutionary approach to understanding personality posits that different levels of personality traits might be more or less adaptive in different environmental conditions (Nettle, 2006). Consider the trait of neuroticism—a tendency toward anxiety and a low threshold for detecting threats. Relatively high levels of this trait might aid survival in dangerous environments. Indeed, being anxious and cautious might have prevented ancestors of modern humans from being injured or killed by predators. However, there are also physiological costs to being on high alert for much of the time. Humans who are chronically anxious might be more susceptible to illness and miss out on important opportunities for doing the kinds of things that also matter for evolutionary success, like reproducing. Such people might not be fun to be around or make for especially good romantic partners. The point is that there are trade-offs associated with high or low levels of all traits, and these trade-offs may depend on the environment in which a person lives. Table 2 lists some of the potential costs and benefits of the Big Five traits that might impact survival and reproductive success.

The key to understanding why there might be variation in a current trait in the population from this perspective is to recognize that humans have exploited a wide range of environmental niches and thus faced a wide range of environmental conditions. Given the vast diversity in environments, there might be no single trait level that is universally optimal for survival and

Table 2 Potential costs and benefits associated with the big five domains

Trait domain	Potential costs	Potential benefits
Neuroticism	Physiological stress; impairment of relationships	Vigilance; protection from threats
Extraversion	Risky behaviors	Exploration, mating success
Openness	Unusual beliefs	Creativity
Conscientiousness	Compulsive tendencies	Long-term goal pursuit
Agreeableness	Exploitation by others	Co-operation, potential to bolster reciprocal relationships

Note. Based on Nettle (2006).

reproduction. The optimal level for a trait depends on the context. Thus, evolutionary theorists might argue that there isn't a strong selective pressure for a specific trait level that is consistent across all people. The variety of environments that exist and the trade-offs that these environments create explain why variation persists in the trait for a population.

Evolutionary psychology and the development of personality

Some evolutionary psychologists try to explain the adaptive significance of variability in the light of the varied environments that humans inhabit, as we described in the last section. Other evolutionary psychologists try to explain individual differences in personality characteristics from a more developmental perspective. One approach is known as life-history theory (e.g., Belsky, Steinberg, & Draper, 1991; Chisholm, 1993; Figueredo et al., 2006). The basic idea is that humans have a limited amount of time and energy to invest in growth, parenting, and reproduction, and therefore, humans must divide their efforts between these different strategies for ensuring that their genes "survive" into future generations. For instance, if someone invests a considerable amount of energy in caring for offspring (i.e., parenting), there will be less energy available for finding new mating partners. (Please note that there is no requirement of conscious awareness of how resources are allocated in these evolutionary perspectives. In fact, most evolutionary perspectives argue that people are generally unaware of the deep-seated evolutionary considerations that might shape thoughts, feelings, and behaviors in the present. In other words, people are not usually aware of the evolutionary motivations behind their behaviors.)

According to one version of life-history theory, the relative preferences individuals have for investing their resources are set early in the life span based on immediate conditions. A harsh upbringing marked by instability in the family and limited resources might predispose individuals toward a "fast" life-history strategy, which entails faster biological maturation, a relative preference for mating over parenting (i.e., having more children but investing less energy in their upbringing), and a more risk-taking personality profile. A more stable upbringing with cues that resources are plentiful might predispose people toward a "slow" strategy, which entails slower biological maturation, more emphasis on parenting (i.e., having fewer children but investing a considerable amount of energy on upbringing), and a less risk-taking personality.

This perspective has proven to be controversial, but it suggests that humans might have a great deal of initial flexibility about how they allocate efforts to growth, mating, and parenting. These investment strategies may be affected by the range of potential human environments that people are exposed to during childhood; the initial flexibility is channeled by local environmental conditions during development. This approach therefore offers a broader perspective on how early upbringing might shape the course of human development; it helps explain certain patterns of behavior from the perspective of survival and reproduction.

You might notice that this developmental perspective seems to conflict with the results of the twin studies we discussed earlier. Recall that such studies often suggest that common rearing environments (i.e., family-wide factors that make children who grow up in the same home similar to one another) are not especially powerful influences on personality. This tension is something that researchers are currently struggling to rectify (see also Bouchard & Loehlin, 2001). It is somewhat unfortunate that researchers in these two strands (behavioral genetic and evolutionary psychology) are often working in parallel with each other, and a resolution of these two strands of evidence has yet to emerge. One way to think about the issue is that the environmental factors that channel efforts toward growth, mating, and parenting might be unique to each member of a family.

Conclusion

We briefly described two areas in which evolutionary psychology and personality research intersect. We hope these two lines of thinking show how evolutionary perspectives could be useful for thinking about personality variability. Thus, we think it is an academic myth to argue that evolutionary psychology is irrelevant to personality psychology.

We would be remiss if we did not end this chapter with a few caveats, given the controversy that is sometimes is attached to evolutionary approaches. First, scientific explanation is not equal to moral justification. For example, researchers might try to explain why some children could be predisposed to bullying from an evolutionary perspective. These researchers are not justifying bullying in a moral sense. Explaining how bullying might be adaptive in an evolutionary sense is not equivalent to arguing that bullying behaviors are morally acceptable, biologically unavoidable, or necessarily positive. This distinction between explanation and understanding, on the one hand, and moral justification on the other is easy to see in medical research. No cancer researcher would argue that cancer is "good" in any moral sense and studying why it exists and the processes through which cancer cells operate are never interpreted as a moral acceptance of cancer as a virtuous entity. Cancer researchers are not justifying the acceptability of cancerous growths by studying cancer. Unfortunately, critics of evolutionary psychology sometimes confuse explanation with justification.

Second, there is no reason to assume that all human variation has relevance for survival and reproduction. Just because an interesting feature of human psychology exists does not mean it has a clear and direct link with survival and reproduction in the evolutionary sense. One job of the evolutionary personality psychologist is to develop empirical tests of any conjecture about the evolutionary functions of human thoughts, feelings, and behaviors. This is how science works.

The point of this chapter was to counter the myth that the science of evolutionary psychology is irrelevant to personality. We hope we made the case in these few short pages. The broad theme of this book about skepticism is also worth repeating here as well. There is every reason to be as skeptical of evolutionary explanations for specific personality traits as for any finding in the field. However, there is probably no reason to be especially skeptical of an idea just because it was derived from an evolutionary perspective. We hope that you keep an open mind to the possibility that evolutionary thinking is valuable while also maintaining a critical perspective on particular arguments and ideas.

References

Banks, M. S., Sprague, W. W., Schmoll, J., Parnell, J. A., & Love, G. D. (2015). Why do animal eyes have pupils of different shapes? *Science Advances*, *1*, e1500391.
Belsky, J., Steinberg, L., & Draper, P. (1991). Childhood experience, interpersonal development, and reproductive strategy: An evolutionary theory of socialization. *Child Development*, *62*, 647–670.

Bouchard, T. J., Jr., & Loehlin, J. C. (2001). Genes, evolution, and personality. *Behavior Genetics, 31*, 243–273.

Buss, D. M. (1991). Evolutionary personality psychology. *Annual Review of Psychology, 42*, 459–491.

Buss, D. M. (2009). How can evolutionary psychology successfully explain personality and individual differences? *Perspectives on Psychological Science, 4*, 359–366.

Buss, D. M., & Hawley, P. H. (Eds.) (2011). *The evolution of personality and individual differences*. New York, NY: Oxford.

Chisholm, J. S. (1993). Death, hope, and sex: Life-history theory and the development of reproductive strategies. *Current Anthropology, 34*, 1–24.

Darwin, C. (1871). *The descent of man, and selection in relation to sex*. New York, NY: Appleton.

Figueredo, A. J., Vásquez, G., Brumbach, B. H., Schneider, S. M., Sefcek, J. A., Tal, I. R., … Jacobs, W. J. (2006). Consilience and life history theory: From genes to brain to reproductive strategy. *Developmental Review, 26*, 243–275.

Nettle, D. (2006). The evolution of personality variation in humans and other animals. *American Psychologist, 61*, 622–631.

Neuberg, S. L., Kenrick, D. T., & Schaller, M. (2010). Evolutionary social psychology. In S. T. Fiske, D. T. Gilbert, & G. Lindzey (Eds.), *Handbook of social psychology, Vol. 2* (5th ed., pp. 761–796). New York, NY: Wiley.

Tooby, J., & Cosmides, L. (1990). On the universality of human nature and the uniqueness of the individual: The role of genetics and adaptation. *Journal of Personality, 58*, 17–67.

5 PEOPLE COME IN DISCRETE PERSONALITY TYPES

As we have emphasized in this book, personality psychology is generally about human variation. It is the science of differences in characteristic ways of thinking, feeling, and behavior. A fundamental question, then, for this science of individual differences is in finding useful ways of characterizing such differences. What are the basic units of a science of personality?

Two broad, almost philosophical approaches to addressing this question have emerged in personality psychology: approaches focused on dimensions versus those focused on types. Dimensions are attributes that vary across people, such as personality traits like extraversion, agreeableness, conscientiousness, neuroticism, and openness (i.e., the Big Five). Dimensional approaches assume that all people can be characterized using any given dimension; people would simply vary in how much of that dimension they have. In contrast, personality types are constellations of qualitatively different attributes that seem to go together within individuals in clear packages. For instance, when a researcher claims that some people are introverts whereas others are extraverts or that some people have Type A (driven and ambitious) personalities whereas others have Type B (relaxed and even-keeled) personalities, they are drawing clear, qualitative distinctions between people who fall into each of the two opposing groups. The question we tackle in this chapter concerns which of these two approaches is the more valid and useful way to organize the field of personality. If you read popular accounts of personality, you will see the typological approach emerging quite often. However, we think the basic assumption of this approach is largely a myth. In light of

Great Myths of Personality, First Edition. M. Brent Donnellan and Richard E. Lucas.
© 2021 John Wiley & Sons, Inc. Published 2021 by John Wiley & Sons, Inc.

our reading of the state of the science, it is a myth to argue that people come in discrete types. This is especially true if one claims that types are as different from each other as dogs are from cats.

Nonetheless, the typological approach has, throughout history, captured the imagination of the general public. One of Aristotle's students, Theophrastus, offered a description of 30 different character types. Likewise, the Roman physician Galen talked about specific personality types that resulted from mixtures of what were thought to be critical biological substances—black bile, blood, phlegm, and yellow bile. These substances gave rise to four widely known temperament types: melancholic (introverted and traditional), sanguine (cheerful and optimistic), phlegmatic (calm and tranquil), and choleric (driven and ambitious) people. Typological thinking is not relegated to the ancient world, however. The familiar Myers–Briggs approach to personality assessment (see Chapter 8) is a contemporary example of a popular typological approach (spoiler alert—the validity of the Myers–Briggs typological approach will be questioned as another widely believed myth).

Popular approaches to measuring personality online and in print magazines are also based on typological thinking. Consider, as an example, the kinds of quizzes that ask people about their personality characteristics to sort them into different houses associated with the *Harry Potter* franchise. For such an approach to have an acceptable degree of validity, there has to be evidence that (a) people actually come in types, and (b) those personality types that exist in nature match up well with the characters associated with the various houses in the books and movies. You might already be skeptical of the second requirement, but it turns out that even the first question is somewhat dicey. Such an idea has provoked heated disagreements in the field (see Donnellan & Robins, 2010, for an accessible review), and the result of these debates is that current personality researchers generally focus on dimensions rather than types.

Why discrete types are a myth

Personality researchers use typologies in two different ways. The "types-as-distinctive forms" approach is based on an extremely strong claim that personality types actually exist in nature, and the job of personality psychologists is simply to identify these naturally occurring groups. Advocates of this approach believe that the differences between the Type A and Type B person are as clear-cut as the differences between gophers and chipmunks (two different species of animals you might find in the woodlands of, say, Michigan or Minnesota). Personality types in this framework are intended to "carve nature at its joints" or to sort people into categories that are true natural categories (Meehl, 1992).

This idea that types exist as distinctive forms is largely considered to be a myth in personality psychology; very little empirical evidence supports this version of the typological approach. The arguments against this perspective range from simple and intuitive to highly technical critiques based on statistical algorithms. At the basic level, there seems to be too much gradation in personality attributes to cleanly divide people into tidy categories like extravert or introvert. Few people represent prototypical extraverts and introverts, and most people fall somewhere in the middle of what looks like a continuous distribution. This seems to hold for most of the various types that have been proposed for human personalities. Compare the ambiguities of classifying the people you know into distinct extravert or introvert categories with the task of classifying woodland creatures—chipmunks are clearly distinct from squirrels, who are clearly distinct from gophers. This impressionistic classification is backed by clear differences in physiology, appearance, genetics, and behavior. Rarely (if ever) would someone have a hard time telling the difference between these different kinds of animals. These different species are close to what philosophers might consider "natural kinds" (forms that exist in nature and not just human minds). Aliens visiting the planet Earth would also likely consider the chipmunk to be a different type of animal than a squirrel.

In addition to the simple thought experiment pointing to problems with personality types as distinctive forms, there is a long line of technical attempts to identify personality or character types using statistical tools. Without delving into statistical arcana, there is a statistical signature that is produced when researchers are dealing with qualitatively distinct types (see Ruscio, Haslam, & Ruscio, 2013). The majority of statistical attempts to isolate personality types (both using normal and abnormal personality attributes) have failed to find evidence of this signature (Aslinger, Manuck, Pilkonis, Simms, & Wright, 2018; Edens, Marcus, Lilienfeld, & Poythress, 2006; Fraley, Hudson, Heffernan, & Segal, 2015; Fraley & Spieker, 2003; Fraley & Waller, 1998; Marcus, Lilienfeld, Edens, & Poythress, 2006). In other words, it has been difficult to find replicable evidence for neat and tidy distinctions between people based on statistical methods. Given these converging lines of argumentation, few researchers endorse the distinctive-forms approach to types.

One alternative to the distinctive-forms perspective is the "types-as-label" approach (Meehl, 1992). This is a less rigorous use of the concept of a type that simply views types as useful labels. No deep claims about whether personality types are truly distinct from one another in the same ways that dogs and cats are different kinds of animals is intended. Types are seen as useful fictions that offer a short-hand way of referring to different configurations of personality information within people in an efficient and reasonable easy to communicate labels. So, for instance, it could be useful to talk about the unique combination of traits (i.e., hostility, a sense of urgency, and a tendency to be driven and hard-working) that make up the "Type A personality," even if people who have this collection of characteristics aren't qualitatively different from those who might have high levels of hostility and a high sense of urgency but are not driven or hard-working.

If types are considered to be useful fictions (at best), a follow-up question then becomes, what are types useful for? In other words, this is a question of whether identifying and using type-focused labels have any practical utility over dimensions in terms of the statistical prediction of consequential outcomes (Asendorpf, 2003; Costa, Herbst, McCrae, Samuels, & Ozer, 2002; Van Leeuwen, De Fruyt, & Mervielde, 2004). The objective here is to compare the statistical efficiency of dimensions (i.e., trait scores) with type membership (i.e., whether someone falls into a particular personality category). To come back to the example of people who can be categorized as having "Type A personality," it is possible to ask whether there is something that we learn about the person from this unique combination of traits that we wouldn't know just by learning their scores on the underlying dimensions of hostility, urgency, and drive. It turns out that most of the time, there does not seem to be much of an advantage to putting people into categories if researchers have access to their scores on basic dimensions. So, if the utility question is framed around prediction, types don't seem that useful beyond dimensions. This might be seen as yet another blow for personality types.

Types, however, might still have some advantages when thinking about different applications besides prediction. At a somewhat superficial but still important level, types get people interested in personality psychology and personality measurement. Although typologies may reflect scientifically problematic oversimplifications, they might reflect a "kernel of truth" about what a person is like; learning about these descriptions can be fun. Thus, types might be a "gateway drug" for getting people to appreciate individual differences and the complexities of psychological assessment. In this sense, types might be useful for advancing personality psychology.

For those who are already accustomed to thinking about personality dimensions, types might also be useful for getting them to think about how trait dimensions are organized within people in interesting ways. Indeed, individual traits do not exist in isolation from the other aspects of a person's personality. People have different levels of many different traits, and the precise pattern of these differences is an important part of what makes people unique; these precise patterns can be an important part of people's identity or life story. Thus, interesting combinations of personality traits might exist and be worth considering both from a scientific viewpoint and a purely descriptive exercise in better understanding people. Types offer a convenient way to do this because they naturally shift the focus from isolated dimensions to combinations of traits that might interact. Some argue that types help researchers to adopt a so-called "person-centered approach" that takes a more holistic approach to what people are like and how they differ from others (Laursen & Hoff, 2006).

Types as useful fictions in current personality psychology

Thus far, we have tried to make two broad points about personality types: Types as "natural kinds" probably do not exist, but types might still prove useful to personality psychology as long as their limitations are acknowledged. In that spirit, we now consider a specific approach to personality types that has some proponents in the literature. This approach helps illustrate both of the points we hoped to convey: It does not make strong claims about "true" differences between the different types, but it does point out how type-based labels can help the field.

A pioneering personality psychologist named Jack Block (e.g., Block, 1971) developed a personality typology based on a long-term research program he pursued with his spouse (see Block & Block, 2006, for a summary of their work). According to Block, there are three replicable personality types: resilient, overcontrolled, and undercontrolled (e.g., Asendorpf, Borkenau, Ostendorf, & Van Aken, 2001; Asendorpf & van Aken, 1999; Robins, John, Caspi, Moffitt, & Stouthamer-Loeber, 1996; Steca, Alessandri, & Caprara, 2010; see also York & John, 1992).

The resilient type includes people who are high in emotional stability (low neuroticism), high in extraversion, and high in conscientiousness. They have direction, energy, and self-confidence. Members of the overcontrolled type are low in extraversion and emotional stability (high neuroticism). They are sensitive, tense, and introverted. The undercontrolled type is low in agreeableness and contentiousness. Members of this group seem impulsive and antagonistic to others. Robins et al. (1996) found that type membership was associated with positive and negative life outcomes in expected ways. For instance, overcontrolled individuals have relatively higher levels of what are called internalizing problems—the types of problems, like anxiety and depression, in which negative thoughts and behaviors are directed inward toward oneself. Undercontrolled individuals, on the other hand, seem to experience relatively high levels of internalizing and externalizing problems (psychological problems that might be directed outward like aggression and substance abuse).[1] Resilient individuals have relatively higher levels of performance in achievement contexts.

These three types are the most commonly discussed types in the current literature. However, not all studies find compelling evidence for the existence of these three types. Indeed, Asendorpf (2003, p. s2) noted that the "consistency of personality types across different studies is however far from being perfect." It is also the case that different statistical methods for extracting types might yield different solutions. So, it is probably safest to conclude that these types are a tentative starting point for developing more extensive and exhaustive taxonomies that can begin to chart interesting personality trait configurations.

Summary

The idea that people's personalities fit into discrete categories that reflect natural kinds is a myth. In other words, there is little support for the idea that personality types are distinctive forms. People differ from one another as a matter of degree and not kind. Nonetheless, personality types might prove useful as a shorthand for summarizing salient individual differences especially in terms of patterns of different levels of particular traits within a person. In that spirit, three types have been discussed in the academic literature and seem to have empirical support (resilient, overcontrolled, and undercontrolled). Researchers have studied whether type memberships outperform dimensions in predicting consequential

---

[1] Although terminology like internalizing and externalizing problems is common in clinical psychology, it is also the case that this dichotomy is itself a bit fuzzy. Some forms of psychopathology might create both intrapsychic distress (internalizing problems) as well as issues of concern for others (externalizing problems). In short, depression and anxiety are commonly considered internalizing problems and aggression and substance use are considered externalizing problems.

outcomes, and most studies fail to find compelling support that types enhance prediction beyond dimensions like the Big Five. Types might still be useful for other reasons as a way to motivate interest in personality psychology and as a way to motivate researchers to think about the complex ways that traits and other dimensions are arranged within individuals.

References

Asendorpf, J. B. (2003). Head-to-head comparison of the predictive validity of personality types and dimensions. *European Journal of Personality*, *17*(5), 327–346.

Asendorpf, J. B., Borkenau, P., Ostendorf, F., & Van Aken, M. A. (2001). Carving personality description at its joints: Confirmation of three replicable personality prototypes for both children and adults. *European Journal of Personality*, *15*(3), 169–198.

Asendorpf, J. B., & van Aken, M. A. (1999). Resilient, overcontrolled, and undercontroleed personality prototypes in childhood: Replicability, predictive power, and the trait-type issue. *Journal of Personality and Social Psychology*, *77*(4), 815.

Aslinger, E. N., Manuck, S. B., Pilkonis, P. A., Simms, L. J., & Wright, A. G. (2018). Narcissist or narcissistic? Evaluation of the latent structure of narcissistic personality disorder. *Journal of Abnormal Psychology*, *127*(5), 496–502.

Block, J. (1971). *Lives through time*. Berkeley, CA: Bancroft Books.

Block, J., & Block, J. H. (2006). Venturing a 30-year longitudinal study. *American Psychologist*, *61*(4), 315.

Costa, P. T., Jr., Herbst, J. H., McCrae, R. R., Samuels, J., & Ozer, D. J. (2002). The replicability and utility of three personality types. *European Journal of Personality*, *16*(S1), S73–S87.

Donnellan, M. B., & Robins, R. W. (2010). Resilient, overcontrolled, and undercontrolled personality types: Issues and controversies. *Social and Personality Psychology Compass*, *4*(11), 1070–1083.

Edens, J. F., Marcus, D. K., Lilienfeld, S. O., & Poythress, N. G., Jr. (2006). Psychopathic, not psychopath: Taxometric evidence for the dimensional structure of psychopathy. *Journal of Abnormal Psychology*, *115*(1), 131.

Fraley, R. C., Hudson, N. W., Heffernan, M. E., & Segal, N. (2015). Are adult attachment styles categorical or dimensional? A taxometric analysis of general and relationship-specific attachment orientations. *Journal of Personality and Social Psychology*, *109*(2), 354.

Fraley, R. C., & Spieker, S. J. (2003). Are infant attachment patterns continuously or categorically distributed? A taxometric analysis of strange situation behavior. *Developmental Psychology*, *39*(3), 387.

Fraley, R. C., & Waller, N. G. (1998). Adult attachment patterns: A test of the typological model. In J. A. Simpson & W. S. Rholes (Eds.), *Attachment theory and close relationships* (pp. 77–114). New York, NY: Guilford Press.

Laursen, B., & Hoff, E. (2006). Person-centered and variable-centered approaches to longitudinal data. *Merrill-Palmer Quarterly*, *52*(3), 377–389.

Marcus, D. K., Lilienfeld, S. O., Edens, J. F., & Poythress, N. G. (2006). Is antisocial personality disorder continuous or categorical? A taxometric analysis. *Psychological Medicine*, *36*(11), 1571–1581.

Meehl, P. E. (1992). Factors and taxa, traits and types, differences of degree and differences in kind. *Journal of Personality*, *60*(1), 117–174.

Robins, R. W., John, O. P., Caspi, A., Moffitt, T. E., & Stouthamer-Loeber, M. (1996). Resilient, overcontrolled, and undercontrolled boys: Three replicable personality types. *Journal of Personality and Social Psychology*, *70*(1), 157.

Ruscio, J., Haslam, N., & Ruscio, A. M. (2013). *Introduction to the taxometric method: A practical guide*. New York, NY: Routledge.

Steca, P., Alessandri, G., & Caprara, G. V. (2010). The utility of a well-known personality typology in studying successful aging: Resilients, undercontrollers, and overcontrollers in old age. *Personality and Individual Differences*, *48*(4), 442–446.

Van Leeuwen, K., De Fruyt, F., & Mervielde, I. (2004). A longitudinal study of the utility of the resilient, overcontrolled, and undercontrolled personality types as predictors of children's and adolescents' problem behaviour. *International Journal of Behavioral Development*, *28*(3), 210–220.

York, K. L., & John, O. P. (1992). The four faces of Eve: A typological analysis of women's personality at midlife. *Journal of Personality and Social Psychology*, *63*(3), 494.

6 PERSONALITY IS TOO COMPLICATED TO BE MEASURED

Whatever exists at all exists in some amount. To know it thoroughly involves knowing its quantity as well as its quality

(Thorndike, 1918)

Earlier in the book, we tackled the question of whether personality even exists and whether it is strong and stable enough to affect behavior in the face of strong situational pressures from the people, objects, and events around us (Chapters 1 and 2, respectively). We noted that after a strong challenge in the 1960s, personality researchers were able to demonstrate that personality is, in fact, relatively consistent across situations, and that the effects of personality characteristics are often as strong as, and sometimes stronger than, the typical effect of situational forces. Thus, understanding personality is a worthwhile endeavor, both for academic researchers interested in the science of behavior and for nonscientists who just want to understand (and perhaps even change) their own and others' behavior.

There is a catch, however, and it might turn out to be a big one. To study personality, one must be able to measure it, and the process of measuring personality raises a huge number of challenges. People are complex, and their personalities may simply be too complicated to measure with much accuracy, even if these personalities do have powerful effects on behavior and other outcomes. For instance, if you received feedback on your personality in the past, you may have felt as though the description you received was vague, superficial, or just plain wrong. Or alternatively, even if you thought that the description had some kernel of truth, you might have felt as though it did not capture the complexity of who you are. In this chapter, we address the myth that this complexity is so great that

Great Myths of Personality, First Edition. M. Brent Donnellan and Richard E. Lucas.
© 2021 John Wiley & Sons, Inc. Published 2021 by John Wiley & Sons, Inc.

useful measures of personality cannot be created. This myth periodically comes up in practical settings where people question the legitimacy of selecting employees based on personal attributes. We will discuss well-established steps—steps that are not unique to personality psychology but are instead common across many branches of science—that can be used to develop and evaluate measures of personality. Finally, we will cover a series of intuitive questions one can ask about personality measures to determine whether or not they are of any value. Hopefully in doing this, we can convince you that carefully constructed personality measures can capture some of the complexity that exists in human personality.

One source of skepticism about our ability to measure personality characteristics is that personality can't be seen. The technical term for this is to say that these characteristics are *latent*—they exist, but they cannot be observed directly. People can only perceive imperfect indicators of those latent or unobservable characteristics. Moreover, personality reflects a person's distinctive pattern of thoughts, feelings, and behaviors, but no single behavior captures the entirety of that person's personality and there's no specific place in a person's brain where personality can be found. Because of this, some may conclude that personality—this invisible thing that can only be inferred from the pattern of behaviors that a person exhibits—cannot be measured. However, if you think carefully about this problem, you realize that many other fields have tackled similar problems with demonstrated success. As we will explain, personality psychologists have proceeded by following these well-established procedures for studying things that may be difficult to observe.

For instance, let's take an example from physics: how to measure temperature. Try to imagine what it would be like to experience temperature before physicists really understood the physical principles related to heat. You might notice that things simply felt different in the summer than in the winter. You might notice that the sensation of the summer sun on your skin was similar to (but not exactly the same as) the sensations created by a roaring fire or even a thick blanket. You might be able to describe these feelings and communicate them to others, but you could not really "see" these differences in temperature, and you would certainly not know what (at a physical level) was causing them. So how would a naïve physicist approach this phenomenon to begin developing sophisticated theories of heat and temperature?

The first step might simply be to document people's perception about objects and environments that differ in temperature. In short, early physicists could take advantage of people's subjective impressions of the phenomenon of temperature to begin to assess it in increasingly sophisticated ways. If people think that the summer is hotter than the winter or that a room with a fire is warmer than a room without, early physicists could begin to document these subjective impressions. These subjective impressions could be put to various tests to see whether people's impressions were meaningful. A basic step might be to test for agreement across people in their impressions. For instance, if everyone agrees that ice is colder than liquid water, which is in turn colder than boiling water, then it suggests that the subjective perception of temperature corresponds to something "real" in the world, rather than something that exists solely in people's minds. At the very least, it might be surprising that so many people could agree about the relative coldness of water if it was all "just" in the minds of the perceivers. So establishing that there is some agreement in these perceptions of temperature is one way to begin measuring temperature so that it can be studied scientifically.

Once this agreement has been established, it is possible to look for objective characteristics that are "out there" in the world that seem to correspond to the subjective evaluations of temperature. For instance, early physicists might notice that when water is placed in a room that people agree is subjectively very cold, it turns to ice, whereas putting ice in a room that is subjectively very hot makes the ice turn to liquid. Documenting such real-world consequences further helps to validate the idea that temperature really exists outside of people's heads. In addition, it helps to develop measures that might go beyond just subjective ratings. The fact that water has specific freezing and melting points can be used to establish the temperature with a great deal of certainty. Furthermore, once substances (such as the mercury that was once commonly used in thermometers) whose volumes change systematically with temperature are identified, this fact can be used to develop even more precise ways to assess temperature across a broader range. In short, physicists can "pull themselves up by their bootstraps" to develop increasingly precise measures of a phenomenon that was first identified because people noticed something interesting about the world.

This same general outline applies to personality measurement. Basically, personality psychologists start with the idea that if people perceive stable characteristics in themselves and the people around them, then perhaps their perceptions reflect something real that is "out there" in the world. If so, then such subjective impressions can be used to "bootstrap" a way to better and better measures. Of course, there is the possibility that what people perceive is not actually a true picture of someone's personality (and perhaps it really could be all in their minds; recall our prior discussion of this issue in Chapter 1), but researchers can test the possibility that it does reflect something real in increasingly sophisticated ways. So one of the first steps that psychologists can take to measure personality is to ask people about their subjective impressions of their own and other people's personality and then test whether there is evidence that these subjective ratings have meaning.

For instance, researchers can test whether there is agreement among observers about a particular target person's personality. In addition, we can test whether these subjective ratings correspond to consequential outcomes in the world. Are people judged to be conscientiousness and dutiful more likely to be promoted to higherlevel positions in an organization? The idea is to test for agreement and then to see if the consensus ratings predict things they should. Researchers might ask five people to rate Bill on his levels of conscientiousness and then test those ratings for agreement and then to see if those ratings predict his GPA next year.

In general, research supports the idea that agreement about people's personalities exists (at least to a nonzero degree) and that the measures that result do, indeed, predict outcomes. As just one example, Connelly and Ones (2010) conducted a meta-analysis (remember, this is a study that summarizes results from many different studies) on the usefulness of observer reports of personality for prediction. They showed that observers tended to agree with one another, with the ratings that the target person himself or herself provides, and with actual behavior that the person exhibits. This suggests that people's subjective impressions of their own and others' personality characteristics reflect real patterns in behavior that are being observed. Ideally, this process of testing should allow psychologists to create better and better measures of personality, perhaps ultimately resulting in measures that do not require subjective evaluations at all (though we are currently a long way off from this, at least as a primary measure of personality).

The term *psychometric* is used to describe this type of investigation into the properties of psychological measures. Two specific psychometric properties that researchers typically evaluate are called *reliability* and *validity*. Reliability refers to the extent to which a measure is free from random errors of measurement. Precision is a quality of measure associated with reliability. Validity refers to the extent to which a measure actually tests what we think it tests. Basically, do scores mean what researchers think they mean? Accuracy is a quality of a measure associated with validity. Reliability and validity may sound similar at first, so let us describe these concepts (and the processes used to test them) in more detail.

First, reliability focuses on the extent to which a measure is free from what is called *random measurement error*. Imagine that you were taking a paper-and-pencil personality measure where you were asked to indicate whether a variety of statements (like "I enjoy parties") applied to you. Typically, respondents are asked to use yes-or-no responses or numeric rating scales like "1—*does not describe me at all*" to "5—*describes me perfectly*." In this case, however, imagine that when reading the item "I rarely get my work done on time" (an item that might measure the personality trait of conscientiousness), you read too quickly and think that it says "I get my work done on time" (notice the missing "rarely"). In this case, you might give a score of 5 instead of the 1 that you would have given had you read the item correctly. This type of mistake—one that is unlikely to be repeated in exactly the same way if you answered the same question at a different time—is a random error that makes you appear less conscientious than you really are. (You answered that rarely getting your work done on time describes you perfectly!) Other similar errors occur if you mistakenly mark 1 instead of 5, if you put the correct response on the wrong line of the answer sheet, or if you accidentally omit a response. These types of errors occur because of random flukes and don't systematically bias your results one way or the other; sometimes they may make you score higher on a trait and other times lower. However, they are errors because they make you appear different than you really are. Reliability is a concept that helps psychometricians (those who study psychometric properties) evaluate the impact of these errors.

If we can't see personality, and therefore can't tell what the right answer should have been for any particular item, how do we know how much random measurement error there is? In general, tests of reliability focus on how consistent or repeatable a response is. Again, thinking about the example above, where you might have misread the item "I rarely get my work done on time," this specific error is unlikely to occur in the exact same way on a different occasion. One way to test reliability is simply to administer the same test on more than one occasion to see whether the answers are the same. To the extent that they are, the measure is reliable; to the extent that they deviate, the measure is unreliable. This is commonly done when people are checking their weight on a scale at the gym. People might step on and off the scale to take repeated measures in quick succession to document that the scale is giving the same reading. This basic principle extends to other ways of testing reliability in psychology. For instance, perhaps there are two items about getting one's work done on time. Even if you make a mistake on the first one, you probably won't make the same mistake on the second. Any inconsistencies across these similar items provides an indication of how unreliable a measure is. Or researchers might give you the same questionnaire on two different days to make sure you give the same responses. Psychometricians use many such procedures to test whether a measure is reliable.

Notice that with these tests of reliability, there is no consideration that people are providing the "correct" answer, just that they are providing consistent answers. You might be a terribly unconscientious person who lies on a personality questionnaire and responds consistently to items that indicate high conscientiousness. So your responses would contribute to high reliability, even though they did not reveal anything useful about your personality. Likewise, a scale designed to measure weight might consistently give the same number, but that number might not actually represent your true weight. This kind of distinction reflects the difference between reliability and validity. Reliability generally focuses on whether a personality measurement is consistent or repeatable; validity gets at the more difficult question of whether that personality measure is measuring what it is really supposed to measure. Reliability is about precision. Did the scale at the gym give you the same output reading the five different times you stepped on the scale in quick succession? As you can imagine, questions about validity are somewhat more difficult to answer than questions about reliability, given that personality attributes are latent entities.

Difficult does not mean impossible, though, and again, there are established techniques for evaluating how much validity is exhibited by personality measures. In general, tests of validity require a bit more judgment on the part of the person who is conducting these tests. Researchers need to have an idea about how the measure should behave before it is possible to conduct tests of validity. Again, let's go back to the example of temperature. Imagine that you were an early physicist (one who had only an inkling of the physical principles that govern heat) who had recently developed a new mercury-based thermometer. You noticed that mercury expanded when the temperature felt warm and that it contracted when the temperature felt cold. Because of this, you thought that perhaps mercury could be used as a more precise indicator of temperature than your own subjective judgment. But before you could rely on this newfangled technology, you had to evaluate its validity. To do this, you would see whether the mercury thermometer corresponded well to the existing (but imperfect) measures that you already had, such as your own subjective ratings. You could also use it to see whether water turned to ice or began to boil when the mercury reached the same point on the new thermometer. In short, you would have certain expectations for how this new thermometer should behave, and you could test these expectations to see whether the measure appeared to be working well, even though you had no gold-standard measure of temperature with which to compare.

This is exactly how the development of personality measures proceeds. If the construct under investigation (say, a trait like conscientiousness) already has existing measures against which the new measure can be compared, then the scale developer will typically test whether the two measures provide similar results. If no measure exists, then the scale developer must have a well-specified theory about how people who vary along the characteristic of interest should behave, and he or she will then show that the new measure actually predicts these differences in behavior. Because there is no gold-standard criterion available, there is no single test that proves the validity of a measure. Rather, scale developers build up more and more evidence that the measure seems to be capturing the individual difference of interest.

It is not possible within the scope of this chapter to review the evidence regarding the reliability and validity of all personality measures. Instead, what we hoped to do was to provide the basic logic by which these measures are developed and evaluated to show that it is possible to create measures that capture some of the complexity of personality. It is up to the developers of the scales themselves (and the researchers who find value in the scales for their own research) to do the studies that evaluate reliability and validity; in general, when measures are first made available, they are accompanied by such evidence.

Despite the fact that a comprehensive review is beyond the scope of this chapter (and indeed, of the book), we can make a few general observations that counter the myth that personality is too complex to measure. First, measures of personality are reliable. We once conducted a study with one of our graduate students (Anusic, Lucas, & Donnellan, 2012) in which about 220 participants completed the same Big Five personality measure every week for about 8 weeks. Scores on the measures were highly correlated from week to week and from the first week to the last week. Consider scores for conscientiousness. The correlation from week 1 to week 2 was 0.82, and the correlation from the first week to the last was 0.80. As you know, these correlations are not perfect (remember, a correlation of 1.0 is a "perfect" correlation), but these figures are quite high. High reliabilities suggest that random measurement error does not have a substantial effect on the scores that the measures provide. Random measurement will almost always exist, but these high reliabilities show that researchers' efforts to reduce the effect of measurement error can be successful.[1]

Second, as we outlined in Chapter 2, scores on personality measures are frequently correlated with consequential outcomes in ways researchers expect. For example, conscientious individuals tend to get better grades, avoid risky behaviors that harm health, and live longer than those who are less conscientious. This pattern is exactly what we would expect given expectations about the nature of this specific trait domain. If you want an impressive single example of the long-term correlates of traits like conscientiousness, read the paper by Moffitt et al. (2011). They showed that childhood measures of conscientiousness (what they called self-control) statistically predicted a wide range of adult outcomes such as income, problems with substances, and physical health using a sample of more than 1,000 people followed from birth until their 30s. These effects were not explained away by IQ or family SES. It is hard to understand how those researchers could have found such results if self-control or conscientiousness were too complex to measure for any degree of accuracy.

All of this discussion and myth busting in this chapter should not be interpreted to mean that personality measurement is easy or ideal or without flaws. Personality measures probably do lag behind the reliability and validity of measures of intelligence, memory, or other cognitive abilities. Psychological measures are not as clear-cut as measures of temperature. Thus, there is room for improving personality measures. Indeed, this is an active area of study.

For example, researchers are trying to figure out how to deal with "faking" in employment selection contexts (or online dating contexts), where people probably try to make their personalities look better than they actually are in real life (see Chapter 7). People might want to make themselves appear nicer and more outgoing than they actually tend to be so as to impress an employer or potential dating partner. Other researchers try to figure out how to deal with "malingering" in medical contexts, where people might try to make themselves look worse than they actually are to receive more attention from medical personnel. For example, some people might wish to look like they have attention deficit problems to gain access to medications. Researchers who use informant reports try to deal with

---

[1] One of the simplest ways to deal with random measurement is to use long surveys so random errors on single items cancel out when all of the many items are averaged together. We only used four items to measure conscientiousness each week in our study to reduce response burden, so some of the measurement errors could have been reduced if we used a longer survey. The problem with long surveys, however, is that they can be boring for participants. Boredom can also contribute to random errors in responding.

problems of bias in these reports. If people are allowed to nominate who they would like to serve as informants, people may only ask those who they know have a positive impression to submit reports. Still other researchers try to improve survey designs to reduce respondent burden and motivate honest and engaged participation. Or they may try to find clever ways to detect when people are responding carelessly to survey questions.

It is also important to remember that personality measures do not necessarily require people—targets or their informants—to answer questions about personality. For example, researchers who study personality in children use lab-based tasks. When participants are too young to complete surveys, these types of observational studies can be quite useful. The list of potential methods goes on and on. Our point is that researchers are actively working to improve the technology of personality measurement.

As a final note, we return to the possibility that the myth that personality is too complex to be measured might come from people's own experiences receiving feedback about their personality. As we noted at the beginning of this chapter, this experience can sometimes be disappointing, because the feedback that we receive may not capture everything about who we are (or who we think we are). It is impossible to expect a small set of numbers or paragraph-length response to capture the full essence and complexity of how people see themselves. So, in that sense, yes, the totality of your entire personality may be too complex to be measured by a single questionnaire or a single interview.

It is important to remember, though, that developing a complex and perfectly complete description of each and every stable characteristic that a person has is not the primary goal of most of personality psychology. Instead, personality researchers want to capture specific characteristics that people may have and to investigate the processes underlying those characteristics. That may not allow them to know every detail about who a person is, but such investigations will provide a deeper understanding of why people do the things they do, and it can help predict broad patterns of future behavior that may have important real-world consequences. So part of our goal in refuting this myth is to point out that sometimes expectations for what personality measures can do are too high, and that psychometrically sound personality measures can tell psychologists quite a bit of important information about what a person is like, even if they do not tell everything. If you want to learn more about the science of creating personality surveys, there is an accessible and excellent paper by Simms (2008) that is well worth reading (see also Flake, Pek, & Hehman, 2017).

References

Anusic, I., Lucas, R. E., & Donnellan, M. B. (2012). Dependability of personality, life satisfaction, and affect in short-term longitudinal data. *Journal of Personality, 80*(1), 33–58.

Connelly, B. S., & Ones, D. S. (2010). An other perspective on personality: Meta-analytic integration of observers' accuracy and predictive validity. *Psychological Bulletin, 136*(6), 1092–1122.

Flake, J. K., Pek, J., & Hehman, E. (2017). Construct validation in social and personality research: Current practice and recommendations. *Social Psychological and Personality Science, 8*(4), 370–378.

Moffitt, T. E., Arseneault, L., Belsky, D., Dickson, N., Hancox, R. J., Harrington, H., … Sears, M. R. (2011). A gradient of childhood self-control predicts health, wealth, and public safety. *Proceedings of the National Academy of Sciences, 108*(7), 2693–2698.

Simms, L. J. (2008). Classical and modern methods of psychological scale construction. *Social and Personality Psychology Compass, 2*(1), 414–433.

Thorndike, E. L. (1918). The nature, purposes, and general methods of measurements of educational products. In G. M. Whipple (Ed.), *The seventeenth yearbook of the National Society for the Study of Education, Part II: The measurement of educational products* (pp. 16). Bloomington, IL: Public School Publishing Co.

7 PERSONALITY MEASURES CAN BE FAKED SO THEY ARE NOT VALID

Many of the topics discussed in this book focus on academic research related to personality characteristics. Personality researchers want to know, for instance, whether the intuition that personality traits are stable over time is correct; or they might want to know whether major life events affect people's personality in dramatic ways. To answer these questions, researchers typically ask people about their personality (using personality measures evaluated in psychometric terms; see Chapter 6) and then test whether their responses are consistent over time or whether they are related to the experience of various life events. These academic studies are not *high-stakes* testing settings, where the scores have direct implications for the test taker in terms of selection, advancement, or diagnosis. In such high-stakes settings, scores have implications for whether one is picked for a position or a promotion or is designated as having a medical condition with treatment implications. However, personality measures can be used in high-stakes settings, and that requires care. Some critics of personality research suggest that people might actively lie about their personalities in ways that would dramatically compromise the validity of the results in high-stakes testing. We briefly talked about faking in Chapter 6, and we acknowledge that worries about faking are greatly magnified in high-stakes settings where scores do matter.

Indeed, we have also noted that there are *applied* researchers who wish not just to understand personality characteristics and the processes that underlie them but also to use these measures in settings where knowing something about a person's personality might lead to better decisions regarding that specific individual. One of the most common applied

Great Myths of Personality, First Edition. M. Brent Donnellan and Richard E. Lucas.
© 2021 John Wiley & Sons, Inc. Published 2021 by John Wiley & Sons, Inc.

contexts for personality research is in selection settings. Employers may want to know, for instance, whether job candidates' personalities can help determine who will be a successful employee. If so, then personality tests might be an important selection tool that could help employers determine which of the candidates they should hire.

Using personality measures in applied settings follows from a long tradition of using cognitive tests for selection purposes. It is not uncommon, for instance, to have to take an intelligence test or more specific aptitude tests that are directly related to the tasks of a job when applying for a position. However, researchers and practitioners alike recognize one fundamental difference between these cognitive measures and personality tests—namely, the latter could be more susceptible to faking than the former. To accurately select the most desirable answer on an intelligence test (i.e., the correct one), one must have the abilities that the test is designed to assess. There actually has to be a correct answer! However, for personality tests using survey-type items, it might be much easier to figure out which answer is the most desirable answer and to select it even if it is not an accurate description of a person's personality. In selection contexts, there might be great pressure to answer personality questions in ways that maximize the desirability of the candidate, and therefore, faking is an important concern. This chapter addresses the idea that personality measures are so easily faked that they have no validity. Although we address faking both in research and in selection settings, it is obviously the latter situation where faking is of greatest concern.

As we have often emphasized throughout this book, there is typically an important kernel of truth to all the myths we address, and there is no clearer example of this than the issue discussed in this chapter. Although we present the idea that personality measures can be faked to such an extent that measures are worthless as a myth (because there are certain aspects of this claim that are certainly false), it is one of the myths about which personality researchers might disagree with each other most forcefully. Thus, we will present the various issues that arise when studying faking on personality tests and then give an overview of which issues have been resolved and which still lead to debate.

First, we need to clarify what we mean when we talk about faking in the context of personality tests. When discussing this issue, Morgeson et al. (2007) noted that one way to define faking is as "a deliberate attempt by an individual to mislead another person by concealing or falsifying information" (p. 691). In other words, people would be "faking" their scores on a personality questionnaire when they chose response options that they did not actually believe represented an accurate description of what their personality was like. One clear example of a situation in which this might be likely to occur would be in job application settings, where it might be obvious to applicants that they should portray themselves as being highly conscientious, even when they might actually be lazy and disorganized.

This definition is important because explicit faking can be distinguished from a different form of problematic responding, which occurs when people have inaccurate perceptions of what their personality is really like. For instance, some people may really believe that they are extremely organized and hard-working even when they are not. Thus, if these people were to respond affirmatively to personality questions that tap into the trait of conscientiousness, we wouldn't say that they were lying per se or even faking. In other words, such people are not trying to portray themselves as someone they know they are not in real life. This person just happens to suffer from a lack of self-insight. Nonetheless, this lack of self-insight would have the same negative impact on the accuracy of an assessment. These two types of incorrect responding are often conflated. It is hard to know, for example, when people are faking or simply deluded about their own attributes.

It is also important to point out that in most cases, faking is only an issue insofar as different people do it to a different extent. For instance, if in selection situations all applicants exaggerated how conscientious they were (relative to some absolute truth), then this would not be a problem, as the most conscientious people would still be selected. If everyone pumped up his or her score by the same amount, it wouldn't ultimately matter so long as the ordering of people from lowest to highest was preserved. Faking on personality tests is most likely to be a problem if some people do it and others do not. If so, then this changes the rank ordering on a personality trait, making some people look like they score higher on a trait more than others because of differences in honesty or self-insight. What is especially problematic is that more dishonest people would effectively look better on the test, a situation that can prove disastrous for organizations selecting employees. So, in a selection context, the person low in conscientiousness who fakes his or her responses may end up looking like a better fit for a job than someone who is actually quite high in conscientiousness but responds to the personality tests honestly. Thus, much research on "faking" in personality assessment focuses on identifying who is most likely to fake and whether steps can be taken to correct for this propensity.

Personality researchers attempt to detect faking and correct for it using a number of different approaches. First, to determine whether faking can be a problem, researchers often compare groups of people who take personality tests in "low-stakes" settings (such as in a research study, where the scores will not be used to make decisions about the individual taking the test) to groups who take the same measures in "high-stakes" settings (such as when applying for a job). The idea is that those in the low-stakes testing situation have little motivation to fake, and thus, this comparison should provide evidence regarding the size of the problem when personality measures are used in these settings. This approach assumes that very little faking goes on in typical research settings (a point we will address later in the chapter). These studies suggest there is faking, but the size of the effect (and consistency across studies) is not as dramatic as might be expected (Morgeson et al., 2007).

Comparing high-stakes to low-stakes testing situations is useful for determining whether people fake their scores on average, but it does not help determine who is faking. To do this, researchers must turn to alternative strategies. The most common of these is to create scales designed to detect the tendency to fake. For instance, one common strategy is to incorporate questions into the test that sound desirable but that few people would actually endorse. For instance, respondents may be asked whether they agree with the statement "I have never told a lie in my life." Although endorsing this item would be seen as desirable (because honesty is a valued characteristic, especially for employers who are searching for good employees), few if any people can truly say that they have never told a lie. Thus, if some respondents respond affirmatively to a large number of items that describe these desirable-but-extremely rare behaviors, then we may assume that these people are faking. The hope is that the scores on these faking measures can be used to "correct" the measures of more substantive personality traits to obtain a more accurate picture of what the person is like.

Although the idea behind the use of faking scales is sound, in practice they pose some difficulty. For instance, if faking scales are to be useful, studies should show that once faking is statically adjusted for in complex models, the ability to predict some criterion (like a verifiable behavior) from self-reports improves (recall faking per se is a concern using self-report measures). However, most research on this topic suggests that this is not the case. In one study, McCrae and Costa (1983) included a scale designed to detect faking along with both self-reports and informant reports of personality. If people were "faking good," then once this tendency was taken into account with statistical tools, there should be better agreement between self and informant ratings. Instead, the opposite was true; once "faking" was controlled or adjusted for, agreement between self and informant ratings often decreased. Indeed, in a meta-analytic review, Ones, Viswesvaran, and Reiss (1996) found that controlling for scores on measures designed to detect faking rarely increased the correlations between personality and relevant behavioral criteria and often reduced them.

This is a surprising result—statistically controlling for measures designed to detect faking often impairs validity. Why might this be the case? Part of the reason is that although the idea of creating questions that can identify fakers sounds simple enough, this task is actually quite difficult. Research into the nature of these questions shows that there may actually be multiple reasons why people respond affirmatively to them. For instance, Paulhus (1984) showed that questions designed to assess faking generally map on to two different underlying dimensions, one that reflects more of an intentional attempt to present oneself in a favorable light (a dimension called "impression management") and a second that appears to reflect self-deception rather than actual lying. Importantly, this tendency toward self-deception appears to be associated with actual positive personality characteristics. This makes sense: People who want to look good for others may actually have desirable attributes and show signs of positive adjustment. For instance, Diener, Sandvik, Pavot, and Gallagher (1991) showed that people who score high on measures of social desirability tend to be rated by others as being happy. When researchers control for this tendency, they may be controlling for valid individual differences that are actually related in meaningful ways to behavioral outcomes.

In addition, even if we focus just on the impression management component, it is possible that those people who know what the "right thing to say" is on a personality questionnaire may actually have greater ability to perform the desired behavior in important situations like a job. In other words, those who strive to create good impressions on job-related personality questionnaires (even when the result is an inaccurate report of their true personality) may also be able to maintain this good behavior if and when they are actually hired for the job. So it is possible that even the narrower construct of impression management may be positively associated with characteristics that actually predict real-world behavior in positive ways. A person who has no clue as to what his or her employers actually want in their employees might turn out to be kind of a disaster in the workplace. Thus, controlling for impression management could harm the predictive correlations of relevant attribute.

The large body of research that focuses on faking leads to a few important conclusions. First, in low-stakes settings, including those that are typical for personality research, there is little evidence that people fake their responses in ways that dramatically affect the validity of the measures.

People may exaggerate the extent to which they perform desirable behaviors, but the tendency to do this is itself a personality characteristic that is associated with positive outcomes. Accordingly, statistically controlling for this tendency does not consistently improve the validity of personality measures.

Second, more faking does occur in high-stakes settings than in low-stakes settings (Morgeson et al., 2007). In other words, people provide more positive responses to personality questionnaires when those measures are administered as part of a job interview than as part of a simple research study. However, even here, it is not clear how much of an effect this has on the validity of the measures. Although we would not go so far as to say that the idea that validity can be impaired (even a little) in selection settings is a myth, the research that has been conducted on this topic does not clearly show that validity is substantially impacted. Indeed, when the same approaches described above are used to assess the effect that faking has on validity in high-stakes settings, the evidence is quite mixed (Morgeson et al., 2007).

We should note, however, that just because faking has not been shown to invalidate personality measures in selection settings, this does not mean that personality measures are free from problems when used for this purpose. Indeed, when a group of editors of journals related to personnel selection got together to discuss the impact that faking had on validity, most agreed that the effect was minimal, but this was partly due to the fact that the ability of personality measures to predict objective job outcomes is relatively modest in the first place (Morgeson et al., 2007). To be sure, personality predicts consequential outcomes (as we discussed in Chapter 2). Yet despite this fact, personality questionnaires may still not be sensitive enough to unambiguously distinguish between a good employee and a bad employee, even in the best of circumstances. In addition, although faking is perhaps not a major problem for personality tests, the potential for faking is much greater with personality tests than with cognitive tests like those that assess intelligence. Therefore, if organizations started to use personality tests more frequently to select their employees, then a set of "correct" or "desired by employers" answers could easily be revealed on the Internet, and unscrupulous job candidates could simply memorize and report these desirable responses.

The solution to these problems might be found in refining the personality measures used for selection in applied contexts and in clarifying the reasons why employers might want to select particular kinds of employees for certain kinds of tasks. People applying for jobs have incentive to be honest because it is unpleasant to be selected for a job that is a poor match for your personality. If you are not especially extraverted and outgoing, a job in sales might be miserable. If you are not especially high on conscientiousness and attention to detail, an accounting job might also be miserable. Selection based on personality assessment might be improved by using multiple measures of personality and by recognizing that employers probably want to select applicants who excel at a range of behaviors. These behaviors are themselves multiply determined (see Chapter 1). Certain personality characteristics might be helpful for some job duties but harmful for others. All of this is just a brief way of saying that personnel selection is complicated.

In summary, it is a myth to assert that faking on personality tests in research settings is widespread and that this behavior completely invalidates the use of personality measures in research or applied settings. As we have discussed elsewhere, personality tests are not perfect, but they have some degree of validity that allows them to be used fruitfully in research settings. As personality psychologists move into more applied settings, faking becomes a bigger concern. Currently, evidenced is mixed as to whether validity is affected in these settings, but concerns are large enough that research continues in this area. And we reiterate the possibility that employees also have an incentive to be honest when thinking about long-term success in a job. A mismatch between employees and their position creates problems for both organizations and the individual.

References

Diener, E., Sandvik, E., Pavot, W., & Gallagher, D. (1991). Response artifacts in the measurement of subjective well-being. *Social Indicators Research*, 24(1), 35–56.

McCrae, R. R., & Costa, P. T. (1983). Social desirability scales: More substance than style. *Journal of Consulting and Clinical Psychology*, 51(6), 882–888.

Morgeson, F. P., Campion, M. A., Dipboye, R. L., Hollenbeck, J. R., Murphy, K., & Schmitt, N. (2007). Reconsidering the use of personality tests in personnel selection contexts. *Personnel Psychology*, 60(3), 683–729.

Ones, D. S., Viswesvaran, C., & Reiss, A. D. (1996). Role of social desirability in personality testing for personnel selection: The red herring. *Journal of Applied Psychology*, 81(6), 660–679.

Paulhus, D. L. (1984). Two-component models of socially desirable responding. *Journal of Personality and Social Psychology*, 46(3), 598–609. doi:10.1037/0022-3514.46.3.598

8 THE MYERS–BRIGGS TYPE INDICATOR IS THE BEST APPROACH FOR ASSESSING PERSONALITY

Thus far, we have noted that personality attributes have potential value because they are associated with consequential outcomes in people's lives. If personality traits reflect stable, internal characteristics that influence the choices that people make and the behaviors they exhibit, then being able to assess these characteristics efficiently would be extremely useful. Employers often want to know whether a specific person will perform well on the job, and school admissions officers want to know whether a potential student is likely to thrive at a particular university; personality measures might help identify qualified candidates in these situations. Indeed, even those of us who are simply curious about our personalities might find scientifically valid feedback about our traits to be enlightening. This feedback might provide useful insight into the patterns of behavior that we exhibit and might aid us in preparing for future experiences. So it should be no surprise that many employers, supervisors, teachers, and managers use personality measures to get to know their applicants, students, and employees better. People complete measures of personality to learn about themselves.

Those of you who have come across personality measures being used for these purposes might have experience with one famous measure, the Myers–Briggs Type Indicator (MBTI) (Myers, 1962). The MBTI is based, at least loosely, on a theory of personality proposed by Carl Jung in the early 20th century (Jung, 1971). Jung was initially a follower and colleague of Freud's, and like Freud, he emphasized the effect of unconscious

Great Myths of Personality, First Edition. M. Brent Donnellan and Richard E. Lucas.
© 2021 John Wiley & Sons, Inc. Published 2021 by John Wiley & Sons, Inc.

processes on thoughts, feelings, and behaviors. We will not go into his theories in much detail, other than to note that they do not play a large role in modern personality research. Students often learn about Jung in the context of the history of psychology rather than as a figure whose thinking actively shapes new research.

The MBTI was designed to assess four dichotomous characteristics that were linked with ideas that Jung proposed in his writing (the measure was not designed by Jung himself). People who take the MBTI get one of two "letters" or scores for each of these four characteristics, leading them to be classified into one of 16 distinct types that are based on the combination of scores they receive. Specifically, people receive scores for whether they take an extraverted or introverted (E vs. I) approach to the world (a characteristic that reflects whether they attend to and are influenced by things "out there" in the world or ideas inside their head), whether they rely on a sensing or intuitive approach to perception (S vs. N), whether they rely on a thinking or feeling approach to judgment (T vs. F), and whether they tend to use a judging or perceptive approach to the world (J vs. P). Presumably, the scores that people receive provide information about the types of jobs for which they might be most suitable. For instance, McCaulley (2000) compared the distribution of types for a group of counselors and managers. The managers tended to be classified as sensing, thinking, and judging, whereas the counselors tended to be classified as intuiting, feeling, and perceiving (there appeared to be a mix of extraverted and introverted types across the two occupations).

Although the MBTI is widely used in applied settings, it is hardly ever used within academic psychology (McCrae & Costa, 1989; Pittenger, 2005). This fact alone does not mean that the measure has little value. It is quite possible that a measure would be unpopular within academic circles because it does not fit with popular theories even though it might have utility for those who use it in applied settings. However, it is usually the case that tools that have applied value also attract interest from researchers (if the tool works, academics want to know why), and many applied users hope that evidence in support of the validity of their preferred tools actually exists. Thus, before considering the feedback you might receive from the MBTI, it is important to understand the criticisms and concerns that research psychologists have raised about the measure.

The biggest concern about the MBTI is the typological approach on which it is based. Remember from Chapter 5 that there was a debate within psychology about whether personality characteristics should be considered as dichotomous types or continuous traits. When psychologists speak of types, they are typically referring to distinct groups of people—people within a type are very similar to one another and are categorically different from those of a separate type. In contrast, when psychologists speak of continuous traits, they usually talk about a distribution, where there are people at all levels of a given trait (e.g., extremely low to extremely high). So, if introversion–extraversion reflects two dichotomous types, then there should be a group of people who were very clearly introverted, and this group should be quite different from a separate group of people who were highly extraverted; few people should be in the middle. In contrast, if introversion–extraversion is a continuous trait, then the dimension would reflect a continuum of scores, and people could score anywhere along this distribution.

As we noted in Chapter 5, most personality attributes generally exhibit a continuous distribution rather than a binary distribution with two extreme poles. In fact, as we discussed in that chapter, it is difficult to find any personality characteristics that clearly display the features of discrete types. In addition, most scores on trait measures are reasonably normally distributed, which means that most people tend to fall toward the middle of the dimension, with increasingly smaller numbers of people at the extremes. So, although people (scientists and nonscientists alike) may talk informally about extraverts and introverts, the truth is that most people are in the middle of a distribution ranging from extremely extraverted to extremely introverted, with relatively few people falling at these extremes.

So, at a minimum there is very little evidence that the dimensions that underlie MBTI scores have distributions that support a typological conceptualization of personality traits (Pittenger, 2005). This may seem like a minor issue, but it can be quite serious. Psychologists have long advised against taking continuous dimensions and simplifying them by turning them into dichotomous types (MacCallum, Zhang, Preacher, & Rucker, 2002). Some of the reasons can be illustrated by considering how type-based measures might be used in applied settings.

Imagine that you were taking a personality questionnaire and you accidentally responded "yes" to a question that was supposed to measure the trait of extraversion when you really meant to respond "no." Remember from Chapter 6 that this is a mistake that would affect the reliability of the measure because it contributes to measurement error. Normally, this error would not make much of a difference; you might get a slightly higher extraversion score than you otherwise would have, but as long as there were many other items, then this error wouldn't dramatically affect your score. But for a measure like the MBTI, such errors can move someone from one dichotomous category all the way to the other. So with inappropriate dichotomization, very small errors can lead to major misclassifications. These errors are even more likely to occur among people who have scores near the middle of the scale. If managers tried to assign employees to specific tasks based on their scores on the MBTI, this could be a big problem. Two people who are actually very similar to one another (both scoring near the middle of the scale) could be classified completely differently, leading to different assignments for two people with quite similar personalities.

Again, think about it this way: If most people are not highly extra-verted or introverted but rather score near the middle of the scale, then very subtle influences may move their scores up or down slightly at any given assessment. However, this also means that if they were to take the measure again, those same influences may push them subtly in the oppo-site direction, leading to an entirely different classification. Pittenger (2005) noted that the test–retest reliabilities of the MBTI subscales are often lower than what would be expected given the underlying theory (which states that these characteristics should be consistent in adult-hood). So, the psychometric properties of the MBTI are not as optimal as one might hope.

Thus far, we have focused on the utility of the typological approach to each individual dimension of the MBTI (remember respondents get four such scores). In other words, we have been asking whether it makes sense to think of those scoring high on the extraversion subscale as being cat-egorically different than those who score low on this scale. However, a second, related issue concerns what, precisely, the combination of MBTI scores tells us about a person. As McCrae and Costa (1989) noted in their critique of the MBTI, the authors of the MBTI posited that this combina-tion of scores provides information that goes beyond what the individual scores can tell us. This is somewhat of a tricky idea, so let us explain it in more detail.

Imagine you took the MBTI and received scores for each of the four subscales; let's say that like McCaulley's (2000) sample of managers, your score was E for extraverted, S for sensing, T for thinking, and J for judging. According to the developers of this measure, this combination of scores is thought to be informative, independent from what we know about the four individual scores that contribute to this categorization. In other words, we know that extraverts might be different from introverts and that thinking people may be different from feeling people; but the MBTI approach suggests that the unique combination of characteristics tells us something beyond what the individual components tell us. McCrae and Costa (1989) argued that there is very little evidence that this is true.

The concerns we have talked about so far are reservations on what are called *psychometric properties* of the scales included in the MBTI. These concerns focus very narrowly on the precision of a measure and how good of a job the measures do in assessing what they are supposed to assess (again, see Chapter 6 for a fuller discussion of these issues). However, one can also criticize the MBTI on conceptual grounds. We focus on two of them here.

First, remember that the MBTI is based on theories proposed by Carl Jung in the early 20th century. Jung developed these theories well before modern personality psychology emerged as a field. Thus, he developed his ideas without the benefit of a strong program of empirical research where hypotheses are formally operationalized and tested against results from large samples. Classic psychoanalytic thinking was often based on case studies and what amounted to hunches about human nature. In comparison to more modern models of personality, very little empirical work had been conducted to verify the basic tenets of this model at the time the MBTI was developed. Thus, beyond the methodological concerns about the MBTI, modern researchers may question the theoretical and empirical foundation on which it is based.

In contrast, alternative models of personality have been based on a stronger empirical tradition. For instance, the most widely accepted model of personality trait structure today is the Big Five model, which consists of five broad trait domains: extraversion, neuroticism, agreeableness, conscientiousness, and openness to new experiences (John, Naumann, & Soto, 2008; McCrae & Costa, 2003). Although this model is not free from controversy, it was developed through multiple approaches that ultimately converged at a similar answer about the general structure of human personality. For example, early researchers searched the dictionary to identify all words that could be used to describe people's personality. Noting that many of these were synonymous, researchers used a variety of statistical techniques to reduce redundancy, arriving over and over again at the answer that five broad traits provided a reasonable description of human personality.[1] Other researchers looked at broad ranges of existing personality questionnaires to see whether they could be summarized with a smaller number of dimensions, and again, they arrived at a similar answer. Thus, many personality psychologists have used a variety of robust methods to try to identify what personality traits exist and are needed to describe people's personality, and these efforts typically

---

[1] If you are interested in a critical but technical perspective on the Big Five, consult Block (1995).

led to similar conclusions. No similar effort underlies the development of the MBTI. Importantly, McCrae and Costa (1989) showed that the scores from the MBTI can be subsumed by the broader, more empirically supported Big Five model. Because the psychometric properties of these alternative measures are stronger, and because the Big Five model captures a broader range of characteristics, a convincing case can be made that both academic and applied users should prefer established alternatives to the MBTI.

So does this mean that you can safely ignore the results you obtain from the MBTI because they tell you absolutely nothing of value? We won't go that far. Indeed, if you look closely at the items on the MBTI, many of them probably look a lot like those that you find in a measure of the Big Five. And, as we discussed above, McCrae and Costa (1989) showed that the individual MBTI scales—at least when scored continuously—correlate reasonably strongly with measures of the Big Five. Thus, people interested in personality attributes can glean better kinds of information from other approaches.

We believe that the most fundamental problem with the MBTI is that better alternatives exist for understanding personality. The use of dichotomous scoring procedures limits the ability of the MBTI to tell us something useful about people's personality, and measures based on alternative models probably provide a more comprehensive picture of what people are like. Thus, we think it is far more profitable to think about dimensions of personality and leave the MBTI behind. Next time someone asks you about which four letters best represent you, you might try to explain to them where you stand on the Big Five domains.

References

Block, J. (1995). A contrarian view of the five-factor approach to personality description. *Psychological Bulletin, 117*(2), 187–215.

John, O. P., Naumann, L. P., & Soto, C. J. (2008). Paradigm shift to the integrative Big Five trait taxonomy. In O. P. John, R. W. Robins, & L. A. Pervin (Eds.), *Handbook of personality: Theory and research, Vol. 3* (pp. 114–158). New York, NY: Guilford Press.

Jung, C. G. (1971). *Psychological types.* Princeton, NJ: Princeton University Press.

MacCallum, R. C., Zhang, S., Preacher, K. J., & Rucker, D. D. (2002). On the practice of dichotomization of quantitative variables. *Psychological Methods, 7*(1), 19–40.

McCaulley, M. H. (2000). Myers-Briggs type indicator: A bridge between counseling and consulting. *Consulting Psychology Journal: Practice and Research, 52*(2), 117.

McCrae, R. R., & Costa, P. T., Jr. (1989). Reinterpreting the Myers-Briggs type indicator from the perspective of the five-factor model of personality. *Journal of Personality, 57*(1), 17–40.

McCrae, R. R., & Costa, P., T., Jr. (2003). *Personality in adulthood, a five-factor theory perspective* (2nd ed.). New York, NY: Guilford Press.

Myers, I. B. (1962). *The Myers-Briggs type indicator*. Palo Alto, CA: Consulting Psychologists Press.

Pittenger, D. J. (2005). Cautionary comments regarding the Myers-Briggs type indicator. *Consulting Psychology Journal: Practice and Research, 57*(3), 210.

9 PROJECTIVE TESTS ARE THE BEST APPROACH FOR MEASURING PERSONALITY

> The Rorschach is held in great esteem by many psychologists for its ability to access intrapsychic material, whereas others point to the Rorschach as a prime example of unscientific psychological assessment.
>
> (Hunsley and Bailey, 1999, p. 266)

As we discussed in Chapter 6, personality attributes are not directly observable in the same ways that characteristics like height and weight are observable. Personality characteristics are not as easily assessed as physical traits. Consider how straightforward it is to assess a person's weight by having him or her step on a scale. The resulting number is rendered in commonly understood units such as pounds or kilograms, and most scales give about the same answer about a person's weight if that person steps on one again right after stepping off (modern scales are precise or highly reliable, to use psychometric terminology). Moreover, a person might not like the number shown on a scale—and he or she might step back on the scale to verify the number—but few people are willing to say that the number lacks validity. Most people accept the accuracy of the readout that a scale provides, and very few would question the whole enterprise of stepping on scales to measure their weight. If only personality measurement were this straightforward!

As it stands, there is no equivalent to a scale for measuring weight that can tell psychologists very precisely how extraverted or conscientious a person is, using units that are commonly understood and objectively

Great Myths of Personality, First Edition. M. Brent Donnellan and Richard E. Lucas.
© 2021 John Wiley & Sons, Inc. Published 2021 by John Wiley & Sons, Inc.

defined. Having tackled the question of whether personality can be measured in Chapter 6 and the question of whether one particular measure—the Myers–Briggs Type Indicator—is valid in Chapter 8, we now turn to a question of whether an entire class of measures has utility for the field. This class of measures is a set called *projective tests*.

The basic idea of a projective test is to have research participants, clients, or patients look at standardized images such as inkblots (as in the case of the famous Rorschach test) or evocative drawings or photographs (as in the case of the less famous but still used Thematic Apperception Test) and narrate how they interpret the images.[1] This process is usually done in a quiet room where responses are recorded and later transcribed by the person administering the projective test. Responses are then sometimes scored by standardized procedures or otherwise coded, such as the Exner (2003) system for the Rorschach inkblots. The ambiguous images or photos serve as stimuli that evoke responses that are thought to be diagnostic of people's personality. The idea is that a person's characteristic thoughts and feelings—in other words, features of his or her personality—are, in a sense, projected onto the ambiguous images (hence the name projective tests).[2] For instance, a person who feels alienated and rejected by the world might be more likely to see images as scary, violent, and hostile, whereas a secure and well-adjusted person would not (at least according to the basic theory underlying projective tests).

---

[1] This chapter will focus on data regarding the Rorschach test as this projective (or performance) test has been more extensively debated than the Thematic Apperception Test and other similar measures. However, we do want to caution that our conclusions about the Rorschach may not apply to the Thematic Apperception Test (see, e.g., Schultheiss, 2007; Schultheiss & Pang, 2007).

[2] Some authors object to the term *projective* (e.g., Meyer & Kurtz, 2006) in reference to these kinds of tests. The arguments often boil down to two major concerns. First, projection refers to a specific type of Freudian defense mechanism that may not be the actual mechanism behind responding to all ambiguous stimuli such as inkblots. Second, the term projective is often contrasted with the term objective in the literature in ways that appear pejorative to projective tests and privileging to self-report, clinician-report, or informant-report methods (see Meyer & Kurtz, 2006). Objectivity is a critical element of science, and thus no one wants his or her method to be considered anything less than objective. This raises the issue of what then to call these kinds of assessments, and no single label appears to satisfy all concerns. One option gaining traction in the literature is to call projective tests as performance assessments of personality (e.g., Bornstein, 2011b; Mihura, Meyer, Dumitrascu, & Bombel, 2013). The idea is that participants perform certain behaviors (i.e., provide a verbal description of an inkblot) in response to stimuli. Although we respect the arguments raised by Meyer and Kurtz (2006), we use the term projective throughout this chapter given its historical usage when referring to the Rorschach. If the term projective is bothersome, feel free to use performative in this chapter. We think our points will hold up.

Again, proponents of projective tests often believe that what someone sees in an ambiguous stimulus provides insights into how that person's mind works. In more psychological terms, the idea is that test takers use their *schemas*—their representations of concepts in memory—about themselves and their social world to interpret the ambiguous stimuli. Proponents of this method may also believe that projective tests are a way to measure elements of personality about which a person may not be consciously aware. People might know if they are extraverted or not, but they may be less aware, for instance, of their tendencies to depend excessively on other people (see Bornstein, 2011a). Thus, projective tests might be more useful in cases where people lack understanding of their own personalities or in cases where people may be prone to self-deception. Moreover, projective tests might be harder to actually fake (see Chapter 7) given that there is no obviously correct answer to provide when evaluating ambiguous images.

Addressing the myth

The use of projective tests in psychology turns out to be somewhat controversial. The primary concern is that such measures may have psychometric deficiencies (e.g., Lilienfeld, Wood, & Garb, 2000). In other words, these measures may lack reliability and validity. One response to this concern is that any method for measuring personality such as projective tests (the subject of this chapter), self-reports (i.e., asking the person questions about his or her personality), or informant reports (i.e., asking people who know a target well such as spouses, friends, parents, or coworkers) has both strengths and weaknesses. The particular mix of strengths and weaknesses might depend on the personality attribute in question and the intended purpose of the scores (e.g., is the goal to predict job performance or to understand the correlates of happiness in basic research?). Self-reports might be adequate for some purposes but not others. Accordingly, it is impossible to unequivocally proclaim that one method is universally superior to all others when it comes to measuring personality.

Nonetheless, this response of hesitancy to proclaim any method of measuring personality absolutely superior to another provides a way to approach the issue by considering the relative merits of projective tests against other approaches for assessing personality. This perspective also means that researchers can consider specific attributes and intended purposes and then decide whether projective tests are better than alternatives such as self- or informant-report measures. Put differently, any answer about the strengths and weaknesses of a measure has to take into account the way the measure will be used.

The most common method for assessing personality is self-report. When using self-report methods, researchers simply ask people a series of questions about their personality using responses that can easily be translated to numbers. These responses can then be summarized numerically to quantify a person's standing on a personality attribute. This is a quick and efficient method for assessing personality because no interpretations of the basic responses are needed. For instance, many contemporary personality measures assess specific attributes like extraversion using simple self-report items like "I am talkative" or "I get a lot of excitement and positive energy from going to parties." Scores are directly derived from the self-reports rather than from transcribing and then coding verbal descriptions of how someone views ambiguous stimuli.

Considering the evidence

There is a large literature comparing the performance of self-report measures to projective tests like the Rorschach as methods for assessing personality. This literature has been summarized in several meta-analyses (i.e., a statistical summary of the existing studies in a defined literature). Before describing those results, we need to digress a bit and say something about how to interpret a literature when different meta-analyses reach different conclusions.

Conflicting meta-analyses are a normal part of science, and the existence of discrepant meta-analytic results often requires experts to review each meta-analysis to see if the decisions and conclusions made by the authors of the meta-analysis are reasonable. Sometimes, a meta-analysis is clearly flawed because of poor decision rules for finding studies or coding effect sizes (see Chapter 2), whereas in other cases the issues are less clear-cut. For example, there are ongoing discussions about how meta-analyses should handle research studies that were conducted but never published; does the fact that they were not peer reviewed and published in a journal mean that they can safely be ignored (Ferguson & Brannick, 2012; but see Rothstein & Bushman, 2012)? If they should not be ignored, how can meta-analysts make sure they have located research that may not be found in empirical journals? Different answers to these questions can lead to differences in results across multiple meta-analyses focused on the same underlying questions. Sometimes different meta-analyses have no obvious flaws but still come to different conclusions, a situation that suggests that further research is needed to resolve the question. Hopefully the different meta-analytic results are at least useful in providing good hints for what kinds of additional research is needed to provide a more definitive answer.

So, what do meta-analytic summaries say about the relative merits of projective tests like the Rorschach? A relatively early but influential meta-analysis by Parker, Hanson, and Hunsley (1988) seemed promising. They summarized studies from 1970 to 1981 published in two journals. The point was to compare the psychometric properties of the Rorschach to a widely used measure of personality in clinical settings called the Minnesota Multiphasic Personality Inventory (MMPI). The authors concluded that the Rorschach had what is called *convergent validity* with the MMPI—this means that results from the two measures tended to agree with one another. However, this meta-analysis also found that there weren't many studies from which strong conclusions could be drawn: The authors were only able to locate five studies to include in their meta-analysis. The authors of this early (and limited) meta-analysis concluded that the "Rorschach and MMPI have acceptable and roughly equivalent psychometric properties when used in appropriate circumstances" (p. 372).

Garb, Florio, and Grove (1998) identified potential concerns with the Parker et al. (1988) meta-analysis. They conducted their own meta-analysis with an eye toward expanding the number of studies that were included in the statistical summary (while also improving other statistical decisions), and they found that the Rorschach seemed to do worse than the MMPI when judged using standard psychometric criteria. They ultimately concluded that "validity is better for the MMPI than for the Rorschach" (p. 404). Later, in 2001, Meyer and Archer conducted yet another analysis of the Parker et al. (1988) dataset and concluded that the evidence pointed to equivalence of the MMPI and the Rorschach. Thus, at best there seems to be little reason to proclaim the Rorschach as a superior method for assessing personality at a global level.

The contradictory meta-analyses provide a broad-strokes perspective on the literature, but they do not address a more specific issue about the assessment of particular personality attributes (see Garb, Wood, Lilienfeld, & Nezworski, 2005). The Rorschach can be scored in different ways to measure different attributes. There are some indications that ways of scoring the Rorschach measure have the ability to detect psychosis (a severe impairment of thoughts and emotions in which the individual has lost contact with reality), whereas the ability of Rorschach measures to detect depressive symptoms is less clear (Mihura et al., 2013, p. 557). Mihura et al. conducted a meta-analysis and suggested that there was empirical support for Rorschach scales designed to detect psychosis as well as cognitive complexity. Moreover, the authors suggested that the Rorschach scales would improve upon self-report measures of these attributes. Thus, projective tests might have some utility for certain kinds of psychological disorders and especially those related to disorganized thinking that might be harder to measure with self-reports.

Summing up

The Rorschach is a controversial measure that evokes passionate feelings in some quarters of psychology. The safest reading of the existing data is to conclude that (a) there is no single best method for assessing personality, (b) multiple methods are generally superior to any single method, and (c) the strengths and weaknesses of any method likely depend on the personality dimension in question. If anything, the Rorschach seems to be useful for detecting psychosis (Mihura et al., 2013), but the evidence does not support statements about the superiority of projective tests as the single best method to assess personality. For many kinds of questions, self-reports and informant reports will do much better and turn out to be much more efficient.

References

Bornstein, R. F. (2011a). An interactionist perspective on interpersonal dependency. *Current Directions in Psychological Science, 20*, 124–128.

Bornstein, R. F. (2011b). Toward a process-focused model of test score validity: Improving psychological assessment in science and practice. *Psychological Assessment, 23*, 532–544.

Exner, J. E. (2003). *The Rorschach: A comprehensive system* (4th ed.). New York, NY: Wiley.

Ferguson, C. J., & Brannick, M. T. (2012). Publication bias in psychological science: Prevalence, methods for identifying and controlling, and implications for the use of meta-analyses. *Psychological Methods, 17*, 120–128.

Garb, H. N., Florio, C. M., & Grove, W. M. (1998). The validity of the Rorschach and the Minnesota Multiphasic Personality Inventory: Results from meta-analyses. *Psychological Science, 9*, 402–404.

Garb, H. N., Wood, J. M., Lilienfeld, S. O., & Nezworski, M. T. (2005). Roots of the Rorschach controversy. *Clinical Psychology Review, 25*, 97–118.

Hunsley, J., & Bailey, J. M. (1999). The clinical utility of the Rorschach: Unfulfilled promises and an uncertain future. *Psychological Assessment, 11*, 266–277.

Lilienfeld, S. O., Wood, J. M., & Garb, H. N. (2000). The scientific status of projective techniques. *Psychological Science in the Public Interest, 1*, 27–66.

Meyer, G. J., & Archer, R. P. (2001). The hard science of Rorschach research: What do we know and where do we go? *Psychological Assessment, 13*, 486–502.

Meyer, G. J., & Kurtz, J. E. (2006). Advancing personality assessment terminology: Time to retire "objective" and "projective" as personality test descriptors. *Journal of Personality Assessment, 87*, 223–225.

Mihura, J. L., Meyer, G. J., Dumitrascu, N., & Bombel, G. (2013). The validity of individual Rorschach variables: Systematic reviews and meta-analyses of the comprehensive system. *Psychological Bulletin, 139*, 548.

Parker, K. C., Hanson, R. K., & Hunsley, J. (1988). MMPI, Rorschach, and WAIS: A meta-analytic comparison of reliability, stability, and validity. *Psychological Bulletin, 103*, 367–373.

Rothstein, H. R., & Bushman, B. J. (2012). Publication bias in psychological science: Comment on Ferguson and Brannick (2012). *Psychological Methods, 17*, 129–136.

Schultheiss, O. C. (2007). A memory-systems approach to the classification of personality tests: Comment on Meyer and Kurtz (2006). *Journal of Personality Assessment, 89*, 197–201.

Schultheiss, O. C., & Pang, J. S. (2007). Measuring implicit motives. In R. W. Robins, R. C. Fraley, & R. E. Krueger (Eds.), *Handbook of research methods in personality psychology* (pp. 322–344). New York, NY: Guilford Press.

10 UNSTRUCTURED INTERVIEWS ARE THE BEST APPROACH FOR MEASURING PERSONALITY

How should managers go about selecting employees for a specific job? Should they rely solely on applicants' past experience? Should applicants' grades in school matter? How about personality attributes; should they play a role? And if personality is a factor, should personality traits be assessed with self-report measures or something else? What about personal interviews, when the manager sits down with applicants, hoping to assess whether each person does or does not have the skills and temperament necessary to be successful at the job? When we've polled our students about these issues, many think that these personal meetings—what we call here "unstructured interviews"—are the best source of information in this type of selection context. It turns out that human-resources professionals (those people in an organization who are often responsible for hiring or provide input on hiring) tend to agree (Highhouse, 2008). Unfortunately, the idea that unstructured information provides the best approach for assessing personality, in a selection context or otherwise, is a myth—one that has important consequences for who gets hired into a job and who does not. This myth also has consequences for organizational efficiency.

The term *unstructured interview* refers to a type of interview where a person or committee (e.g., a boss, potential coworkers, or a representative from an organization's human-resources office) sits down with applicants and asks questions about skills and qualifications without a specific plan.

Great Myths of Personality, First Edition. M. Brent Donnellan and Richard E. Lucas.
© 2021 John Wiley & Sons, Inc. Published 2021 by John Wiley & Sons, Inc.

This free-flowing approach to gathering insights about a person has flexibility to tailor questions to different applicants. Applicants may be asked to list specific experiences they've had that have prepared them for the job or specific skills that they have; but the defining characteristic of the unstructured interview is just that: it is unstructured. The interviewer may have a rough idea about what information he or she wants to obtain, but the questions may differ from person to person, follow-up questions may change, and responses may lead to a global "impressionistic" picture of what the applicant is like. Highhouse (2008), after surveying human-resources professionals, noted that these experts believe that unstructured interviews allow them to "read between the lines" when selecting candidates. In other words, those experts believe that evaluating prior experience and identifying candidates with specific, objective skills are only part of the goal in selecting employees. Managers also want "team players" and "go-getters" and "self-starters"—people who match a variety of buzzword-worthy personality traits that all good employees are supposed to have. Is this true? Can people identify these hard-to-detect personality traits from unstructured interviews?

Employee selection is a high-stakes setting for both parties—the organization and the applicant. Organizations who pick "bad" applicants risk wasting money on training. In addition, there are opportunity costs for missing out on better candidates. Bad employees also affect morale and hurt organizations by engaging in so-called counterproductive work behaviors, such as skipping work, being lazy, or even stealing from the organization (e.g., Robinson & Bennett, 1995; Spector et al., 2006). For the applicant, there are obvious consequences if interviewers fail to accurately judge their potential: These applicants might miss out on an opportunity to earn money and advance their career.

Rational managers want to use effective tools to evaluate the personality attributes of applicants, so how should they proceed? We have suggested that unstructured interviews may not be ideal, but what are the alternatives? One possibility is to use a more constrained version of the interview, the *structured interview*. Unlike the unstructured interviews we've been discussing (where interviewers might change the questions they ask and how they ask them across different applicants), structured interviews occur when applicants are asked to address the exact same set of questions in a standardized format. Which approach—the structured or unstructured interview—is superior?

For the most part, research has shown that structured interviews are generally superior to their unstructured counterparts (McDaniel, Whetzel, Schmidt, & Maurer, 1994; Schmidt & Hunter, 1998; Wright, Lichtenfels, & Pursell, 1989; Schmidt, Oh, & Shaffer, 2016). For example, after meta-analytically summarizing existing empirical evidence, Schmidt and Hunter (1998) concluded that the validity correlation for predicting overall job performance was .51 for structured employment interviews versus .38 for unstructured interviews (these can be interpreted as correlations, so higher scores mean that an approach is more effective at predicting job performance). McDaniel et al. (1994) also conducted a meta-analysis and reported that structured interviews had higher predictive power than unstructured interviews. They concluded quite succinctly that "Structured interviews, regardless of content, are more valid (.44) than unstructured interviews (.33) for predicting job performance criteria" (p. 608). Such results would seem to bust the myth that unstructured interviews are superior to structured interviews. But let's dig a little deeper and consider some big-picture issues about human judgments.

Subjective judgments or statistical algorithm: which is best?

The idea that people's idiosyncratic processes for evaluating other people's personality—in other words, their ability to "read" people—is better than more standardized approaches reflects a broader belief that people make better decisions when relying on their intuition and subjective judgments than when using a structured, methodological approach that mechanically weights information. Is this belief warranted? We are skeptical.

A large body of research has examined the relative merits of using a strict formula to weight information versus relying on gut-level judgments. For instance, there is a long literature comparing doctor's holistic judgments to more systematic methods for making medical diagnoses (e.g., Ægisdóttir et al., 2006; Dawes, Faust, & Meehl, 1989; Grove, Zald, Lebow, Snitz, & Nelson, 2000; Meehl, 1954). The tension between these two approaches reflects a debate about the relative merits of *clinical judgments* and *actuarial/mechanical predictions* (see Grove & Meehl, 1996). The term *clinical* refers to the idea of a clinician who takes in various pieces of information and then forms a diagnosis based on a holistic impression. The clinician in this scenario does not necessarily rely on a systematic formula that weights information in precisely the same way, case after case. Rather, judgments are more flexible, and different pieces of information are given different weights based on the details of a specific case. And it does not have to be the case that the clinician is actually a clinical psychologist or medical professional. The clinician could refer to any sort of "expert" who is making decisions from the available information, such as a baseball scout picking players for a team or a hiring professional picking an employee. In contrast to clinical judgments, actuarial or mechanical predictions occur when specific pieces of information are entered into a statistical model that combines this information in the same way, case after case. Little or no judgment is involved in mechanical prediction once the information is entered into the formula.

Consider the task of a college admissions officer (see Sarbin, 1942). One officer might use a simple formula of weighting high-school GPA and standardized test scores to predict how well a prospective student will do in college. Students with high predicted performance would be given priority in admissions over those with lower predicted scores. The only two pieces of information that are used to make this prediction are high-school GPA and test scores. Another officer—one who relies on clinical judgment—might read interview transcripts, personal statements, and even look at test scores but would then use this information to generate an admissions decision based on the overall gestalt of the record. The popular book and movie *Moneyball* (Lewis, 2004) demonstrated the tensions between clinical judgment and actuarial prediction when it comes to selecting baseball players. Should teams use computer formulas to select players based on their performance on a set of common indicators such as on-base percentage, or should they use the gut-level judgments of professional scouts? In other words, which approach is better—clinical or mechanical prediction?

The general conclusion across a range of studies and reviews is that actuarial/mechanical methods are as good if not better than clinical judgments. Dawes et al. (1989), after reviewing the literature, reached this conclusion: "In virtually every one of these studies, the actuarial method has equaled or surpassed the clinical method, sometimes slightly and sometimes substantially" (p. 1669). A little over a decade after that paper, Grove et al. (2000) conducted a meta-analysis of more than 130 studies that compared clinical and mechanical prediction. They also concluded that mechanical predictions were generally as good as or even more accurate than clinical predictions. Moreover, they could not find systematic factors that qualified their conclusions. For instance, their conclusions held regardless of the domain of the judgment (medicine vs. education vs. personality, for instance) and even when using trained judges. It seems that across the board, systematic approaches are as good or better than holistic judgment. This would seem to be a big strike against unstructured interviews.

What accounts for this finding that clinical judgments are rarely if ever superior to mechanical/actuarial approaches? One suggestion is that human judges are susceptible to a number of biases and heuristics that undermine their performance (see Garb, 1989; Goldberg, 1970; Kahneman, Slovic, & Tversky, 1982; Lewis, 2016; Tversky & Kahneman, 1974). People often inappropriately weight information when making judgments and fail to critically evaluate why their judgments are successful as opposed to unsuccessful. There is a tendency to take too much credit for successful judgments and to explain away poor judgments. This makes it difficult for judges to learn from their mistakes and might lead to overconfidence. In contrast, actuarial methods are not susceptible to these human foibles. Formulas don't have egos.

In light of these considerations, we rarely extol the virtue of clinical judgment over actuarial methods. However, we think it is important to remember another critical point about the debate about clinical and actuarial prediction: Both approaches are far from perfect. Judging personality, selecting employees or students, picking all-star baseball players, making medical diagnoses for rare conditions, evaluating the likelihood that a paroled former inmate will commit another crime, and all the other judgments that have been studied are challenging tasks (see also Highhouse, 2008). Dawes et al. (1989) make a point well worth remembering: "An awareness of the modest results that are often achieved by even the best available methods can help to counter unrealistic faith in our predictive powers and our understanding of human behavior" (p. 1673). Human behavior is complicated, so there are limits to the ability to predict it. This might be a sobering reality; but acknowledging this reality might be a useful step toward curbing overconfidence and ultimately making better decisions. Intellectual humility is a virtue.

Let's now return to the debate over structured and unstructured interviews. If managers and human-resources officers want to learn about personality characteristics that are relevant for job success, should they ask everyone the same set of questions and weight responses by a standard formula, or should they just come up with interview questions "on the fly"? The first approach reflects mechanical prediction, whereas the second relies on clinical judgment. Structured approaches rely on standardized information from all applicants so that the same information can be weighted the same way across applicants. This is likely to improve prediction over haphazard unstructured approaches that seem far more likely to suffer from the limits of human judgments when it comes to the influence of biases and heuristics.

In fact, intriguing preliminary evidence exists that suggests that the specific type of information that is gleaned from unstructured interviews can make judgments worse because people who rely on clinical judgment may pay too much attention to extraneous information (Dana, Dawes, & Peterson, 2013). This extraneous information undermines what good information the person who is making the evaluation was able to acquire (Nisbett, Zukier, & Lemley, 1981). Imagine a situation where an employer has references from five former coworkers who all suggest an applicant is bright, energetic, and motivated. Now imagine this employer conducts an unstructured interview with this candidate that goes poorly; the applicant might be nervous and might fail to develop good rapport with the interviewer over the course of 45 minutes. The concern is that the positive predictive information from the references might be overshadowed by the impression that was made in the unstructured interview. In other words, the irrelevant information from the interview might dilute the value of the more relevant references. Some intriguing research suggests this happens. And if this is the case, unstructured interviews might be considerably worse than structured interviews.

Summing up

Judging personality attributes is a difficult task. Likewise, selecting job applicants on the basis of those traits is a major challenge. It is easy to find instances where someone will proclaim the value of unstructured interviews over structured when picking an employee. Likewise, it is easy to find people who advocate for clinical judgments over actuarial methods for all sorts of predictive contexts. People like to have the freedom to rely on their gut-level intuitions when those intuitions conflict with predictions from more systematic approaches. However, when researchers pit the predictive value of unstructured and structured approaches, there is little consistent evidence that unstructured approaches are optimal. More broadly, when considering clinical judgments against mechanical predictions, there is little evidence that clinical judgments are consistently superior. Limits to human judgments undermine predictions. Structured interviews by virtue of their systematic nature place constraints on how such biases can be introduced into the judgment. Accordingly, it is a myth to argue that unstructured approaches to judging personality are superior to structured approaches. In fact, unstructured approaches might lead people to discount good information!

References

Ægisdóttir, S., White, M. J., Spengler, P. M., Maugherman, A. S., Anderson, L. A., Cook, R. S., ... Rush, J. D. (2006). The meta-analysis of clinical judgment project: Fifty-six years of accumulated research on clinical versus statistical prediction. *The Counseling Psychologist, 34*(3), 341–382.

Dana, J., Dawes, R., & Peterson, N. (2013). Belief in the unstructured interview: The persistence of an illusion. *Judgment and Decision Making, 8*(5), 510–520.

Dawes, R. M., Faust, D., & Meehl, P. E. (1989). Clinical versus actuarial judgment. *Science, 243*(4899), 1668–1674.

Garb, H. N. (1989). Clinical judgment, clinical training, and professional experience. *Psychological Bulletin, 105*, 387–396.

Goldberg, L. R. (1970). Man versus model of man: A rationale, plus some evidence, for a method of improving on clinical inferences. *Psychological Bulletin, 73*(6), 422.

Grove, W. M., & Meehl, P. E. (1996). Comparative efficiency of informal (subjective, impressionistic) and formal (mechanical, algorithmic) prediction procedures: The clinical–statistical controversy. *Psychology, Public Policy, and Law, 2*(2), 293.

Grove, W. M., Zald, D. H., Lebow, B. S., Snitz, B. E., & Nelson, C. (2000). Clinical versus mechanical prediction: A meta-analysis. *Psychological Assessment, 12*(1), 19.

Highhouse, S. (2008). Stubborn reliance on intuition and subjectivity in employee selection. *Industrial and Organizational Psychology, 1*(3), 333–342.

Kahneman, D., Slovic, P., & Tversky, A. (1982). *Judgment under uncertainty: Heuristics and biases.* Cambridge, UK: Cambridge University Press.

Lewis, M. (2004). *Moneyball: The art of winning an unfair game.* New York, NY: Norton.

Lewis, M. (2016). *The undoing project: A friendship that changed our minds.* New York, NY: Norton.

McDaniel, M. A., Whetzel, D. L., Schmidt, F. L., & Maurer, S. D. (1994). The validity of employment interviews: A comprehensive review and meta-analysis. *Journal of Applied Psychology, 79*(4), 599–616.

Meehl, P. E. (1954). *Clinical vs. statistical prediction: A theoretical analysis and a review of the evidence.* Minneapolis: University of Minnesota Press.

Nisbett, R. E., Zukier, H., & Lemley, R. E. (1981). The dilution effect: Nondiagnostic information weakens the implications of diagnostic information. *Cognitive Psychology, 13*(2), 248–277.

Robinson, S. L., & Bennett, R. J. (1995). A typology of deviant workplace behaviors: A multidimensional scaling study. *Academy of Management Journal, 38*(2), 555–572.

Sarbin, T. L. (1942). A contribution to the study of actuarial and individual methods of prediction. *American Journal of Sociology, 48*, 593–602.

Schmidt, F. L., & Hunter, J. E. (1998). The validity and utility of selection methods in personnel psychology: Practical and theoretical implications of 85 years of research findings. *Psychological Bulletin, 124*(2), 262.

Schmidt, F. L., Oh, I. S., & Shaffer, J. A. (2016). *The validity and utility of selection methods in personnel psychology: Practical and theoretical implications of 100 years of research findings.* Retrieved from https://testingtalent.com/wp-content/uploads/2017/04/2016-100-Yrs-Working-Paper-on-Selection-Methods-Schmit-Mar-17.pdf

Spector, P. E., Fox, S., Penney, L. M., Bruursema, K., Goh, A., & Kessler, S. (2006). The dimensionality of counterproductivity: Are all counterproductive behaviors created equal? *Journal of Vocational Behavior, 68*(3), 446–460.

Tversky, A., & Kahneman, D. (1974). Judgment under uncertainty: Heuristics and biases. *Science, 185*(4157), 1124–1131.

Wright, P. M., Lichtenfels, P. A., & Pursell, E. D. (1989). The structured interview: Additional studies and a meta-analysis. *Journal of Occupational and Organizational Psychology, 62*(3), 191–199.

11 MOST PERSONALITY QUIZZES IN MAGAZINES AND ON WEBSITES PROVIDE ACCURATE INFORMATION ABOUT YOUR PERSONALITY

Chances are, you have some interest in personality (you are reading this book, after all). And for many people, that interest is more than just academic. People are typically more interested in figuring out their own personalities and the personalities of their friends and family members than in understanding personality theories or the statistical machinery behind correlations or meta-analyses. Because of this interest, you may have investigated your personality by taking quizzes that you've found online. But can such quizzes tell you anything meaningful? In Chapter 6, we addressed the myth that personality is too complicated to be measured with any accuracy. If you remember, we countered this claim by showing that personality measures do a pretty good job of capturing something important about the distinctive and characteristic patterns of thoughts,

Great Myths of Personality, First Edition. M. Brent Donnellan and Richard E. Lucas.
© 2021 John Wiley & Sons, Inc. Published 2021 by John Wiley & Sons, Inc.

feelings, and behaviors that make up people's personalities. Specifically, we discussed how it is possible to follow standardized steps for measuring difficult-to-observe characteristics (steps that are not unique to personality psychology). And when psychologists use these procedures, the result is a personality measure that has some degree of reliability and validity, two characteristics that are essential for good measurement.

One of the main claims we made in Chapter 6 was that the process of evaluating the quality of personality measures is relatively straightforward and mostly uncontroversial. The steps that one would take are—at least at an abstract level—the same as those used by other fields, and so long as they are followed very carefully and deliberatively, decent measures of personality can be produced. Indeed, the personality measures that have been developed through this process have been used widely, not only by research psychologists but also by teachers, clinicians, managers, and employment recruiters to identify people with characteristics that might predict real-world, future outcomes. Thus, the personality measures that have been developed using these techniques have proven their worth in a variety of important settings.

This does not mean, however, that the process of developing personality measures is quick, easy, or without need of specific expertise. We raise this issue because a negative consequence of the fact that most people have increasing familiarity with personality measures is that it might lead them to believe that anyone can devise a personality measure that provides meaningful results. We can say with some degree of certainty that it is harder and more frustrating than it looks. Indeed, if you took a quick look at well-validated personality measures, you would find that they were typically developed by personality researchers over a period of many years. That kind of research might seem boring to some, but it is necessary work. We will describe the steps involved in developing a personality measure in this chapter, and we hope this information convinces you of the work in terms of conceptual analysis, evidence gathering, and evidence interpretation that is required to develop a personality measure that has acceptable levels of precision and validity.

To be fair, questionnaires you find in magazines or on websites that purport to describe and explain your personality might look like legitimate personality measures. Both may ask you to describe whether you like parties, tend to get your work done on time, or worry a lot. If these measures often look the same, then can the questionnaires you see in magazines or on websites that claim to "reveal your true personality" or that will allow you to "find out what you are really like" provide you with any useful information? Unfortunately, the answer is in most cases, probably not. The careful research needed to bolster the case for reliability and validity is typically missing. There is more to personality assessment than coming up with clever questions! Thus, we think it is a myth to trust the personality measures that one finds in casual settings.

One reason why the feedback you receive from online questionnaires is rarely useful is that the people who create these measures usually do not have well-developed norms that help clarify the meaning of the scores you receive. Scale norms reflect information about how people typically score on the measure. To develop scale norms, personality measures are often administered to large groups of respondents—ideally respondents who are selected to be representative of some broader population—and then information about the distribution is recorded and perhaps published. With such norms, researchers can provide very specific feedback about where you stand relative to other people. Is your response typical or more extreme than most other responses? Without such norms, it is hard to interpret scores on personality measures, and as a result, the specific feedback that you might get from an online quiz can be almost meaningless. An average score of 3.5 on a bunch of questions typically lacks any inherent meaning.

There are other reasons why the information from these popular quizzes is suspect. In explaining why, we will need to revisit a topic from Chapter 6—the topic of validity. Remember, the validity of a measure refers to the extent to which it accurately assesses the attribute it is intended to measure. A reasonably valid measure of extraversion assesses extraversion (and only extraversion), a valid measure of conscientiousness really assesses conscientiousness (and only conscientiousness), and so on. The problem is that most measures developed for informal settings like magazines or websites were not created with the goal of maximizing validity. As a result, and unsurprisingly, they may not have much validity. Or at the very least, these informal measures have unknown validity. These quizzes are often designed for entertainment purposes only. That might be fun, but they are not likely to lead to self-insight.

To explain this myth, it is necessary to discuss the idea of different types of validity. One type is called *face validity*. Face validity refers to the extent to which a measure looks like it measures what it is supposed to assess. For instance, using an example outside of personality psychology, if you wanted to assess knowledge of the rules of the road for a driving test, an item with face validity might be something like "When a car is merging onto a highway and there is already a car traveling in the right-most lane, which car has the right of way?" In contrast, items that have nothing to do with cars, driving, or the rules of the road would lack face validity for a driving test. It would be clear to see why the item "What is

48 divided by 8?" would probably be inappropriate for a driving test. What does that question have to do with driving at a superficial level? Again, face validity refers to whether an item or test looks like it measures what it is supposed to measure.

A satisfactory degree of face validity is the weakest form of validity that a measure can have. Some face-valid measures of personality constructs are actually quite poor in terms of other more important kinds of validity evidence. In addition, some measures of personality have low face validity yet do surprisingly well at measuring a given attribute. Face validity is often seen as a preliminary form of validity that is emphasized in early stages of scale construction. For instance, if you want to measure extraversion, you might start out with a list of face-valid items like "I enjoy going to parties" or "I spend a lot of time with large groups of people." However, it would be necessary to provide further tests of these items to see whether they really assess what you hope to assess. Validity judgments must ultimately involve empirical results.

Armed with an understanding of face validity, it is possible to reconsider the informal personality measures found in magazines and on websites. And although you might expect there to be a high degree of face validity to many informal surveys, you would quickly find that that is not true. For instance, if you have ever read an astrology chart that tried to describe your personality based on the month in which you were born, then you took a personality quiz that had no face validity. There is no clear link between month of birth and personality, and thus, this measure lacks face validity. Other face-invalid measures might ask you to rate specific foods, or colors, or other objects that have little to do with personality. You should be highly suspicious of the results that such personality quizzes provide.

This is not to say that all personality measures that lack face validity are in fact invalid. Indeed, one of the most famous personality inventories—the Minnesota Multiphasic Personality Inventory (MMPI)—was developed using a procedure that often resulted in low levels of face validity (we discussed this tool in Chapter 9). The MMPI was developed using *criterion-* or *empirical-keying* techniques. In this approach, a broad range of personality items are administered to participants who are known to differ on some characteristic. For instance, the items may be administered to a group of people who had been diagnosed as having major depression and a separate group of people without such a diagnosis. Researchers then identified those items that best distinguished the two groups on purely empirical grounds. The items that were selected may have absolutely no face validity (e.g., "Cats are better than dogs"), but they could still be useful in distinguishing between these groups. The items worked empirically! And that is a higher standard than face-validity judgements. Human judgments are imperfect (see, e.g., Chapter 10). Similar empirical approaches could be used for just about any personality trait. Indeed, researchers often use face-invalid or seemingly nonsense items to identify people who are likely to lie or misrepresent themselves on personality questionnaires. They just need to know items that are rarely endorsed by people to get a set of items that might be useful for identifying people who are providing unusual responses that need to be flagged. Again, the use of items that lack face validity can often be useful because respondents may not know what the items are supposed to measure, which means that they will be less likely to change their answers to make themselves look better.

Thus, face validity is not a necessary feature of personality measures. However, especially for measures without face validity, it is essential that a strong theory, or even better, a strong theory and strong empirical evidence exist to link responses to the questionnaire to the underlying trait that is being assessed. Most informal personality measures on websites and in magazines lack such theories and empirical evidence. For instance, there is little evidence that your astrological sign is linked in any meaningful way to your personality. Therefore, any time you see a personality quiz that lacks face validity, you should look closely for citations to scientific articles that can help explain how the responses that you provide might be linked to personality characteristics. Without this evidence, you should be highly suspicious.

A second form of validity that is also relatively easy to understand is what is called *content validity*. Content validity reflects the extent to which the measure in question samples all the relevant content associated with an attribute. To illustrate, let's go back to our earlier example of the driving test. If a driving test has content validity, it would sample from all the various types of information that a person should know to be a good driver. It might include questions about speed limits, rules for merging on to roads, road signs, and parts of the car. Those who administer the test want to ensure that all of this content is included because if some critical set of items is omitted, they may end up giving driver's licenses to people who have no idea what a stop sign means or what to do when they see a yellow light. So a driving test that had high levels of content validity would have questions about all the most relevant domains of knowledge that were important for this task. A driving test would also not include content that is irrelevant for measuring attributes of driving ("I like salty pickles"). So content validity is about covering all aspects of the attribute in question without including extraneous or irrelevant content.

Content validity is especially likely to be a problem for informal measures because the people who created these measures rarely start from a scientific understanding of the trait they hope to assess. Instead, they often start from their own idiosyncratic ideas about what that trait is supposed to be. If this perspective does not map on to scientifically established constructs, then the person who constructs the quiz is likely to omit some important category of items that is relevant for the trait in question. Or they might include random things that do not belong.

For instance, people are often interested in knowing where they stand on the trait of extraversion/introversion. This is a construct that has been studied by personality psychologists for almost a century. However, psychologists have come to a relatively strong consensus regarding the features of this trait. According to one prominent definition, extraversion consists of multiple distinct but related components, including a desire to be with others (gregariousness), a tendency to have high levels of energy and be active, a tendency to seek out exciting activities, a tendency to be warm and friendly with others, a tendency to be relatively assertive and self-confident, and a tendency to experience positive emotions. Importantly, personality psychologists did not simply decide that these were the components, they based this conceptualization on empirical evidence regarding different thoughts, feelings, and behaviors that tend to go together. Thus, most extraversion measures tap into a broad range of characteristics that reflect the diverse ways that someone can be extraverted.

Although lay people's view of what extraversion is may be similar to the empirically informed definition that psychologists use, it may not be precise enough to result in a content-valid measure of the trait. For instance, a journalist who has not studied the topic may equate extraversion with a tendency to enjoy parties. Constructing a measure to tap this narrow construct would result in something much different than the broad trait of extraversion that personality psychologists typically study. So if you were to take such a scale, you may find out how much you like parties relative to other people, but this would not give you a reasonable overview of how extraverted you were because the measure omits many of the components of extraversion that are important for the trait. Determining whether a measure has content validity is only possible if there is a clear definition of the various components, and informal measures such as magazine and website quizzes rarely start with such a definition.

The first two forms of validity both can be evaluated by looking at the items that are included in the measure. However, psychologists who develop new measures typically go through a number of additional steps to test whether their questionnaire measures what they hope it measures. This is because even highly face-valid and content-valid measures may still have problems when it comes to actually assessing the underlying trait.

The biggest problem is that even with items that have a high degree of face validity, it is not always possible to predict how people will respond. As a result, the items may not do a good job measuring the trait of interest. Let's take the trait of agreeableness, which reflects whether you are mild mannered and tend to treat people nicely. Agreeable people get along well with others. To develop a measure of agreeableness, we might think of some things that agreeable people do or do not typically do and then write items that tap into those behaviors. However, if we were to rely on our own judgments about what is a good item, the measure we came up with could be quite problematic. For instance, because agreeable people tend to be nice, it is probably safe to assume that those who are high on agreeableness have never killed anyone. However, if we were to write an item for our personality questionnaire that read "I have never killed anyone," it would be quite problematic, to put it mildly. First, it is extremely unlikely that many people in a sample actually have killed anyone, so in most cases everyone who took your measure would respond identically. If we are using personality questionnaires to try to distinguish people on some underlying continuum, items with no variance (i.e., where everyone provides the same answer) are useless. Although the example of killing someone is extreme, you might also obtain little to no variance with less extreme items like "I have gotten in a fistfight in the past month." Thus, even items with face validity can have problems if they are so extreme that nobody exhibits the behavior that is described.

A second problem is that even if you had a murderer in your sample, he or she may be unwilling to actually admit to killing someone. Of course, personality items that can implicate someone in a crime are rare and easily avoided, but this concern applies even for less extreme items. Put another way, items that reflect thoughts, feelings, or behaviors that are either very high or very low in *social desirability* may cause people to report doing approved things more than they really do, or these items may cause people to underreport the disapproved things that they do. Thus, it is important to pick items to which people are likely to respond honestly and accurately.

In addition to these concerns, psychometricians (people who study psychological measures) have identified numerous problems that can affect the validity of items. The wording of the items can be awkward, or the vocabulary can be difficult. If so, participants' responses may reflect a misunderstanding or misinterpretation of the item rather than their true beliefs. Items can be "double-barreled," which means that they are asking two different things at once. An example of this would be a survey question such as "I am very organized and tend to get my work done on time." It is possible that someone might be organized but not very punctual (or vice versa). All of these issues can be overlooked by those creating informal measures.

So what do psychologists do to ensure that the measures they develop really do tap into the underlying construct of interest? In general, they use a variety of procedures that build on the ideas developed in Chapter 6. Specifically, psychologists often see how well the items and measures they develop correlate with other things. If the measures are good, then they should correlate strongly with other variables that reflect the trait under investigation. This is part of the empirical work needed to justify claims of validity.

For instance, if other measures of the trait already exist, one easy step to take is to test whether the new measure correlates with this existing measure. This is a test of *convergent validity*—it tests whether the answers we get from the new measure converge with those we get from existing measures. Convergent validity is useful when researchers are developing new measures that are thought to improve upon existing measures or that change them in ways that make them more appropriate for specific research situations.

If an existing measure is unavailable, it is possible to select relevant criteria to see whether the new measure predicts them. For instance, if a psychologist believes that extraverts should be more likely to serve in leadership positions than would introverts, then it would be possible to measure experience in leadership positions to see whether the new extraversion measure predicts this criterion. In fact, the name of this type of validity is *criterion validity*, because it is a form of validity that focuses on whether the new measure predicts some relevant criterion. For some constructs, the criterion of interest is clear. For instance, if we go back to our example of the driving test, we hope that a new driving test would predict how many car accidents a person got into and their number of traffic violations. If the test creators actually collected this information, this would be a test of criterion validity. Or, to take another example from outside personality psychology, any time the creators of the SAT and ACT tests examine whether their measures predict future college grades, they are conducting a test of criterion validity. They are examining whether their measure (the SAT or ACT) predicts a criterion (or relevant outcome)—the grades a student gets over the course of his or her college career. Thus, tests of criterion validity often show the real-world utility of a measure. Again, informal measures such as those found in magazines and websites rarely go through this rigorous process of validation.

The final form of validity is probably the most difficult to describe. This is the form of validity that psychologists label *construct validity*. In short, construct validity reflects that total body of evidence that supports the ability of the measure in question to assess a construct. Usually, when scientists measure something that is difficult to observe, they have some theory about what it is they are trying to measure. In the example from Chapter 6, it was heat; in many of the examples we've used throughout this chapter, it is extraversion. Although these constructs are difficult if not impossible to see directly, scientists have theories about them. For instance, scientists know that if they put an ice cube in an environment with a lot of heat, then the ice cube will melt. Similarly, scientists expect that if you put an extravert in a social situation—something like a party—then this person should be comfortable and enjoy the experience. Importantly, scientists—including personality psychologists—have theories that make a broad range of predictions. Construct validity reflects the total body of evidence regarding the extent to which the measure behaves the way the underlying construct should. So, if a measure of extraversion provides results that match with existing theories of extraversion, this provides support for the construct validity of the trait. The reason that this concept is so difficult is because there is no single step that establishes whether a measure has construct validity. Instead, the process of construct validation is ongoing and extensive and draws on many strands of evidence and theoretical reasoning. As you can imagine, people who construct quizzes for magazines and websites rarely go through the processes required to establish this form of validation, which is why you might be suspicious of the results you obtain from such a quiz.

Before closing this chapter, one qualification is in order. Although you should be suspicious of quizzes that you find on the Internet, not all of them are mostly invalid and problematic. We suspect that at least some of these are measures created by psychologists using the procedures described in this chapter that have been adopted by websites for popular use. In fact, some such websites are run by personality psychologists who want to provide nonscientists with valid feedback. So our primary advice is to use the information in this chapter (along with the background material provided with the quizzes you find) to determine whether the quizzes you are taking are likely to have evidence of validity. Unfortunately, many of the quizzes you will find have gone through few, if any, of the validation procedures discussed here. Thus, we close with the famous dictum of caveat emptor—let the buyer beware. Have fun with those informal measures but do not get too worked up about the results! And if you are picking measures for your own projects, be highly skeptical.

12 PERSONALITY TRAITS DO NOT HAVE MUCH CONSISTENCY ACROSS THE LIFE SPAN

Personality psychologists focus on characteristics that are thought to be a part of the psychological makeup of the individual. As discussed in Chapter 1, if people changed dramatically from one moment to the next, and the behaviors they exhibited today had no relation to the behaviors they will exhibit a week from now, there would be no good reason to study personality characteristics. Therefore, the concept of stability is central to the field, and as we noted in Chapter 1, the idea that behavior lacks such stability is probably the most important myth that we address in this book.

After decades of research, it is now clear that personality is at least somewhat stable over short periods of time and across different situations. However, there remains an important question regarding how long these individual differences persist. In other words, your personality today may be quite like the personality that you have tomorrow and the day after that, but will you have the same personality next year or even two decades from now? If the things that happen to us—the events that occur, the people we meet, the jobs we perform—all affect our personality, is it reasonable to expect that our personality will change as these events accumulate? Or are there some core features that remain constant and that result in some level of stability, even over extremely long periods of time? In this chapter, we address the myth that the

Great Myths of Personality, First Edition. M. Brent Donnellan and Richard E. Lucas.
© 2021 John Wiley & Sons, Inc. Published 2021 by John Wiley & Sons, Inc.

cumulative effect of life experiences results in virtually no long-term stability in personality traits across the life span.

You might be asking whether anyone believes this myth. This is a good question, and it might be something that only academic psychologists ever consider as a possibility. In many ways, this is just a specific case of the argument that personality itself does not exist. As we talked about in Chapter 1, this perspective is something that has a surprising degree of currency in some academic quarters. For example, Lewis (2001) concluded that "longitudinal studies, for the most part, found only weak correlations of personality variables over time" (p. 79). He further noted, "Given our strong belief in personality—that is, that characteristics are stable over time—such weak findings raise doubt as to meaning of personality" (p. 79). Even if one does not go as far as Lewis, a less extreme version of this myth is the belief that people change dramatically from one year to the next. This version grants that there is some stability in terms of days and weeks, but that this stability vanishes when considering longer intervals. Indeed, we believe that many different people hold different intuitions about how much people change over time. Thus, we think it is reasonable to consider this myth even if you might be worried a bit that we have created a straw person. Indeed, we suspect that the Lewis (2001) piece would find many sympathetic readers today.

Before we discuss the evidence for personality consistency over the life span, we need to point out that when we talk about stability and change, there are at least two types of stability that we could mean: *mean-level stability* and *differential stability* or *rank-order stability*. Mean-level stability refers to the extent to which average levels of personality change or stay the same in groups of people as they age. For instance, research that focuses on mean-level stability might ask whether older people in general are more conscientious than younger people or whether average levels of neuroticism decline as people age. This type of research is useful for determining whether there are certain normative or typical changes (either internal or external) that occur over the life course and that affect people's personality in similar ways. Questions about mean-level stability (or change) are about the attributes of a population and framed in terms of average levels. Differential stability, on the other hand, refers to the extent to which individual differences in personality traits are maintained over time (Ferguson, 2010; Roberts & DelVecchio, 2000). In other words, differential stability will be high when the rank order of people on a personality trait is maintained over time: people who are high on a trait at one point in time still score highly in the future; people who are low on a trait at one point in time maintain these low scores at this later point.

Questions about this kind of stability are framed in terms of the correlation coefficient. Differential stability is the focus of this chapter; we will come back to mean-level stability in the next chapter when we discuss the precise types of changes that occur as people age. Notice also that we are talking about trends and generalizations that apply to large groups of people. We are not making strong statements about any individual. In other words, what does the evidence say about people in general?

It is also necessary to first discuss two additional issues that complicate the interpretation of existing data when considering differential or rank-order stability. First, when studying differential stability, researchers need to worry about *measurement error*. As we discussed in Chapter 6, measurement error can result from things like respondents misreading questionnaire items or checking the wrong box on the response sheet. Measurement error reduces the reliability of measures. All measures have error, and these errors affect results. For instance, imagine that the personality trait of extraversion was completely stable over a period of 1 year (nobody ever changed in their level of extraversion), so that the rank ordering of people in a sample would be maintained perfectly from one occasion to the next. People high in extraversion are always high and people low in extraversion always stay that way. People have the exact same standing on the attribute at each time point. This stipulation about perfect stability applies to the construct—we are saying that extraversion is an attribute that is truly fixed across a 1-year period. But this example is about the perfect stability of the latent attribute. Researchers still have to actually measure extraversion, and so let's also imagine that our measure of extraversion has a reasonable amount of measurement error.

Imagine that the person who is truly highest on extraversion carelessly checks the wrong box on a few questions, and these errors reduce his or her score so that it is below that of the person who was the second highest in extraversion. These types of errors are transitory, which means that they will not occur in the same way on each occasion. This is why they are called random measurement errors. But such random errors serve to reduce the observed correlation between two measures given at different times. Thus, even a trait that is perfectly stable over time (in reality) will appear to have less than perfect stability because of the effects of measurement error. Measurement error is a concern for assessing differential stability because differential stability is evaluated by examining the size of correlations between two measures assessed at different points in time (see Ferguson, 2010).

A second issue concerns the ways that personality traits are manifested in behavior. If you were asked to describe an extraverted preschooler and an extraverted college student, would your description be the same? We think it would differ. It's extremely unlikely that the extraverted pre-schoolers that you know are characterized by the extent to which they attend parties on weekends, whereas this may be a defining feature of the extraverted college student. Thus, traits like extraversion may lead to different "signature" types of behaviors at different ages, a fact which complicates our understanding of how these traits change over the wide range of ages that cover the life span. This issue about the same latent traits having different indicators at different ages makes it more difficult to study differential stability from childhood to adulthood, and it becomes less of an issue when studying stability among adults (though the issue does not totally disappear once research participants reach adulthood—can you think of different ways conscientiousness might be demonstrated by a 30-year-old versus a 75-year-old?).

If we need to assess people at least twice to assess differential stability, then that means that we need longitudinal data, preferably longitudinal data from people who have been followed for many years (which allows researchers to test consistency over very long periods of time). Unfortunately, longitudinal data are hard to come by. It is difficult to fol-low people for many years because participants die, they move, or they lose interest in the study. Similarly, it is hard to motivate researchers to conduct these studies because the payoff for all their hard work does not come until many years in the future. As a result, there are fewer longitu-dinal studies than cross-sectional (onetime) studies, and the studies that do exist tend to be smaller in size and from more select samples. However, the studies that exist provide useful information about whether any long-term stability in personality exists.

In one famous study, Conley (1985) assessed the personality of married couples twice, once in the late 1930s and once in the middle of the 1950s (with an average interval of 19 years between the two occasions). Notably, in addition to asking participants to rate their own personalities using self-report methods, he asked the spouses and other acquaintances to pro-vide informant reports. This methodological feature is important because if evidence for stability emerges, we want to make sure that it is not just stability in people's perceptions of themselves but actual stability in their personality traits (remember Mischel's, 1968, suggestion described in Chapter 1 that people have stable beliefs about personality traits that do not map on to reality). Even though the time interval separating these two assessments was relatively long, stabilities were quite impressive, even when different methods of assessment (e.g., self-reports vs. informant reports) were compared. Furthermore, Conley obtained reports of person-ality from a smaller subset of participants 25 years later (for a total interval of almost 45 years), and evidence of personality stability emerged even over this extremely long period, though the correlation coefficients were smaller for this long interval compared to the shorter intervals. Thus, studies like this show that some amount of stability in adult personality does exist, even over very long periods of time. In technical terms, the correlation coefficients tend to get smaller as the interval of time increases from, say, a 1-year interval to a 20-year interval; however, these correlations do not reach zero even when considering the 20-year interval.

As we noted, however, high-quality longitudinal studies over long intervals are rare because they are so difficult to conduct. As a result, many of the long-term longitudinal studies that exist include samples that are small or unusual and that might differ from the broader population in important ways. Therefore, it is difficult to draw strong conclusions from single studies of personality stability and change, and researchers have adopted additional methods for investigating this important question. Specifically, to develop stronger conclusions about long-term personality stability, researchers have used meta-analysis to examine differential stability across multiple studies of different intervals and different levels of quality.

Recall that meta-analysis is a procedure in which many studies are combined quantitatively to get an overall estimate of the size of an effect in the literature. For instance, imagine researchers had conducted five studies examining personality stability over time. Study 1 had 100 participants of varying ages who were followed for 5 years; Study 2 had 50 participants of varying ages who were followed for 15 years; Study 3 had 250 participants in their 20s who were followed for 10 years; Study 4 had 1,000 participants in their 60s who were followed for 5 years; and Study 5 had 300 participants of various ages who were studied for just 2 years. As you can see, the different studies have different strengths and weaknesses. Study 4 has the largest sample size (which is good for coming up with precise estimates of the size of stability coefficients), but it only included people in their 60s, so we cannot determine whether stability differs for those at different ages. Study 2 had participants from different ages and followed people for the longest time, but it only included 50 participants. A meta-analysis would combine the results of all five studies to see what the average statistical effect would be (i.e., the average correlation across time) while addressing the different time intervals of the studies. In addition, using meta-analytic techniques, researchers can determine whether different characteristics of the study, such as the age of the participants or the length of the interval, affect the stability coefficients that are found.

There have now been three prominent meta-analyses of long-term personality stability coefficients (Ardelt, 2000; Ferguson, 2010; Roberts & DelVecchio, 2000). These studies consistently show that personality is relatively stable even over relatively long periods of years. For instance, Roberts and DelVecchio (2000) calculated the average stability coefficient for the average length of time across all studies they found (a period of 6.7 years). As we discuss in more detail in the next chapter, this average stability coefficient varies by age, but even among studies conducted with very young children, stability was moderate (correlations around .35), and among older adults, it was quite high (with correlations around .70). Ferguson (2010) conducted a more recent and updated meta-analysis, one that also corrected for measurement error. This study showed that once measurement error was controlled, stability coefficients were very high, often above .80 in adults. Thus, these meta-analyses convincingly show that personality is quite stable even over very long periods of time.

To fully understand how personality changes over the life span, we would ideally follow a large group of people from birth to death, keeping track of how their personality changes at each stage. Although some such studies exist, they are extremely rare, and they do not always have the information that we would want to test this possibility (remember, some of the most widely supported models of personality were only developed in the last 40 years, which means that measures of these characteristics did not exist before that time). Thus, researchers have had to look at shorter term studies and extrapolate from these data to get a sense of the stability of personality over the life span. These studies provide robust evidence that the personality traits that people have today will, to some extent, be maintained long into the future. There appear to be some core characteristics that we carry with us over time, influencing our thoughts, feelings, and behaviors in similar ways for long periods of time. These characteristics may also contribute to the situations people select for themselves and thus further contribute to personality consistency because of a matching between the person and his or her contexts (although this matching will not likely be perfect). In short, the idea that personality attributes do not have consistency across the life span is certainly a myth. The kernel of truth to this myth, however, is that personality is not perfectly stable, so some changes (at least for some people) are likely to occur. We address a related myth in the next chapter.

References

Ardelt, M. (2000). Still stable after all these years? Personality stability theory revisited. *Social Psychology Quarterly*, *63*(4), 392–405.

Conley, J. J. (1985). Longitudinal stability of personality traits: A multitrait–multimethod–multioccasion analysis. *Journal of Personality and Social Psychology*, *49*(5), 1266.

Ferguson, C. J. (2010). A meta-analysis of normal and disordered personality across the life span. *Journal of Personality and Social Psychology*, *98*(4), 659–667.

Lewis, M. (2001). Issues in the study of personality development. *Psychological Inquiry*, *12*(2), 67–83.

Mischel, W. (1968). *Personality and assessment*. New York, NY: Wiley.

Roberts, B. W., & DelVecchio, W. F. (2000). The rank-order consistency of personality traits from childhood to old age: A quantitative review of longitudinal studies. *Psychological Bulletin*, *126*(1), 3–25.

13 PERSONALITY IS COMPLETELY STABLE (OR SET LIKE PLASTER) AFTER AGE 30

Although stability in personality characteristics is a central assumption for personality psychology, we know that nobody is perfectly stable either from one situation to the next or even across the same situation at different times. As we discussed in Chapter 1, this is partly due to the fact that situations that appear similar may in fact be subtly different to the person experiencing them. In addition, intervening situational factors (including relatively minor factors like a person's mood) may have changed the person or his or her view of the situation across time. Nonetheless, personality shows a surprising degree of consistency across time periods, as we discussed in Chapter 12.

This degree of consistency across time raises the possibility that personality traits might become fixed at some point in the life span. Intuition suggests that more changes in personality may occur in childhood than in adulthood. As we shall see, this intuition is partially born out in the data; some forms of thoughts, feelings, and behaviors change more during childhood and adolescence than at older ages. However, this leads to a critical question of what happens next. Once major physiological developments have taken place and people settle into adult roles, does personality development also end? Given that people may settle into an adult routine starting somewhere in the late 20s or early 30s, can we expect to be the same person at age 70 as we were at age 30?

Some people believed the answer to this question is "yes." For instance, William James, one of the most influential psychologists in history,

Great Myths of Personality, First Edition. M. Brent Donnellan and Richard E. Lucas.
© 2021 John Wiley & Sons, Inc. Published 2021 by John Wiley & Sons, Inc.

famously suggested that personality was set like plaster by age 30 (James, 1985). This idea has also influenced more modern perspectives, with McCrae and Costa (2003) suggesting that in terms of core personality traits (as opposed to more context-specific goals and behaviors or characteristic adaptations that might result from these core traits), change pretty much grinds to a halt once individuals become adults. Any exception would be attributable to atypical events like head injuries or diseases that alter the brain in often catastrophic ways. For example, consider the famous victim of a railway accident, Phineas Gage, who survived an accident where a large metal bar was driven through his brain (Google his name if you don't know this story). Evidence suggests that his personality changed, but this was likely a result of the devastating brain injury that occurred when the steel rod pierced his skull.

Fortunately, the question of whether personality is set like plaster is one of the most widely researched questions in personality psychology, and some of the best data available have been used to answer it. However, before we discuss what this evidence says, we need to take some time to be a little more precise about what we mean when we talk about personality change. There are at least two ways that personality can change, and the answer to the question "Does personality change?" could depend on how one interprets the term "change" (see Caspi, Roberts, & Shiner, 2005).

Remember from Chapter 12 that personality psychologists typically distinguish between *mean-level stability/change* and *differential* or *rank-order stability/change*. Mean-level stability (or change, depending on the focus) refers to the extent to which average levels of a personality trait stay the same over time, whereas differential stability refers to the extent to which the rank ordering of a group of people is maintained over time. It is not difficult to see why these two forms of stability must be investigated separately. The two are potentially independent, and one form of stability could be high whereas the other could be quite low. For instance, it would not be inconceivable to have a trait with very high mean-level stability—on average, 30-year-olds might have the same scores as 80-year-olds—while having very low differential stability—those who are high on the trait at age 30 might not be the same people who are high at age 80.

As is often the case, when trying to answer the question of whether people's personality becomes perfectly stable at some point in their lives, we need to consider some important methodological issues. In addition to the issues discussed in the previous chapter (those involving measurement error and the extent to which the same trait manifests differently at different points in one's life), we need to consider the difficulty of attributing differences between people of different ages to the actual effect of age. Let's look at an example. Imagine you want to know whether 80-year-olds are more conscientious than 20-year-olds, so you do a cross-sectional study in the year 2019 comparing a group of people who are 20 years old at the time of the study (and thus, who were born in 1999) with a group of people who are 80 years old at that time (and thus, who were born in 1939). If you found that the 80-year-olds were indeed more conscientious than the 20-year-olds, could you really conclude that this effect was due to age itself? One alternative possibility was that some other factor that is common to each age group beyond their age might have led to this difference. For instance, all of the 80-year-olds lived through World War II, whereas none of the 20-year-olds did, and perhaps this major historical event changed their personalities. Unfortunately, with this simple cross-sectional design, it is impossible to separate out the effects of age from the effects of history. The issue of isolating aging effects is a difficult one, and there is no easy solution. However, the use of longitudinal data almost always helps. In this design, the same people are observed at multiple ages, so inferences about age-related differences are clearer. Thus, it will be important to consider differences in results from cross-sectional studies as compared to longitudinal studies when evaluating the evidence for mean-level change.

Let's first look at the evidence for mean-level stability. As we noted above, William James (1985) suggested that personality change stops after age 30. At least one prominent model echoes this idea, suggesting that because core traits result solely from biological systems, then change in these traits should stop when the underlying systems reach maturity (which should happen in early adulthood; McCrae & Costa, 2003). In the most recent formulations of this model, the proponents of this model acknowledged that some change does occur after age 30, though they believe that it is slower among older people than younger. Furthermore, they believe that this slow change in adulthood can also be linked to biological changes. At least some evidence for this perspective exists. For instance, McCrae et al. (2000) used cross-sectional data from more than 5,000 respondents from five countries to examine the size of mean differences across various age groups to see whether most of the change occurs before age 30 or after age 30. Although they concluded that these differences were indeed larger before age 30 than after, other researchers have noted that they did not test this difference explicitly (Srivastava, John, Gosling, & Potter, 2003). To be fair, this was difficult to do in their study because even with a sample of more than 5,000 participants, testing for these differences is challenge when the sample is divided across multiple subsamples from different countries.

However, more recent research tested these ideas more explicitly, and some of these studies came to different conclusions from those of McCrae et al. (2000). For instance, Srivastava et al. (2003) used an extremely large sample of Internet respondents ($N = 132,515$), which allowed them to provide much more precise estimates of the age differences that were observed. In their study, there was little evidence that personality differences across ages stopped at age 30 (i.e., there were differences when comparing those who were 35 to those who were 55). Indeed, their results suggest that average levels of conscientiousness tended to be higher in older individuals throughout the age range they studied (ages 21–60). According to their study, neuroticism declines linearly (with bigger changes for women than for men). Openness declines very slightly but linearly throughout the life span. Extraversion was relatively stable across age groups. And finally, agreeableness actually showed larger differences after age 30 than before (with relatively steep increases from age 30 to age 50, after which it declined).

Although the study by Srivastava et al. (2003) was very large, it (like all studies) was not without limitations, most notably that the sample consisted of people who chose to take a personality quiz at an online site. Perhaps those who take such quizzes differ from the general population, which would make it wrong to generalize from their results to the population as a whole. Or more problematically, the types of people who choose to take personality quizzes might actually differ by age, which would dramatically complicate any interpretation of the results. So stronger studies use data generated using scientific sampling plans to help ensure that all participants are representative of the population as a whole; and fortunately, there have been a number of such studies in recent years.

For instance, we have now published numerous studies looking at cross-sectional and longitudinal age differences in personality traits from representative samples of the United States, the United Kingdom, Germany, Australia, and Switzerland (Anusic, Lucas, & Donnellan, 2012; Donnellan & Lucas, 2008; Lucas & Donnellan, 2009, 2011; Wortman, Lucas, & Donnellan, 2012). The sample sizes are generally very large (with some studies reaching into the tens of thousands of participants), and two of the studies were longitudinal. As we have noted, even with longitudinal data, it is not always easy to draw clear conclusions about the effect of age, and the fact that the studies are from different countries and use somewhat different methodologies complicates the matter even further. However, the results from these studies were generally clear and rarely supported the idea that personality reaches near-perfect stability after age 30. Like Srivastava et al. (2003), these studies found that conclusions about the age 30 cutoff varied by trait.

So what, specifically, do these studies show? First, in all studies, there was a tendency for extraversion to decline relatively linearly with age. Trends in neuroticism were more mixed, with most studies showing a slight decline or no change with age, and one study showing slight linear increases with age. Evidence regarding openness was a bit more consistent, with most studies showing a decline and an occasional study showing relatively little change with age. Agreeableness tended to increase with age across the studies, though like Srivastava et al.'s (2003) study, the changes were not linear. However, the precise ages at which the differences were greatest varied across studies. Finally, conscientiousness often showed the greatest amount of change, and here, the pattern was closest to that predicted by the "set-like-plaster" model. In most cases, there were relatively large increases from adolescence to young adulthood, followed by a leveling off, with fewer changes among older adults. However, the peak of the curve often occurred after age 30, and at least some of the studies suggested that conscientiousness levels again decreased among the oldest old. Importantly, the results from the longitudinal studies were not dramatically different from the cross-sectional studies, which suggests that the effects are likely due to age rather than to different experiences that people who have lived through different historical periods may have had.

It is now clear, using data from a wide variety of sources, countries, and methodologies, that at least in terms of mean-level change, personality does not become set like plaster at age 30. Indeed, among the studies that have large enough samples to obtain precise estimates of the changes that occur before age 30 and to compare them to the changes after age 30, most show little evidence of a generalized slowing of change at this critical age. Instead, personality appears to change in similar ways (for most traits) throughout the life span. In terms of the precise nature of this change, some have referred to the *maturity principle* (Caspi et al., 2005). According to this idea, average trait levels change in ways that reflect increasing psychological health and improved capabilities to fulfill adult social roles. This is reflected in replicable increases in conscientiousness and agreeableness, along with somewhat less replicable declines in neuroticism. Extraversion and openness also appear to decline, but these differences are not really reflected in the maturity principle. Clearly, many individual differences in change occur over the life span, but average levels of personality traits do not stop changing at age 30.

What about differential stability? Even if most people become more conscientious as they leave adolescence and approach middle age, are those who were most conscientious at age 20 still the most conscientious at age 40? To answer this question, it is essential that researchers use longitudinal data, which is often hard to come by. However, over the past few years, more and more such data have become available, and again, the answer we get tends to contradict James's ideas about personality being set like plaster (even if there is a gradual increase in stability as one ages).

In the previous chapter we noted that three large meta-analyses have summarized the results from the large number of longitudinal studies concerning differential stability (Ardelt, 2000; Ferguson, 2010; Roberts & DelVecchio, 2000). All three studies agreed that personality stability increases considerably with age, at least until young adulthood. However, beyond this first conclusion, the conclusions differed. For instance, Roberts and DelVecchio (2000) suggested that differential stability continues to increase linearly from infancy through the early 70s, with a peak stability near .70 over a period of several years. In contrast, Ardelt (2000) found that differential stability peaked around age 50 and then declined after that point. Finally, Ferguson (2010) suggested that existing studies underestimate personality stability because they did not correct for the problems of measurement error. Fortunately, procedures allow researchers to correct for this influence, and once Ferguson did this, he found that stability quickly rose to very high levels (e.g., stability coefficients greater than .80) even by the 20s. This last result is a bit more supportive of the set-like-plaster model.

Meta-analysis provides a useful technique for summarizing the many studies that exist in an area of research. However, meta-analyses require high-quality studies to summarize, and as we noted, many of the studies that exist are not ideal. More recently, large-scale, nationally representative panel studies have begun to include personality measures, and some have assessed personality more than once. We have now published two studies that have examined differential stability across different age groups over a period of 4 years (one study was conducted in Germany and one was conducted in Australia; Lucas & Donnellan, 2011; Wortman et al., 2012). In these studies, we were able to correct for measurement error, which allowed us to address Ferguson's (2010) concern about attenuated stability coefficients. In addition, because of the nature of the study, larger numbers of very old participants were included in our studies than had been included in previous studies, which allowed us to determine whether stability declined in old age. Results were remarkably consistent across the two studies.

First, for all five of the Big Five personality traits, personality stability increased from the late teens, reaching a peak in adulthood. Consistent with Ferguson (2010), after correcting for measurement error, the peak of this stability was around .80 (though it did vary by trait; the stability of extraversion reached .90 in one study, whereas the stability of neuroticism and agreeableness was a bit lower). However, consistent with Roberts and DelVecchio (2000), this peak tended to occur later than the 20s or 30s (though again, this varied a little bit by trait). On average, peak stability was reached between the ages of 50 and 60. Finally, consistent with Ardelt (2000), stability declined for all traits in both studies after age 60, showing that there is robust evidence that stability does not remain at its highest levels throughout the life span. Instead, it begins to decline again in late life. This finding makes sense, as these oldest adults may begin to experience physical changes that could influence their personality traits, and they might experience more life transitions (such as the loss of friends and spouses, retirement, and perhaps a move to assisted-living housing), and these transitions may have cumulative effects on their personality.

As we noted early on in this chapter, we probably have more evidence regarding the myth that personality becomes set like plaster than for any other myth discussed in this book. After many studies, some of which have included data from extremely large, representative samples, it is now clear that personality change does not stop at age 30. In terms of mean-level change, there is little evidence that even the rate of change has an inflection point at this age. Instead, for some traits, the change that occurs is linear over the life span or may even increase later in life. In terms of differential stability, the evidence does suggest—consistent with the set-like-plaster model—that stability increases from childhood through adulthood. However, this trend increases past age 30. Furthermore, even after correcting for measurement error, stability is not perfect (though it is quite high, illustrating the importance of stable personality traits). Finally, some recent evidence suggests that stability again declines among the oldest old, perhaps due to increasing biological and environmental changes in this group. Thus, there is strong reason to expect personality development to continue across the life span. It is important to keep this conclusion in the context of the material in Chapter 12. Personality traits can and do change; but evidence also points to consistency as well. So, it would be a mistake to predict that an adult would be dramatically different in 20 years, and it would be a mistake to predict that such an adult would be exactly the same over this interval. This reality is why we think about personality traits as relatively enduring attributes of the person.

References

Anusic, I., Lucas, R. E., & Donnellan, M. B. (2012). Cross-sectional age differences in personality: Evidence from nationally representative samples from Switzerland and the United States. *Journal of Research in Personality, 46*(1), 116–120.

Ardelt, M. (2000). Still stable after all these years? Personality stability theory revisited. *Social Psychology Quarterly, 63*(4), 392–405.

Caspi, A., Roberts, B. W., & Shiner, R. L. (2005). Personality development: Stability and change. *Annual Review of Psychology, 56*, 453–484.

Donnellan, M. B., & Lucas, R. E. (2008). Age differences in the Big Five across the life span: Evidence from two national samples. *Psychology and Aging, 23*(3), 558–566.

Ferguson, C. J. (2010). A meta-analysis of normal and disordered personality across the life span. *Journal of Personality and Social Psychology, 98*(4), 659–667.

James, W. (1985). *Psychology: The briefer course*. Notre Dame, IN: University of Notre Dame.

Lucas, R. E., & Donnellan, M. B. (2009). Age differences in personality: Evidence from a nationally representative Australian sample. *Developmental Psychology, 45*(5), 1353–1363.

Lucas, R. E., & Donnellan, M. B. (2011). Personality development across the life span: Longitudinal analyses with a national sample from Germany. *Journal of Personality and Social Psychology, 101*(4), 847–861.

McCrae, R., & Costa, P. (2003). *Personality in adulthood, a five-factor theory perspective* (2nd ed.). New York, NY: Guilford Press.

McCrae, R. R., Costa, P. T., Jr., Ostendorf, F., Angleitner, A., Hřebíčková, M., Avia, M. D., … Smith, P. B. (2000). Nature over nurture: Temperament, personality, and life span development. *Journal of Personality and Social Psychology, 78*(1), 173.

Roberts, B. W., & DelVecchio, W. F. (2000). The rank-order consistency of personality traits from childhood to old age: A quantitative review of longitudinal studies. *Psychological Bulletin, 126*(1), 3–25.

Srivastava, S., John, O. P., Gosling, S. D., & Potter, J. (2003). Development of personality in early and middle adulthood: Set like plaster or persistent change? *Journal of Personality and Social Psychology, 84*(5), 1041–1053.

Wortman, J., Lucas, R. E., & Donnellan, M. B. (2012). Stability and change in the Big Five personality domains: Evidence from a longitudinal study of Australians. *Psychology and Aging, 27*(4), 867–874.

14 TRAUMATIC LIFE EVENTS DRAMATICALLY RESHAPE PERSONALITY

One of the most interesting things about studying personality is checking whether our intuitions about personality characteristics track with scientific evidence. Indeed, much of this book is about the ways that common intuitions can steer people to conclusions about the world that are too strong, too certain, or sometimes just plain wrong. Sometimes people strongly believe in some specific cause of behaviors that is not supported by scientific evidence, such as the idea that most situations overwhelm personality traits when predicting behavior. Indeed, as we have discussed throughout this book so far, many of the ways that common intuitions are wrong relate to beliefs about the relative importance of internal versus external influences on psychological processes and behavior.

For instance, imagine yourself as a child growing up in a stable home with two parents. You suddenly experience an incredible loss—both your parents are killed in a car accident. Because of this event, you are subject to enormous upheaval, including a new family, a new school, quite likely new friends, and many experiences that you would not have had if your parents were still alive. Or alternatively, imagine as an adult working at a stable job, you are suddenly laid off, forced to seek new employment, perhaps in an entirely new field in an entirely new state. Would these major life events lead to dramatic differences in your personality? Would the external changes cause you to be a different person—or at least to have a different personality—than you would have otherwise had?

Great Myths of Personality, First Edition. M. Brent Donnellan and Richard E. Lucas.
© 2021 John Wiley & Sons, Inc. Published 2021 by John Wiley & Sons, Inc.

Most of us would probably assume that the answer to this question would be an unequivocal "yes." You might be able to point to examples of events in your own life—hopefully none as extreme as those mentioned above—that you believe have influenced your personality traits. You might be able to point to a critical job or educational experience that changed the way you focused on work or school to make you more conscientious. Or you might remember a good friend or family member who was such an important role model that you were inspired to become better, nicer, and more agreeable. However, the fact that you believe you understand the processes that led to the development of your current personality does not necessarily mean that your ideas are correct. Research shows that people often come up with completely plausible theories about the explanations of their behaviors, even when those explanations are demonstrably false (Nisbett & Wilson, 1977). People are good storytellers, especially when it comes to explaining the causes of their own personality. Given this human tendency to tell coherent (and often self-serving) life stories, it is important to consider the empirical evidence.

Interestingly, one line of research has shown that perceptions of personality change are often inaccurate. For instance, although it is often difficult to determine why a person's personality has changed, a number of studies allow us to determine whether his or her personality has changed. And once such a study has been undertaken, it is also possible to compare the amount of change that has occurred with the person's perceptions of that change. Somewhat surprisingly, perceptions often do not map on to reality. In one study, Herbst, McCrae, Costa, Feaganes, and Siegler (2000) followed more than 2,000 people for between 6 and 9 years and then asked them whether they thought they had stayed the same, changed a little, or changed a lot. Most people believed that they had stayed pretty much the same (which, as we have described elsewhere in this book, is likely not so far from the truth). To be fair, the accuracy of these judgments does vary, perhaps with the age of the people studied (Robins, Noftle, Trzesniewski, & Roberts, 2005). But the point is that even when evaluating whether change has occurred, people often have trouble arriving at perfectly accurate judgments. When people consider the cause of that change, the task becomes even more difficult. After all, do you really know why you are the way you are?

As with many of the questions we have tackled in this book, determining whether major life events, traumatic or otherwise, influence personality trait change turns out to be extremely difficult to address in a conclusive fashion. Just imagine what type of study would be needed to answer this question. Putting aside the issue of establishing causality in a definitive way (experimental studies that actually created traumatic events for some people but not others are gravely unethical), the most feasible design would be to follow large groups of people for long periods of time and examine what happens when some of those people experience traumatic events and others do not. However, traumatic events are thankfully very rare, so even in the largest studies, such events are unlikely to happen to many of the participants. This is a good thing for people in the studies but poses a problem for researchers.

Because of this difficulty, alternative approaches to examining this question must be used, and most have serious limitations. For example, the most common approach to examining the impact of childhood life events is to ask a large group of people what their personality is like and then ask them whether they have had any traumatic experiences. However, although you might think that traumatic experiences can be remembered and reported with some amount of accuracy, the process is somewhat tricky. For instance, it is possible that the events that would rise to the level of being "traumatic" may differ for different individuals. Different people might define traumatic differently. And more importantly, a person's current personality may be related to the tendency to classify things this way. People who are high on neuroticism, for instance, may exaggerate or be more affected by objectively similar events as compared with individuals who are low on neuroticism. And no matter how objective sounding the events that are to be remembered may be, there is always room for interpretation. Thus, studies that rely on retrospective reports of traumatic events or other major life changes are difficult to interpret. It becomes a chicken-and-egg problem in terms of separating personality traits from the perceptions of traumatic events.

Because of the limitations of studies that rely on retrospective reports, combined with the difficulty of doing large longitudinal studies in which enough people experience major life events to provide statistical precision, alternative designs are often used. Specifically, researchers may rely on relatively large, cross-sectional samples of participants who are willing to report on their personality as it is right now. These researchers can then identify ways of obtaining objective information about prior traumatic events. For instance, if both parents say that their adult child experienced a certain event when young, then it is quite likely that that event actually occurred as described. Similarly, certain types of events (like the death of a parent, being a victim of a crime, or experiencing a traumatic health problem) may result in objective records that can be verified later on in life. If we were to find in such studies that the experience of life events was associated with differences in personality, this might provide stronger evidence for the importance of these events.

However, even here there is a challenge to the conclusions that can be drawn. This is due to the fact that life events do not occur randomly. The hypothetical study that we just described is correlational—the researchers observe a correlation between the past occurrence of a major event and current differences in personality. Even though that event occurred before the assessment of personality, it is possible that something about one's personality made the event more likely to occur. Or alternatively, there may be some third variable that caused both the event itself and the personality of the participant. What could such a third variable be? The most likely possibility would be the personality of the parents themselves. People with certain personalities may be more likely to experience certain types of events, and the children of those people would be more likely than average to experience those events and to have personality traits similar to their parents. Thus, with such a correlational study, it is still difficult to conclude that the events caused the personality to change.

Indeed, a number of studies have found that such factors are at work in the experience of major life events. How do we know? One way is by studying twins. We have discussed twin studies a few times throughout this book. This method is especially powerful for determining whether external factors are responsible for current characteristics of the people who are being studied. For example, if we want to know whether extraversion is due to our genes or the way we were raised, we can study identical twins who were separated at birth and reared by different parents. If genes matter, these separated twins should be quite similar in extraversion; if environment matters, they should be quite different. As we have described elsewhere, in terms of personality traits, it appears that genes are a significant factor, whereas life events shared by twins in the same family do not seem to matter nearly as much for personality.

The twin methodology can be used to study whether the events that happen to people are, themselves, heritable. Again, using the logic described above, if the events that occurred to people were due to chance or to the environments that they grew up in, then identical twins who were reared apart should not be very similar in the types of events that occur to them. If, in contrast, something about the person pulls for these events, then even identical twins who were raised by different parents may experience similar types of events across their lives. It appears that the evidence supports at least some genetic effect on the events that tend to occur (Afifi, Asmundson, Taylor, & Jang, 2010; Jang, Dick, Wolf, Livesley, & Paris, 2005; Jang, Stein, Taylor, Asmundson, & Livesley, 2003). To be sure, genes are not the only factors at work here. Most studies that use twin designs to examine traumatic events find that the role of genes is measurable but not especially large. In addition, the effect of genes appears to depend on the type of trauma experienced. One study found that assaultive traumas (such as being the victim of a violent crime) were heritable but nonassaultive traumas (such as having one's parent die in a car accident) were not (Jang et al., 2003). (See if you can come up with a theory to explain this pattern of results.)

Importantly, researchers who study these effects are quick to point out that genes do not directly affect the likelihood of experiencing an event. Instead, it is more likely that genes affect broad personality dispositions, which in turn make it more or less likely that a person will be in situations that contribute to these traumatic events (Jang et al., 2003). The point is that it is difficult to interpret a simple association between the experience of life events and specific personality traits; without prospective, longitudinal data, it is impossible to determine which came first.

When examining the links between trauma and personality change, it is not always the case that negative effects are to be expected. Indeed, a relatively large literature focuses on the possibility that trauma can lead to growth (Jayawickreme & Blackie, 2014). The idea behind these investigations is that traumatic events make people reevaluate their priorities, change their life stories, identify strengths that they did not know existed, or develop and appreciate strong interpersonal bonds. And although these benefits are primarily in terms of mental health and well-being, some theories of posttraumatic growth posit that these changes, in turn, lead to true changes in otherwise stable personality traits. In a recent review of the evidence for posttraumatic growth, however, Jayawickreme and Blackie (2014) noted that most research investigating the topic is cross-sectional, precluding strong conclusions about the extent to which such growth occurs.

Thus far, we have focused mainly on research that examines the links between trauma (especially childhood trauma) and personality change. However, this is just one line of research in a broader effort to examine the links between life events and personality characteristics. So, it is possible to turn to this broader effort to determine whether there is evidence that life events can lead to personality change. And to be sure, a number of studies show that personality can be linked with changes in life circumstances (see Luhmann, Orth, Specht, Kandler, & Lucas, 2014, for a review). However, when these studies are examined closely, many of the same issues we described come into play when studying the impact of nontraumatic life events or the impact of events in populations other than children. For instance, Luhmann et al. (2014) noted that few studies use research designs that allow for clear conclusions about the long-term effects of life events on personality. Many studies follow people for short periods of time, which means that the extent to which personality change lasts cannot be determined. Other studies do not assess personality before the event occurs, which means that selection effects cannot be addressed (i.e., the possibility that personality traits channel people toward the experience of certain life events). Finally, even when effects of life circumstances are found, the size of these effects is often not large, and few of the effects that have been identified have been replicated in independent samples. Thus, even when more mundane life events are examined, it is often difficult to find unambiguous evidence that specific life experiences lead to large changes in personality in robust ways.

In 2015, Disney/Pixar released a movie called *Inside Out*. In this movie, the emotional life of a young girl is examined as her family moves to a new home in a new location. Although the movie received attention mainly because of the insightful way that it portrayed emotions and emotional development, it also presented an intuitive view of how personality works and how personality may change. According to the story, personality is developed through the accumulation of emotionally important memories that then provide a guide for future experiences or resources that can be called upon when facing new challenges. Accordingly, personality develops gradually, with the accumulation of new, important memories. In addition, as the movie illustrated, this intuitive view suggests that one's personality can change dramatically if these critical memories are seen in a new light or replaced with different recollections. In short, *Inside Out* does an excellent job describing a plausible, intuitive model of how personality forms and changes over time, and this model leaves open the possibility for dramatic changes in personality as new experiences are encountered.

The problem with this intuitive model, however, is that it ignores the broad array of influences—many of which are hidden, or at least difficult to observe—that affect the characteristic pattern of thoughts, feelings, and behaviors that make up our personality. Although it is probably true that our conscious thoughts about meaningful life experiences can influence the characteristic ways that we deal with the world, this is just one factor—and it is probably not the most important one—that influences our personality. As we have discussed elsewhere in this book, behavioral genetic studies and direct examinations of the physiological systems in the brain and the rest of the body suggest that we are probably born with at least some deep-seated, physiological differences that influence our personalities. Furthermore, even if personality results from experience, it is likely that long-term exposure to constant stimuli in the world around us—constant pressures to act a certain way—play a stronger role in determining our personality than do short-term changes or one-time events. Indeed, some researchers have suggested that personality traits are (somewhat paradoxically) most likely to be exhibited in a strong and unambiguous way when we are exposed to unusual circumstances like trauma or dramatic changes (Caspi & Moffitt, 1993). The idea is that in challenging new circumstances in which a person feels uncertain about how to act, he or she will be especially likely to fall back on the behaviors that have worked in the past, namely, the characteristic behaviors that are most strongly associated with his or her personality traits. Thus, although we typically think of important life events as phenomena that have the potential to "shake up" one's personality traits, this paradoxical hypothesis suggests that it is during these times of transition that our stable personality traits exert their strongest effects.

To sum up, intuitive theories of how personality develops suggest that important life events should dramatically reshape personality characteristics. However, this intuitive model is based on a relatively narrow consideration of the broad array of hidden influences on personality. Biological factors and long-term learning histories likely lead to stable characteristics that are not only resistant to change but that may be especially pronounced in times of change. Moreover, the research we reviewed consistently points to one clear fact about research on life events and personality change: *This research is extremely hard to do.* The ideal study requires large numbers of people to be followed over long periods of time so that rare events can occur and long-term changes can be examined. Unfortunately, too few studies possess these characteristics to allow strong conclusions about the extent to which major life events lead to lasting changes. However, the studies that exist suggest that the effects of life events that have been observed are often not large, and many of these associations have plausible alternative explanations that cannot presently be ruled out. To be sure, as we have discussed in earlier chapters, personality is not completely stable over time, and to the extent that it changes, researchers must strive to understand the causes of that change. Thus, sophisticated research on the links between changes in the environment and changes in personality should continue to be conducted; and researchers and lay people alike should be cautious in interpreting the results of these studies.

References

Afifi, T. O., Asmundson, G. J., Taylor, S., & Jang, K. L. (2010). The role of genes and environment on trauma exposure and posttraumatic stress disorder symptoms: A review of twin studies. *Clinical Psychology Review*, 30(1), 101–112.

Caspi, A., & Moffitt, T. E. (1993). When do individual differences matter? A paradoxical theory of personality coherence. *Psychological Inquiry*, 4(4), 247–271.

Herbst, J. H., McCrae, R. R., Costa, P. T., Feaganes, J. R., & Siegler, I. C. (2000). Self-perceptions of stability and change in personality at midlife: The uNC alumni heart study. *Assessment*, 7(4), 379–388.

Jang, K. L., Dick, D. M., Wolf, H., Livesley, W. J., & Paris, J. (2005). Psychosocial adversity and emotional instability: An application of gene–environment interaction models. *European Journal of Personality*, 19(4), 359–372.

Jang, K. L., Stein, M. B., Taylor, S., Asmundson, G. J., & Livesley, W. J. (2003). Exposure to traumatic events and experiences: Aetiological relationships with personality function. *Psychiatry Research*, 120(1), 61–69.

Jayawickreme, E., & Blackie, L. E. (2014). Post-traumatic growth as positive personality change: Evidence, controversies and future directions. *European Journal of Personality*, 28(4), 312–331.

Luhmann, M., Orth, U., Specht, J., Kandler, C., & Lucas, R. E. (2014). Studying changes in life circumstances and personality: It's about time. *European Journal of Personality*, 28(3), 256–266.

Nisbett, R. E., & Wilson, T. D. (1977). Telling more than we can know: Verbal reports on mental processes. *Psychological Review*, 84(3), 231–259.

Robins, R. W., Noftle, E. E., Trzesniewski, K. H., & Roberts, B. W. (2005). Do people know how their personality has changed? Correlates of perceived and actual personality change in young adulthood. *Journal of Personality*, 73(2), 489–522.

15 ADOLESCENCE IS THE MOST SIGNIFICANT PERIOD OF PERSONALITY DEVELOPMENT

Adolescence is a phase in life characterized by physical, cognitive, and emotional changes.[1] It is often depicted in popular movies and books as a difficult time. Likewise, a long-standing tradition in developmental psychology considered adolescence as a time of storm and stress (Hall, 1904; also see Arnett, 1999; but see Eccles et al., 1993; Petersen et al., 1993), and the idea that adolescence was a time of identity crisis was prominent in the well-known work of Erik Erikson (e.g., 1968). A study in the late 1980s (Holmbeck & Hill, 1988) suggested that college students endorsed beliefs about adolescence consistent with the storm-and-stress view. Surveys of parent and teachers found that they also tended to believe that adolescence was a difficult time of life (Buchanan et al., 1990; see also Steinberg, 2001). It would be interesting to replicate those studies in this century, and we suspect the results would hold up. In view of the tradition of viewing adolescence as a difficult time of life, there is a belief that adolescence is perhaps the time of the life span with most substantial personality development. This is a myth, however. As we discuss below,

---

[1] There is debate about the precise beginning and end of adolescence. We adopt the convention that it encompasses the years between ages 12 and 17 (Arnett, 2000). Nonetheless, delineating the exact time frame for adolescence is not important for this chapter so long as readers accept that it covers the second decade of life.

Great Myths of Personality, First Edition. M. Brent Donnellan and Richard E. Lucas.
© 2021 John Wiley & Sons, Inc. Published 2021 by John Wiley & Sons, Inc.

the reality is that more systematic changes tend to occur in the 20s, a period sometimes referred to as young adulthood. This chapter builds on previous chapters about personality development (especially Chapters 12 and 13) by drawing on many of the same meta-analyses.

The evidence

Roberts, Walton, and Viechtbauer (2006) conducted a meta-analytic review of 92 longitudinal studies tracking personality change over time. They tried to collect all available studies on personality change so they could draw conclusions based on an entire literature rather than just a single study. Their primary focus was on whether average levels of a given trait increased, decreased, or remained the same across substantial periods of time. Specifically, they computed the difference in average personality scores across two times of measurement so that a positive score indicated an average increase with age, whereas a negative score indicated an average decrease.

Roberts and colleagues also evaluated the starting age of each sample to determine when in life the biggest changes tended to occur. Therefore, they could test whether there were more increases or decreases in samples with starting ages in the teens versus the 20s, 30s, and so on. This procedure allowed them to identify the period of life when the most personality change occurs.

The findings from this analysis were somewhat surprising: Roberts and colleagues found that the largest changes occurred for samples with starting ages between 18 and 40 rather than samples with starting ages between 10 and 18. They concluded that "personality traits change most during the period of young adulthood (age 20 to 40), rather than in adolescence" (p. 12). Recall that this conclusion is based on an analysis of multiple studies rather than a single study, so it should be given substantial weight when evaluating the strength of the evidence. Findings from a single study can be suggestive, but conclusions that are derived from multiple studies are often more robust and therefore more persuasive.

The general pattern of mean-level change that occurs is that average levels of traits increase from early adolescence through adulthood in ways that seem to facilitate functioning in adult social roles (see, e.g., Soto, John, Gosling, & Potter, 2011). In other words, as people get older, they really do seem to *mature*: They increase in positive, adaptive traits like conscientiousness and agreeableness, and they tend to decrease in neuroticism. As we discussed in previous chapters, this pattern of change is often called the *maturity principle* of personality development because it reflects a tendency for people to develop personality characteristics that are associated with maturity as they age (Caspi, Roberts, & Shiner, 2005). An accessible discussion of personality and identity development is available in Klimstra (2013). We should also point out that some studies even suggest that personality trait development regresses a bit during adolescence— early adolescents, for example, might have lower levels of agreeableness and conscientiousness than children (see Klimstra, 2013); however, more work is needed on this topic.

Evaluating changes in average levels of personality is one way to approach the study of personality development, and evidence from this type of study suggests that changes in personality are not especially pronounced in adolescence. As we discussed in Chapters 12 and 13, though, another way to think about personality development and change is to consider whether people maintain the same trait standing relative to others over time. When personality psychologists ask questions about relative standing, they are asking whether the people who score highest on a trait at one point in time still score relatively highly at some point in the future. It is possible that average levels of a personality trait may be relatively stable in adolescents, while people's relative position on personality trait measures changes dramatically during this time. Similarly, it is possible for mean levels to change in important ways, while the relative stability remains quite high.

To make this possibility a little more concrete, think about body weight. It seems likely that individuals gain weight as they age. At the same time, individuals might still preserve their relative standing as they age such that relatively light weight people at age 20 weigh less than average at age 40, and similarly, relatively heavy people at age 20 would also be relatively heavy at age 40. As we noted earlier, this kind of personality stability is called *rank-order* consistency, and it is often investigated by correlating scores taken on a sample at one time point with scores at a second time point. Evidence for the idea that personality change is greatest during adolescence would come from studies that showed that over-time correlations are weakest during that period. As we shall see, evidence like this serves as the "kernel of truth" for the myth that adolescence is an especially important time for personality development.

As was true for studies of mean-level change, a number of meta-analyses have been conducted to aggregate evidence about over-time correlations in personality trait scores among people of different ages. This meta-analytic evidence suggests that long-term retest correlations do increase with age (Ardelt, 2000; Ferguson, 2010; Roberts & DelVecchio, 2000). Specifically, these correlations increase from childhood through old age, at least until retirement age, a point at which they may level off or even decline (see, e.g., Lucas & Donnellan, 2011; Specht, Egloff, & Schmukle, 2011; Wortman, Lucas, & Donnellan, 2012). Taken together, the existing data suggest that although some idiosyncratic personality changes do occur in adolescence (changes that result in relatively low rank-order stability during this period of life), there are more systematic, normative changes that occur during the early adult years than during the adolescent years. Thus, if we use the term *personality development* to refer to this more systematic form of change, then it is a myth to say that adolescence is the time of greatest personality change.

The fact that personality traits change beyond adolescence and especially during young adulthood raises interesting possibilities about the processes and mechanisms that are responsible for personality trait changes. Many important life events occur during the early adult years, such as the completion of formal education, movement into the world of work and the adult labor market, the formation of committed romantic unions (e.g., marriage and cohabitation), and, for some, the transition to parenthood (Rindfuss, 1991). It remains to be seen whether these kinds of life events or intrinsic biological changes toward maturity are the primary driving force in personality development (see, e.g., Costa & McCrae, 2006), although life events seem to matter (e.g., Bleidorn, Kandler, Riemann, Angleitner, & Spinath, 2009). Indeed, researchers are actively trying to address this question, and they often focus on the young adult years rather than adolescence proper to study this issue (Bleidorn et al., 2019). All of this is a way to circle back to the central myth of this chapter—perhaps young adulthood and not adolescence is the best time to study personality development!

References

Ardelt, M. (2000). Still stable after all these years? Personality stability theory revisited. *Social Psychology Quarterly, 63*, 392–405.

Arnett, J. J. (1999). Adolescent storm and stress, reconsidered. *American Psychologist, 54*(5), 317–326.

Arnett, J. J. (2000). Emerging adulthood: A theory of development from the late teens through the twenties. *American Psychologist, 55*(5), 469–480.

Bleidorn, W., Hill, P., Back, M., Denissen, J. J. A., Hennecke, M., Hopwood, C. J., … Roberts, B. (2019). The policy relevance of personality traits. *American Psychologist, 74*(9), 1056–1067. doi: 10.1037/amp0000503

Bleidorn, W., Kandler, C., Riemann, R., Angleitner, A., & Spinath, F. M. (2009). Patterns and sources of adult personality development: Growth curve analyses of the NEO PI-R scales in a longitudinal twin study. *Journal of Personality and Social Psychology, 97*(1), 142–155.

Buchanan, C. M., Eccles, J. S., Flanagan, C., Midgley, C., Feldlaufer, H., & Harold, R. D. (1990). Parents' and teachers' beliefs about adolescents: Effects of sex and experience. *Journal of Youth and Adolescence, 19*(4), 363–394.

Caspi, A., Roberts, B. W., & Shiner, R. L. (2005). Personality development: Stability and change. *Annual Review of Psychology, 56*, 453–484.

Costa, P. T., Jr., & McCrae, R. R. (2006). Age changes in personality and their origins: Comment on Roberts, Walton, and Viechtbauer (2006). *Psychological Bulletin, 132*, 26–28.

Eccles, J. S., Midgley, C., Wigfield, A., Buchanan, C. M., Reuman, D., Flanagan, C., & Mac Iver, D. (1993). Development during adolescence: The impact of stage-environment fit on young adolescents' experiences in schools and in families. *American Psychologist, 48*(2), 90–101.

Erikson, E. H. (1968). *Identity: Youth and crisis.* New York, NY: Norton.

Ferguson, C. J. (2010). A meta-analysis of normal and disordered personality across the life span. *Journal of Personality and Social Psychology, 98*, 659–667.

Hall, G. S. (1904). *Adolescence* (Vol. I and II). New York, NY: Appleton.

Holmbeck, G. N., & Hill, J. P. (1988). Storm and stress beliefs about adolescence: Prevalence, self-reported antecedents, and effects of an undergraduate course. *Journal of Youth and Adolescence, 17*(4), 285–306.

Klimstra, T. (2013). Adolescent personality development and identity formation. *Child Development Perspectives, 7*(2), 80–84.

Lucas, R. E., & Donnellan, M. B. (2011). Personality development across the life span: Longitudinal analyses with a national sample from Germany. *Journal of Personality and Social Psychology, 101*(4), 847–861.

Petersen, A. C., Compas, B. E., Brooks-Gunn, J., Stemmler, M., Ey, S., & Grant, K. E. (1993). Depression in adolescence. *American Psychologist, 48*(2), 155–168.

Rindfuss, R. R. (1991). The young adult years: Diversity, structural change, and fertility. *Demography, 28*(4), 493–512.

Roberts, B. W., & DelVecchio, W. F. (2000). The rank-order consistency of personality traits from childhood to old age: A quantitative review of longitudinal studies. *Psychological Bulletin, 126*, 3–25.

Roberts, B. W., Walton, K. E., & Viechtbauer, W. (2006). Patterns of mean-level change in personality traits across the life course: A meta-analysis of longitudinal studies. *Psychological Bulletin, 132*, 1–25.

Soto, C. J., John, O. P., Gosling, S. D., & Potter, J. (2011). Age differences in personality traits from 10 to 65: Big five domains and facets in a large cross-sectional sample. *Journal of Personality and Social Psychology, 100*(2), 330–348.

Specht, J., Egloff, B., & Schmukle, S. C. (2011). Stability and change of personality across the life course: The impact of age and major life events on mean-level and rank-order stability of the Big Five. *Journal of Personality and Social Psychology, 101*, 862–882.

Steinberg, L. (2001). We know some things: Parent–adolescent relationships in retrospect and prospect. *Journal of Research on Adolescence, 11*(1), 1–19.

Wortman, J., Lucas, R. E., & Donnellan, M. B. (2012). Stability and change in the Big Five personality domains: Evidence from a longitudinal study of Australians. *Psychology and Aging, 27*, 867–874.

16 BIRTH ORDER IS AN IMPORTANT INFLUENCE ON PERSONALITY

The Achiever, the Peacemaker and the Life of the Party: How Birth Order Affects Personality

> (title of article in the Huffington Post, 12/23/2013; see: http://www.
> huffingtonpost.com/dr-gail-gross/how-birth-order-
> affects-personality_b_4494385.html)

Of the many factors that could potentially affect personality, one that has attracted a great deal of attention is the order in which people are born into their families. It seems intuitive that there could be systematic differences in the way that parents treat firstborn children relative to laterborn children, and also that these differences in treatment would translate into noticeable differences in personality. But do these intuitions reflect reality? Do intuitions about parental treatment reflect real differences in behavior? And do differences in treatment ultimately cause differences in personality? This topic has generated quite a bit of public interest, and many popular books about birth order suggest that this factor plays an important role in personality development (see Bleske-Rechek & Kelley, 2014).

Behavior genetic researchers have long wondered why children in the same family are so different from one another (Plomin, 2011; Plomin & Daniels, 1987, 2011). This finding has led to the search for environmental factors that could explain why genetically similar individuals differ (i.e., biological siblings). Birth order is an intuitively appealing explanation for why genetically similar siblings are so different (Harris, 2000; Sulloway, 1996). As it turns out, however, the idea that birth order plays a strong

Great Myths of Personality, First Edition. M. Brent Donnellan and Richard E. Lucas.
© 2021 John Wiley & Sons, Inc. Published 2021 by John Wiley & Sons, Inc.

role in personality differences is probably a myth. Before getting into the data, though, it is useful to provide some historical context for this myth.

The neo-Freudian psychotherapist Alfred Adler (see, e.g., Adler, 1928) was a vocal proponent of the idea that birth order was a significant determinant of personality (if you are so inclined you might check out Chapter 9 in his book *Understanding Human Nature: The Psychology of Personality)* (Adler, 1927). Although Adler never carried out systematic research on the topic, he outlined the personality profiles associated with individuals who differ in birth order. Adler's basic observation was that firstborn children start the world at the center of attention in their families. No other siblings exist to divert attention from doting parents. This creates feelings of power in the developing child. Firstborn children are the monarchs of their world until the arrival of a sibling. This centrality in the family would have been a concern for Adler, as his theories often focused on the negative consequences of pampering children (he was also concerned about neglect; balance was something that Adler prized). In other words, firstborn children might receive too much attention and indulgence, at least until the birth of a sibling.

Adler saw the birth of the second child in a family as a major event that produced a sense of dethronement for the firstborn. It is unpleasant to be pushed out of the limelight, and it hurts to move from the center of attention to a supporting character role. Consider the plight of aging athletes who must yield playing time to the younger stars of a team. This change in centrality can be especially challenging, as the older child is still immature psychologically and often expected to help care for the new sibling. Given this family dynamic, firstborn children were thought to be concerned with power and somewhat focused on the past. Nonetheless, they strive for attention and tend to achieve, perhaps thinking that they can regain parental favor by succeeding in school. Firstborns were thought to be conscientious, responsible, and detail orientated as adults. They might also be politically and socially conservative given their admiration of the past.

Because laterborn children never enjoyed the centrality and power of the firstborn, they never experienced a sense of dethronement. Instead, such children might be the perennial "baby" of the family and may have received more coddling from parents and even older siblings. This meant they might be subject to overindulgence. Thus, as adults, they might be dependent on others and somewhat undercontrolled or impulsive.

However, laterborn children could turn out to be overachievers because they had older siblings to serve as models and provide sources of competition (Adler thought that one of the struggles of life was to overcome feelings of inferiority). In more modern treatments of birth order based on evolutionary accounts (Sulloway, 1996), laterborn siblings are thought to be rebellious because their older siblings had already adopted the conventional role in the family. Laterborns could distinguish themselves by taking more risks and adopting more liberal perspectives than their older sibling. For example, laterborns might be more likely to start scientific revolutions (Sulloway, 1996).

These family dynamics meant that middle children were in a privileged position to avoid the psychic injury of dethronement and the ills of being spoiled and indulged (remember that Adler was a follower of Freud, so he was psychoanalytically inclined). Middle children have at least one older sibling to serve as a marker for competition, and thus their cognitive and physical abilities might develop more rapidly. At the same time, they have younger siblings to care for, and there is less of a risk of being the spoiled "baby" of the family. This might mean that as adults, the middle child would be competitive, ambitious, and optimistic. There's a catch, however. If a middle child was unlucky enough to have an exceptionally talented older sibling, competition might be a losing proposition. Thus, the competitive drive of the middle sibling could be thwarted by exposure to an exceptional firstborn.

You might be wondering about only children who are not subjected to sibling influences. The picture here was thought to be mixed. According to Adler's theory, only children are never dethroned and persist as the center of attention in the family. They spend lots of time with adults and were thought to adopt adult attitudes earlier in development. However, like firstborns, only children risk being pampered and spoiled and might be expected to have trouble in school and other settings when they are not the center of attention.

This sketch of birth-order effects inspired by Adler is surprisingly like more modern articles on the subject one might find from a quick internet search. Indeed, the 2013 Huffington Post article mentioned at the beginning of this chapter suggested that firstborns were achievers, middle children were peacemakers (cooperative and flexible but still competitive), and youngest children were the life of the party. Only children are lone wolves. Old ideas are sometimes new again. But do these ideas have strong evidentiary support?

The evidence

Let's cut to the chase: no. Evidence that birth order is a systematic predictor of personality is weak (see Damian & Roberts, 2015; Rohrer, Egloff, & Schmukle, 2015). Ernst and Angst drew this conclusion in 1983 and suggested that birth-order influences were exaggerated (p. 242). Old ideas are new again in psychological science as well! The field of birth-order studies is contentious, and one commentator went so far as to coin the phrase the "birth order trap" (Rodgers, 2000, p. 168). For whatever reason, people want to believe in the power of birth order, but the concern is that any interesting ideas about the influence of birth order are accepted as fact well before adequate tests are conducted. When adequate tests of birth-order effects are performed, the evidence usually fails to support strong birth-order effects on personality.

We should acknowledge that there are a number of methodological complexities involved in testing for birth-order effects (see Ernst & Angst, 1983; Rodgers, 2000; Rodgers, Cleveland, van den Oord, & Rowe, 2000; Wichman, Rodgers, & MacCallum, 2006). For instance, researchers know that SES correlates with how many children are in a family: Wealthier families tend to have fewer children. Because large families have more laterborn children, people who are laterborns tend to come from families with lower SES. This and other confounds make it difficult to compare firstborns from one family to laterborns from a different family. Because of this problem, many researchers believe that the most appropriate research design for studying birth-order effects is to compare siblings within the same family who are presumably exposed to similar shared factors such as income and parental educational levels. However, even this research design is not without challenges. When looking within families, birth order is always completely confounded with age if the study takes place at a single point in time: Firstborns are always older than laterborns, so any effect that is found may simply be an effect of age.

Sulloway (2011) reported a meta-analysis of 10 studies that compared siblings using measures of the Big Five personality traits for within-family designs (i.e., comparisons of siblings within the same family). The largest effect size was for conscientiousness ($r = .18$ based on a sample size of 6,208), which means that conscientiousness scores were higher for those who were born earlier rather than later. The other correlations were between .00 (neuroticism; $N = 4,704$) and -0.13 (extraversion; $N = 5,346$). According to this meta-analysis, laterborns are less conscientious but more extraverted than firstborns. However, the effect sizes of the correlations were small, which undercuts the argument that birth order is the major nongenetic influence on personality. Even so, there might be some differences between firstborns and laterborns according to this work.

More recently, Damian and Roberts (2015) published an exceptionally large test of birth-order effects among 263,713 high school students. They used a between-families design but controlled for sex, age, family size, family structure, and family SES. In contrast to the meta-analytic results from Sulloway (2011), the final correlations (taking into account the control variables) ranged from –.02 (extraversion) to .04 (conscientiousness). The researchers noted that they observed "remarkably small effect sizes" (p. 104) and concluded that "birth order has a negligible relation to self-reported personality traits in a between-family design" (p. 103).

Rohrer et al. (2015) reported a comprehensive set of analyses using large datasets from Germany, the United Kingdom, and the United States. Birth-order position was not associated with any of the Big Five traits except perhaps for openness. When openness was decomposed into more specific facets related to intellect and imagination, an interesting pattern emerged. It seemed that birth order had nothing to do with imagination but was related to intellect (i.e., being quick to understand ideas). Rohrer et al. (2015) noted that this finding might reflect a small effect of birth order on cognitive ability, with firstborns exhibiting a very slight tendency to score higher than laterborn children. Like Damian and Roberts (2015), Rohrer et al. concluded that "birth order does not have a meaningful and lasting effect on broad Big Five personality traits outside of the intellectual domain" (p. 14227).

Summary

The idea that birth order accounts for a substantial amount of the variation in personality differences is a myth. Although the literature is somewhat inconsistent, the effect sizes from the very best studies are small (at best). This indicates that other factors are likely to be much more important than birth order for understanding why people are different from one another (in general) and why children in the same family often have different personalities. Indeed, the statistical control variables used by Damian and Roberts (2015) such as gender and family SES often had larger associations with personality when compared to birth order. Harris (2000) offered a memorable suggestion: "It is time for researchers to look elsewhere—outside the childhood home—for sources of the nongenetic variation in adult personality" (p. 177).

The evaluation of this myth raises interesting questions about the origins of the so-called birth-order trap. Why do people believe that birth order is an important factor in personality development? This could be a fruitful question for future research! We suspect a human tendency to like simple explanations. Indeed, the complete explanation as to why children in the same family have different personalities needs more attention, but the answer is likely to be quite complicated and involve multiple factors.

Furthermore, we suspect the strongly held belief in the power of birth order is really an expression of the intuition that siblings influence one another growing up. However, it is also useful to bear in mind that sibling influences are complicated. Older (and younger) siblings come into the world with different temperaments, and this fact makes it difficult to make blanket statements about the overall effects of siblings. Some older siblings might be conventional, whereas others might be rebellious. These initial tendencies might impact how younger siblings respond to the older sibling. The impact of a sibling on one's personality is likely to be bidirectional and probably depends on a multitude of factors such as gender, the closeness of the sibling relationship, the age gap, and so on. Sorting this out will take time and a great deal of data. Family dynamics and siblings might influence personality development, but it is likely to be a complex process. Regardless, we urge you to watch out for the birth-order trap. The evidence is far from compelling.

References

Adler, A. (1927). *Understanding human nature*. Oxford, England: Greenberg.

Adler, A. (1928). Characteristics of the first, second, and third child. *Children, 3,* 14–52.

Bleske-Rechek, A., & Kelley, J. A. (2014). Birth order and personality: A within-family test using independent self-reports from both firstborn and laterborn siblings. *Personality and Individual Differences, 56,* 15–18.

Damian, R. I., & Roberts, B. W. (2015). The associations of birth order with personality and intelligence in a representative sample of U.S. high school students. *Journal of Research in Personality, 58,* 96–105.

Ernst, C., & Angst, J. (1983). *Birth order: Its influence on personality*. Berlin, Germany: Springer.

Harris, J. R. (2000). Context-specific learning, personality, and birth order. *Current Directions in Psychological Science, 9,* 174–177.

Plomin, R. (2011). Commentary: Why are children in the same family so different? Non-shared environment three decades later. *International Journal of Epidemiology, 40*, 582–592.

Plomin, R., & Daniels, D. (1987). Why are children in the same family so different from one another? *Behavioral and Brain Sciences, 10*, 1–16.

Plomin, R., & Daniels, D. (2011). Why are children in the same family so different from one another? *International Journal of Epidemiology, 40*, 563–582.

Rodgers, J. L. (2000). The birth order trap. *Politics and the Life Sciences, 19*, 167–170.

Rodgers, J. L., Cleveland, H. H., van den Oord, E., & Rowe, D. C. (2000). Resolving the debate over birth order, family size, and intelligence. *American Psychologist, 55*, 599–612.

Rohrer, J. M., Egloff, B., & Schmukle, S. C. (2015). Examining the effects of birth order on personality. *Proceedings of the National Academy of Sciences of the United States of America, 112*(46), 14224–14229.

Sulloway, F. J. (1996). *Born to rebel: Birth order, family dynamics, and creative lives.* New York, NY: Pantheon Books.

Sulloway, F. J. (2011). Why siblings are like Darwin's finches: Birth order, sibling competition, and adaptive divergence within the family. In D. M. Buss & P. H. Hawley (Eds.), *The evolution of personality and individual differences* (pp. 86–119). New York, NY: Oxford.

Wichman, A. L., Rodgers, J. L., & MacCallum, R. C. (2006). A multilevel approach to the relationship between birth order and intelligence. *Personality and Social Psychology Bulletin, 32*(1), 117–127.

17 PARENTING PRACTICES ARE THE MAJOR SOURCE OF PERSONALITY DIFFERENCES

In Chapter 16, we addressed the idea that birth order is an important determining factor for people's personality. As we noted when introducing that topic, the idea that birth order matters is part of a broader tendency to believe that family dynamics are a major influence on personality if not the single biggest influence, overshadowing all others. In this chapter, we turn to a related issue: whether parenting practices systematically affect people's personality traits. As you should be able to guess by now, the point of this chapter will be to critically evaluate strong claims about parenting effects. Put simply, family dynamics are complicated, and we think it is an exaggeration to claim that parenting practices or any other aspect of family dynamics are the primary driver—or even a strong overall predictor—of personality differences.

Do people really believe that parents affect children's personality? If we look at the strong opinions that people have about parenting practices, it seems likely that they do. Think about recent debates regarding the dangers of "helicopter parenting," where parents hover over their children, watching every decision and protecting them from any potential danger, versus the relative benefits of encouraging "free-range children" who are left to make their own decisions and their own mistakes, which hopefully leads to a sense of empowerment and responsibility. Beliefs about the relative merits of these parenting practices presumably arise

Great Myths of Personality, First Edition. M. Brent Donnellan and Richard E. Lucas.
© 2021 John Wiley & Sons, Inc. Published 2021 by John Wiley & Sons, Inc.

because parents think these practices matter for their children's long-term outcomes. If you believe that allowing your children to "roam free" encourages them to become more responsible by learning from their mistakes, then you subscribe to a belief that parenting practices shape personality. Likewise, consider the conversations that occur when people try to explain ill-mannered or delinquent behaviors in teens. Parenting practices are often blamed. It is common to hear that parents were too lax with their children or sometimes even that parents were too harsh and that the teen was rebelling against parental authoritarianism.

Yet if parenting effects were especially powerful, then we might expect to find that children who grow up in the same home (in other words, children who are more likely than average to experience the same parenting practices) are more similar than any two random children in terms of the personality traits that they exhibit. Yet one of the most surprising findings that comes from research that examines this question is that children raised in the same family are often quite different from one another when it comes to personality attributes (Plomin, Asbury, & Dunn, 2001; Plomin & Daniels, 1987, 2011; Turkheimer & Waldron, 2000). In fact, an influential review paper concluded that once genetic similarity is taken into account, "siblings often appear no more alike than individuals selected at random from the population" (Turkheimer & Waldron, 2000, p. 78). This conclusion might be seen as a serious blow for a simple theory that posits the existence of a general parenting style that consistently and strongly shapes the personalities of siblings in the same way.

We've already talked about classic twin designs, but a quick review will make it easier to follow some of the evidence discussed in this chapter. The basic approach in a twin study is to identify pairs of siblings who differ in their genetic similarity and then to see how similar these sets of siblings are for specific attributes like personality traits. For instance, one specific type of sibling pair—monozygotic (MZ) or identical twins—shares 100% of their genes, whereas regular siblings and dizygotic (DZ) or fraternal twins share (on average) 50% of their genes. A simple approach is to compare identical and fraternal twin pairs that have each grown up in the same household. When identical twins are much more similar than fraternal twins, behavioral-genetics researchers infer that genes play a role. Why? If both identical and fraternal twin pairs are raised in the same household, then the household (and presumably, at least some parenting practices, though this secondary assumption is more complicated than it might first seem) is constant across the pairs. Something else beyond parenting practices is needed to explain why the similarity was higher for the identical twin pairs. The higher genetic similarity for identical (MZ twins) as opposed to fraternal twins (DZ twins) is a good explanation.

As an aside, if you are interested in seeing estimates of similarities for identical and fraternal twins for a wide range of variables, there is a fascinating website you can access (http://match.ctglab.nl/#/home). This site collates data from 2,748 twin studies published from 1958 to 2012 (see Polderman et al., 2015) and quickly returns similarity estimates for identical and fraternal twins. In virtually all cases, identical twins are more similar than fraternal twins. Such work points to a broad role for genetics in explaining differences between people for many individual differences—not just personality traits like the Big Five.

Another simple way to evaluate whether genetic factors are relevant for an attribute is to find a natural experiment in which identical twins are separated early in life and grow up in different families. If those kinds of twins show similarity, the most plausible explanation for this similarity is the genes that the twins share. How else could they turn out to be the same given that they grew up in different environments and experienced different life circumstances? Researchers have not found a huge number of these separated MZ twins, but some have been studied, and the results support the idea that powerful genetic influences exist (see Tellegen et al., 1988). MZ twins separated early in life show impressive and sometimes eerie levels of similarity.

Indeed, as we discussed in previous chapters, genetic factors are a part of the explanation of why people have different personalities. More specifically, a large review paper based on a summary analysis of 134 studies concluded that about 40% of the variability in personality traits could be attributable to genetic variance (Vukasović & Bratko, 2015). Of course, the fact that 60% of the variance is not accounted for by genes suggests that environmental factors are important for explaining variability in personality. The interesting caveat, however, is that these environmental factors do not seem to make siblings in the same families similar to one another. In fact, it has been exceedingly difficult to find consistent evidence that environmental factors like SES, neighborhood contexts, or even general parenting styles strongly act to make siblings in the same family similar to one another (Turkheimer & Waldron, 2000). The effects of the environment that are not shared by siblings are called (as you might guess) *nonshared environmental effects*. And these kinds of environmental effects tend to be stronger than the shared environmental effects we have just discussed. (Shared means that the factors are shared by siblings who grow up in the same household and promote similarity.) The stronger power of the nonshared environment in genetically informed studies points to an interesting question—just what are the environmental factors responsible for personality differences?[1]

The task for personality researchers is to identify the specific non-shared environmental factors that contribute to personality differences. This task has proven difficult. At the time we wrote this chapter, researchers had not found strong evidence that any specific environmental factors reliably affect personality trait development with strong and consistent effects. One set of authors even posited a "gloomy prospect" (Plomin & Daniels, 1987; see Turkheimer, 2000) that the environmental factors that are most likely to shape personality might be rare events like traumas, sicknesses, accidents, or positive lucky events (e.g., winning the golden ticket as in the children's story of *Charlie and the Chocolate Factory*). The problem is that these rare events are hard to pin down in scientific research given their low base rates and the range of potential confounding factors that also need to be addressed (e.g., researchers would like to rule out selection effects or the possibility that genetic factors or personality traits are themselves somehow associated with the occurrence of the events). This is why the idea of identifying nonshared influences is considered gloomy—these kinds of events are both hard to study and hard to control. But notice that the prospect is most gloomy for researchers who like to predict things! The fact that these kinds of events seem to matter for individual personality development simply underscores the complexity of human development. This prospect is not necessarily gloomy from the perspective of individual lives (see Turkheimer, 2000).

These two empirical findings—the comparatively strong genetic component to personality and the fact that the strongest environmental effects seem to be found in things not shared by siblings—should lead to caution when someone claims that any specific environmental factor is a powerful cause of personality. Accordingly, this evidence suggests that general parenting practices—practices that are constant across siblings—may not be a substantial driver of personality development. This is why we consider this idea a myth in this chapter.

A few basic issues are important to remember when considering this myth. First, when we say that parenting practices are not systematically related to personality outcomes, we are not saying that parents do not

---

[1] Remember that researchers can estimate the general size of genetic and environmental effects in twin designs, but they cannot pin sources of variance down to specifics such as a particular gene or a specific environmental factor. Thus, when we say that nonshared environmental effects are powerful, we mean this mostly in a statistical sense of a broad factor that accounts for variation even when researchers cannot identify what part of that broad factor is responsible for any observed differences between people.

matter: Parents do matter in many ways and for many things. Parents also matter in a critically important sense. Human babies need an incredible amount of care and investment so they can mature into independent people. An infant without caregivers will die; an infant with neglectful caregivers will suffer. Infants and children who are deprived of nutrition, caring adults, and exposure to stimulating environments show a host of problems. So, it is absolutely the case that parents are necessary for children to develop into productive adults (see Scarr, 1996). The question that is most relevant for this myth is whether variation in the wide range of typical parenting practices observed across families in the same culture has much effect on the personality traits that people ultimately develop (see Scarr & McCartney, 1983).

A second point to remember is that parent–child interactions (including parenting) are the product of a bidirectional relationship between two parties. Parents respond to the characteristics of their children (Bell, 1968, 1979; Ge et al., 1996). Thus, children evoke different responses from parents, and these responses result, at least in part, from the children's own attributes. This leaves open the possibility that the relatively unique ways that the same parents interact with different children (even two or more of their own) may impact those children's characteristics. The thing to remember is that this effect may emerge as part of the nonshared environment because these conditions are not shared by siblings.

A classic study by Anderson, Lytton, and Romney (1986) demonstrates the possibility that children evoke responses from parents. Anderson et al. paired mothers with either their own child or another child for a series of observed interactions. About half of the children in the study had clinically diagnosed conduct disorders so that some of the adults in the study were paired with kids who had serious behavior problems. Results indicated that observed interactions were largely driven by the characteristics of the child. Children with conduct disorder tended to evoke the same kinds of parenting behaviors regardless of whether the interaction was with their own mom or another adult in the study. The authors concluded that the results showed that "interactions are 'driven' mainly by the child and not the mother" (p. 607). This is a potentially extreme example given that some of the children in the study had clinically significant behavior problems; but it illustrates the point that some behavior patterns in children evoke predictable responses in adults. You might want to ask any elementary school teacher if different children can evoke different responses.

Simplistic notions about parenting as a major cause of personality should be critically evaluated in light of the possibility of this type of evocative effect. If parents react to how children typically behave, how should cause-and-effect be evaluated? It often becomes a chicken-and-egg problem when trying to understand the connection between parenting and child attributes. For example, imagine that a research study finds that aggressive children who act out in school tend to have permissive parents who demand very little and rarely enforce punishments. Can we say that this parenting style causes aggressive behavior? It is possible that the reverse direction of effects is really at work. Parents with difficult kids might eventually start to withdraw from making demands of their kids over time. It may simply become too frustrating for parents to repeatedly make demands of a child who refuses to follow directions and who increasingly acts out when demands are made (e.g., Patterson, 1982). It might be less distressing for the parent to stop asking the child to follow directions than to get pulled into unpleasant cycles of having directives ignored and thus escalating conflicts. Thus, lax and permissive parenting may not always be the cause of aggressive behavior and might instead reflect a consequence of having to manage an irascible child. So again, parent–child dynamics are complicated; it can be too easy to project a simple cause-and-effect account on observations of a correlation between parenting and child attributes.

A third point (most certainly related to the second) is to question whether there is even such a thing as a general parenting style that is similar across all kids in the same family. If evocative processes happen and kids have different temperaments (e.g., Caspi, Henry, McGee, Moffitt, & Silva, 1995), is it really the case that parents treat siblings in the same family the same? The evidence here is somewhat mixed, but the idea that consistent parenting styles exist does not seem well supported (Plomin et al., 2001; Plomin & Daniels, 2011). One interesting result from a study of parents and their adolescent children was that parents report greater consistency in their treatment of siblings than do the siblings themselves (Daniels, Dunn, Furstenberg, & Plomin, 1985). This seems to suggest that siblings experience their parents differently and that even the idea of general parenting style is overstated.

In light of all these considerations, it seems unrealistic to think that individuals receive (and perceive) the exact same treatment from their parents regardless of their individual characteristics. Parenting might be a response to personality as much as it is a potential cause of personality. Moreover, parenting itself might not act to make siblings similar because parenting is a function of specific parent–child interactions. What works to motivate and control some kids will not work for others. Thus, parenting dynamics like the sibling dynamics discussed at the end of Chapter 16 are much more complicated than they may appear at first glance.

Summary

Parenting is often invoked in everyday discussions as a major factor in personality development, but evidence from twin studies suggests there is a limit to the effects that general parenting strategies have on personality traits. Having the same parents does not seem to make children growing up in the same household any more similar than they would be expected to be based on genetic transmission alone. When combined with research showing that the attributes of children influence how they are parented, you should be skeptical of the idea that parenting itself is a strong, simple, and straightforward cause of personality differences. None of this means that parents are unimportant to the welfare and well-being of children. In addition, this conclusion does not contradict the idea that some specific behaviors that parents exhibit can have powerful but perhaps idiosyncratic effects on their children's lives and personalities.

Engaging with this myth, however, raises provocative questions about how parents might think about their role in shaping the development of their children. It might be valuable to recognize that children are different from one another and that parenting strategies that work for one child might not work as well for another. Likewise, when you see a parent struggling to control the behavior of his or her child at the grocery store or in an airplane, it might be useful to recall the complexity of the parent–child relationship. It is not always the parent's fault that the child is misbehaving! Thus, understanding the research related to this myth might help foster compassion for parents who end up with a fussy and strong-willed child. And it might give you pause when people are quick to blame parents for their parenting behavior when children and adolescents turn out to have problems.

References

Anderson, K. E., Lytton, H., & Romney, D. M. (1986). Mothers' interactions with normal and conduct-disordered boys: Who affects whom? *Developmental Psychology*, 22(5), 604.

Bell, R. Q. (1968). A reinterpretation of the direction of effects in studies of socialization. *Psychological Review*, 75, 81–95.

Bell, R. Q. (1979). Parent, child, and reciprocal influences. *American Psychologist*, 34(10), 821.

Caspi, A., Henry, B., McGee, R. O., Moffitt, T. E., & Silva, P. A. (1995). Temperamental origins of child and adolescent behavior problems: From age three to age fifteen. *Child Development*, 66(1), 55–68.

Daniels, D., Dunn, J., Furstenberg, F. F., Jr., & Plomin, R. (1985). Environmental differences within the family and adjustment differences within pairs of adolescent siblings. *Child Development, 56*, 764–774.

Ge, X., Conger, R. D., Cadoret, R. J., Neiderhiser, J. M., Yates, W., Troughton, E., & Stewart, M. A. (1996). The developmental interface between nature and nurture: A mutual influence model of child antisocial behavior and parent behaviors. *Developmental Psychology, 32*(4), 574.

Patterson, G. R. (1982). *Coercive family process*. Eugene, OR: Castalia.

Plomin, R., Asbury, K., & Dunn, J. (2001). Why are children in the same family so different? Nonshared environment a decade later. *Canadian Journal of Psychiatry, 46*(3), 225–233.

Plomin, R., & Daniels, D. (1987). Why are children in the same family so different from one another? *Behavioral and Brain Sciences, 10*(1), 1–16.

Plomin, R., & Daniels, D. (2011). Why are children in the same family so different from one another? *International Journal of Epidemiology, 40*(3), 563–582.

Polderman, T. J., Benyamin, B., de Leeuw, C. A., Sullivan, P. F., van Bochoven, A., Visscher, P. M., & Postghuma, D. (2015). Meta-analysis of the heritability of human traits based on fifty years of twin studies. *Nature Genetics, 47*, 702–709.

Scarr, S. (1996). How people make their own environments: Implications for parents and policy makers. *Psychology, Public Policy, and Law, 2*(2), 204.

Scarr, S., & McCartney, K. (1983). How people make their own environments: A theory of genotype→ environment effects. *Child Development, 54*, 424–435.

Tellegen, A., Lykken, D. T., Bouchard, T. J., Wilcox, K. J., Segal, N. L., & Rich, S. (1988). Personality similarity in twins reared apart and together. *Journal of Personality and Social Psychology, 54*(6), 1031.

Turkheimer, E. (2000). Three laws of behavior genetics and what they mean. *Current Directions in Psychological Science, 9*(5), 160–164.

Turkheimer, E., & Waldron, M. (2000). Nonshared environment: A theoretical, methodological, and quantitative review. *Psychological Bulletin, 126*(1), 78–108.

Vukasović, T., & Bratko, D. (2015). Heritability of personality: A meta-analysis of behavior genetic studies. *Psychological Bulletin, 141*, 769–785.

18 HAPPINESS IS COMPLETELY DETERMINED BY SITUATIONAL FACTORS

In the next three chapters, we turn our attention from basic personality traits to a different topic—happiness. It may seem strange to you to see the topic of happiness addressed in a book on personality. But as you will see below, this is actually a natural fit. People differ in their levels of happiness, and these levels of happiness persist over time. Some might even consider happiness to be a personality trait or something that approximates a consistent individual difference. To be sure, questions exist about precisely how stable these individual differences are and the extent to which they are affected by the things that happen to us (indeed, most of the happiness myths we discuss are related to these two questions). But personality researchers—people who deal with these challenging questions on a day-to-day basis—are in an excellent position to tackle these questions.

Happiness is a term that has multiple meanings. In some contexts, the term refers to a short-lived pleasant emotion that might arise in response to a specific event (like winning the lottery or getting a promotion at work). This type of happiness changes from day-to-day and even moment-to-moment. When something good happens, people experience momentary boosts in positive emotions. When very little is going in the moment, people may experience boredom, a lack of emotion, or a relatively "flat" affect. And when something bad happens, happiness may be replaced by less pleasant feelings like sadness, anxiety, or fear. Therefore, it's no myth that this first type of happiness—the *emotion* of happiness—is strongly

Great Myths of Personality, First Edition. M. Brent Donnellan and Richard E. Lucas.
© 2021 John Wiley & Sons, Inc. Published 2021 by John Wiley & Sons, Inc.

determined by situational factors. Daily emotional responses or momentary feelings are clearly tied to situational factors. People feel sad when they hear bad news, upbeat when they get a compliment, and frustrated when their phones run out of batteries.

In contrast to momentary feelings, the term *happiness* can also refer to something broader and much deeper than short-lived emotional experiences. For instance, if you ask parents what they want for their children when they grow up, parents often say that they just want their children "to be happy." It seems unlikely that these parents really mean that they want their children to experience an unending state of joy with no bouts of unpleasant emotions at every moment of every day. Instead, it's more likely that they're using the term "happiness" in a different way, perhaps to refer to a deeper state in which their children have experienced most of the important things that they want out of life and have relatively few psychological scars from the traumas, heartbreaks, and losses that are inevitable in life. This broader meaning of the term "happiness" is captured by the somewhat more unwieldy term "subjective well-being" (Diener, Suh, Lucas, & Smith, 1999). Psychologists typically prefer this more specific term precisely because it allows them to distinguish the narrow emotion of happiness from an overall subjective evaluation of one's life as a whole. It is this latter form of happiness that we address in this chapter.

Specifically, we focus on the question of whether subjective well-being is primarily determined by the things that happen to people in their everyday lives. It seems like people act as if this were true. If stopped and asked to think about why they do the things they do—why they want a great job, why they want to get married or have children, why they feel the need to take a luxurious vacation—people will often fall back on the explanation that they want these things because they think it will make them happier. In short, people often believe that if they make the right decisions in life (and have a bit of luck), then they will end up with a "happy" life.

So, does happiness in this broader sense depend on the life circumstances in which people find themselves? The answer, as you can probably guess, is that happiness depends on situational factors to a lesser extent than many people think. How do we know this? In this chapter, we'll review five pieces of evidence that situations matter less than people expect. Thus, the myth we address is that long-term happiness is primarily determined by situational factors. The upshot is the conclusion that some people seem to have a happy disposition.

First, there is the direct evidence from studies that examine the association between situational factors and reports of subjective well-being.

Early on in the history of research into subjective well-being, psychologists assumed that happiness was determined by external factors. The rationale that guided this belief was that people had certain universal psychological needs that could only be met if certain environmental conditions existed. Just as there were universal physiological needs that could only be met with air, water, and food, psychologists posited that humans might possess a set of universal psychological needs that could only be met through certain objective features of the environment around them. If true, then a state of high well-being could only be attained if one acquired the requisite environmental conditions.

However, once psychologists and other social scientists started conducting empirical studies on the topic, they began to realize that external, situational factors—the things that people strive for and the things that they hope to avoid—did not seem to play a large role in the levels of subjective well-being that research participants reported. For instance, in one of the first broad reviews of the literature, Wilson (1967) examined the correlates of what he called "avowed happiness." After examining the literature, Wilson concluded that the happy person is a "young, healthy, well-educated, well-paid, extroverted [*sic*], optimistic, worry-free, religious, married person with high self-esteem, high job morale, modest aspirations, of either sex, and of a wide range of intelligence" (p. 294). This list includes a few external factors or factors that reflect life circumstances that people might believe matter for subjective well-being (e.g., income or health). However, this list also includes a number of other characteristics, such as being extraverted and optimistic—attributes that seem to have nothing to do with the events that happen to a person.

More importantly, when researchers tried to quantify the size of the associations between happiness and external, situational factors, the correlations were sometimes surprisingly small. For instance, one of the most intuitively appealing predictors of subjective well-being is income. Presumably, money matters because it can be used to purchase all the other things that might be necessary to live a happy, satisfied life. This not only includes luxuries like a large home, a nice car, or expensive vacations but also more mundane things like good health insurance (at least in the United States), transportation that is reliable, and the ability to fix one's home and the things in it when something breaks. Thus, it was quite surprising to find that when large-scale studies were conducted, the correlation between income and subjective well-being was consistently estimated to fall in the range that psychologists typically describe as "small" (Diener & Biswas-Diener, 2002; Myers, 2000).

Importantly, the small size of these situational effects was not limited just to income. Regardless of the demographic factor or external correlate that was studied, the associations were consistently weaker than expected by those who thought situational factors were critically important for happiness. For instance, a number of researchers attempted to explain as much variance in reports of subjective well-being as they could using as many demographic predictors as were available to them, and these researchers consistently concluded that only about 10–20% of the variance in people's happiness could be explained by these factors (Andrews & Withey, 1976; Argyle, 1999; Campbell, Converse, & Rodgers, 1976). This was the first clue that perhaps happiness was not strongly linked to what happened to people in their lives.

The second clue came from research that examined the association between personality traits and subjective well-being. As Wilson's (1967) list of correlates suggests, many factors that appear to be important for well-being are not external to the person. Instead, they reflect stable characteristics of the person. In other words, Wilson's initial list suggested that happiness depends partially on a person's personality. Some people might have a personality profile that predisposes them to happiness, whereas others have a far less sanguine temperament.

Subsequent research verified this initial impression, and a considerable amount of research suggests that personality does in fact matter for subjective well-being (Lucas & Diener, 2008). In particular, of the Big Five personality traits, extraversion tends to be positively associated and neuroticism negatively associated with subjective well-being (especially the more affective components of subjective well-being like tendencies to typically experience good moods and not many bad moods). Traits like agreeableness and conscientiousness also tend to be positively associated with well-being outcomes, though these correlations tend to be a bit smaller (Steel, Schmidt, & Shultz, 2008). Furthermore, additional traits beyond the Big Five (like self-esteem and optimism) are moderately correlated with variables like life satisfaction and positive and negative affect (Lucas & Diener, 2008). These associations are typically larger than the correlation between subjective well-being and even the largest objective, situational characteristics, which has led some researchers to believe that happiness depends more on who you are than on what happens to you.

Consistent with this idea is the third piece of evidence that personality matters more than situations—evidence from behavioral genetic studies. For many years, behavioral genetic researchers have used various methods to determine how much of the variation in happiness that exists is due to genetic factors. For instance, as we discussed in previous chapters, one common approach is to compare similarity across pairs of identical twins to the similarity across pairs of fraternal twins. Identical twins share 100% of their genes, whereas fraternal twins share, on average, 50% of their genes. Therefore, if our genetic makeup affects subjective well-being in a simple way, then we would expect identical twins to be quite similar to one another and fraternal twins to be about half as similar as identical twins (because fraternal twins have half as many genes in common as do identical twins). Furthermore, in some cases, researchers can identify twins who were separated at birth, which provides an even stronger method for isolating more complex genetic and environmental effects.

Research that uses behavioral genetic techniques consistently shows that subjective well-being is moderately heritable (Lykken & Tellegen, 1996; Nes, Røysamb, Tambs, Harris, & Reichborn-Kjennerud, 2006; Røysamb, Harris, Magnus, Vittersø, & Tambs, 2002; Røysamb, Tambs, Reichborn-Kjennerud, Neale, & Harris, 2003; Tellegen et al., 1988). For instance, studies that use twin designs typically find that the heritability of most well-being measures falls in the range of 40–50% (much like personality traits, as we discussed in Chapter 3). In other words, 40–50% of the variability in subjective well-being that exists between people can be accounted for by genetic differences across people. Perhaps even more surprisingly, growing up in the same household rarely leads to increased similarity in happiness, suggesting that the features of the environment that are shared by siblings play a very small role in their happiness (at least by adulthood). As we discuss in the next chapter (and in Chapter 17), these behavioral genetic findings need to be interpreted carefully, and the implications of these estimates for our own behavior are not clear, but the relatively high estimates of heritability suggest that genetic factors that people are born with play a significant role in determining people's well-being in a big picture sense.

A fourth piece of evidence that situations may not matter as much as people think comes from studies that directly examine the stability of well-being scores over time. Presumably, as people live their lives, circumstances change. If life circumstances matter, then changes in these circumstances should be associated with changes in well-being. The results from an increasing number of longitudinal studies that assess people at different time points show that some amount of stability exists in levels of happiness, even when people's lives change in dramatic ways.

For instance, one way to use longitudinal studies to address this issue is to simply assess well-being at multiple times over many years to see whether people tend to stay the same. Such studies examine the stability of happiness to provide a descriptive answer of whether happiness does indeed change for a typical person. The research from these studies shows that some amount of change occurs (Fujita & Diener, 2005; Lucas & Donnellan, 2007; Schimmack & Oishi, 2005). In addition, the more time that has elapsed, the more change that occurs. However, even over very long periods of time, some amount of stability exists. For instance, we (Lucas & Donnellan, 2007) looked at the stability of life satisfaction in a sample of tens of thousands of Germans followed for 20 years, and we found that year-to-year stability was about .60 (a relatively strong correlation). Even over a period of 20 years, stability coefficients were about .25, which means that people who were happy early on were at least somewhat likely to maintain that level of happiness many years later. We later replicated these findings in three additional large-scale, longitudinal studies, with remarkably consistent results (Lucas & Donnellan, 2012). Thus, those people who are especially satisfied with life right now are likely to be more satisfied than average even 20 or 30 years later.

A second way to examine the stability of well-being is to look closely at people who actually experience major life events to see whether their levels of subjective well-being change from before to after the event. Although it would seem likely that such major changes would lead to large and lasting changes in a person's happiness, the changes that actually occur are often not as large as one might expect. Sometimes the results were downright shocking!

Brickman, Coates, and Janoff-Bulman (1978) conducted one of the most famous studies to address this question (though one that did not actually follow people before and after an event). They compared the happiness of a group of lottery winners to a group of patients with spinal cord injuries and a group of control participants who had not experienced any recent major life event. Although this study did not look specifically at change, by comparing the groups, the authors hoped to isolate the impact of the two events they studied. Presumably, those who won the lottery would otherwise have had happiness levels similar to the control group had they not experienced this event. The authors concluded that neither the lottery winners nor the spinal-cord-injured patients were very different from the control group in terms of the happiness that they reported. The interpretation was that adaptation had occurred, and that people had reverted to whatever level of happiness they had experienced before the event.

Looking back on this study from a modern perspective, it seems to have many flaws. The sample sizes were small, the selection procedures used to obtain their samples were imprecise (and therefore, there may be differences between groups beyond the event that occurred), and the authors' description of the results was somewhat impressionistic and open to alternative interpretation. For instance, although it was true that the lottery winners were quite similar to the control group in their level of happiness, the patients with spinal cord injuries were significantly (and substantially) lower in happiness than the controls or lottery winners. Nonetheless, this famous study highlighted the fact that research on life events was needed and that many life events do not lead to the very large changes in well-being that might be expected in one adopts the view that situations trump all when it comes to happiness.

Finally, as a fifth piece of evidence, starting in the 2000s, researchers have begun to use large-scale longitudinal studies to actually assess change that occurs in people who experience life events. For instance, Lucas, Clark, Georgellis, and Diener (2003) used the same large German study described earlier in the chapter to examine the life satisfaction of people before and after they married. Although marriage is a positive event that most people who experience the event want to occur, Lucas et al. (2003) found that on average, people adapted back to their original baseline level of life satisfaction within a few years after the event. Later studies have qualified these findings a bit (e.g., Yap, Anusic, & Lucas, 2012), though the main finding that satisfaction levels do not change much following marriage has been confirmed. Similarly, although many people strongly desire having children and believe that doing so will make them happier (Lyubomirsky & Boehm, 2010), research from large-scale panel studies shows that having children does not, on average, lead to large, lasting boosts in life satisfaction (Dyrdal & Lucas, 2013; Yap et al., 2012). Thus, many of the events that people expend great effort pursuing are not associated with lasting changes. As we will discuss in the next chapter, this does not mean that happiness cannot change; it's just that many of the events that we expect to be associated with large changes are not. This might be a pretty shocking result, indeed!

The lesson to be learned here is this: People seem live their lives as if each decision will have important implications for their happiness (at least people in Western industrialized countries that tend to prioritize individualism). People often believe that the choices they make will have direct and lasting effects on their subjective well-being. And although it's true that short-term changes in the emotion of happiness are likely to occur when positive events happen, much research suggests that the lasting effect on the broader form of happiness—the form that psychologists call subjective well-being—will be shorter lived and less intense. This is in part due to the fact that people's personalities also influence these long-term levels of well-being, perhaps directly or maybe through the life choices associated with personality. Regardless of the reasons (which are still being explored), long-term levels of happiness depend less on the situational factors than many people think.

References

Andrews, F. M., & Withey, S. B. (1976). *Social indicators of well-being: Americans' perceptions of life quality.* New York, NY: Plenum Press.

Argyle, M. (1999). Causes and correlates of happiness. In D. Kahneman, E. Diener, & N. Schwarz (Eds.), *Well-being: The foundations of hedonic psychology* (pp. 353–373). New York, NY: Russell Sage Foundation.

Brickman, P., Coates, D., & Janoff-Bulman, R. (1978). Lottery winners and accident victims: Is happiness relative? *Journal of Personality and Social Psychology, 36*(8), 917–927.

Campbell, A., Converse, P. E., & Rodgers, W. L. (1976). *The quality of American life: Perceptions, evaluations, and satisfactions.* New York, NY: Russell Sage Foundation.

Diener, E., & Biswas-Diener, R. (2002). Will money increase subjective well-being? *Social Indicators Research, 57*(2), 119–169.

Diener, E., Suh, E. M., Lucas, R. E., & Smith, H. L. (1999). Subjective well-being: Three decades of progress. *Psychological Bulletin, 125,* 276–302.

Dyrdal, G. M., & Lucas, R. E. (2013). Reaction and adaptation to the birth of a child: A couple-level analysis. *Developmental Psychology, 49,* 749–761.

Fujita, F., & Diener, E. (2005). Life satisfaction set point: Stability and change. *Journal of Personality and Social Psychology, 88*(1), 158.

Lucas, R. E., Clark, A., Georgellis, Y., & Diener, E. (2003). Reexamining adaptation and the set point model of happiness: Reactions to changes in marital status. *Journal of Personality and Social Psychology, 84*(3), 527–539.

Lucas, R. E., & Diener, E. (2008). Personality and subjective well-being. In O. John, R. Robins, & L. Pervin (Eds.), *Handbook of personality: Theory and research* (pp. 171–194). New York, NY: Guilford Press.

Lucas, R. E., & Donnellan, M. B. (2007). How stable is happiness? Using the sTARTS model to estimate the stability of life satisfaction. *Journal of Research in Personality, 41,* 1091–1098.

Lucas, R. E., & Donnellan, M. B. (2012). Estimating the reliability of single-item life satisfaction measures: Results from four national panel studies. *Social Indicators Research, 3,* 323–331.

Lykken, D., & Tellegen, A. (1996). Happiness is a stochastic phenomenon. *Psychological Science, 7*(3), 186–189.

Lyubomirsky, S., & Boehm, J. K. (2010). Human motives, happiness, and the puzzle of parenthood: Commentary on Kenrick et al. (2010). *Perspectives on Psychological Science, 5*(3), 327–334.

Myers, D. (2000). The funds, friends, and faith of happy people. *American Psychologist*, 55(1), 56–67.

Nes, R., Røysamb, E., Tambs, K., Harris, J., & Reichborn-Kjennerud, T. (2006). Subjective well-being: Genetic and environmental contributions to stability and change. *Psychological Medicine*, 36(07), 1033–1042.

Røysamb, E., Harris, J., Magnus, P., Vittersø, J., & Tambs, K. (2002). Subjective well-being: Sex-specific effects of genetic and environmental factors. *Personality and Individual Differences*, 32(2), 211–223.

Røysamb, E., Tambs, K., Reichborn-Kjennerud, T., Neale, M. C., & Harris, J. R. (2003). Happiness and health: Environmental and genetic contributions to the relationship between subjective well-being, perceived health, and somatic illness. *Journal of Personality and Social Psychology*, 85(6), 1136–1146.

Schimmack, U., & Oishi, S. (2005). The influence of chronically and temporarily accessible information on life satisfaction judgments. *Journal of Personality and Social Psychology*, 89(3), 395–406. doi:10.1037/0022-3514.89.3.395

Steel, P., Schmidt, J., & Shultz, J. (2008). Refining the relationship between personality and subjective well-being. *Psychological Bulletin*, 134(1), 138–161.

Tellegen, A., Lykken, D., Bouchard, T., Wilcox, K., Segal, N., & Rich, S. (1988). Personality similarity in twins reared apart and together. *Journal of Personality and Social Psychology*, 54(6), 1031–1039.

Wilson, W. (1967). Correlates of avowed happiness. *Psychological Bulletin*, 67(4), 294.

Yap, S. C., Anusic, I., & Lucas, R. E. (2012). Does personality moderate reaction and adaptation to major life events? Evidence from the British Household Panel Survey. *Journal of Research in Personality*, 46(5), 477–488. doi:10.1016/j.jrp.2012.05.005

19 HAPPINESS IS UNRELATED TO MAJOR LIFE EVENTS

In Chapter 18, we covered the myth that "Happiness is Completely Determined by Situational Factors." As we noted when introducing this myth, intuition might suggest that people work for the things that they want in life because they believe that these accomplishments will generate lasting happiness, but this highly intuitive belief turns out to be a myth. Happiness levels (specifically, levels of what psychologists call "subjective well-being") are more strongly correlated with measures of personality traits than with measures of life circumstances, reports of happiness are relatively stable (but not perfectly stable) even over long periods and even in the face of changing life circumstances, and twins who were separated at birth (and who, presumably, have had different life experiences) report similar levels of happiness and life satisfaction. So clearly, something internal to the person—something related to personality—plays a role in happiness.

In this chapter, we are going to tackle a myth that is the polar opposite of the idea that situations are the primary determinant of happiness. Specifically, we'll address the extreme view that people's ability to adapt to changes in life circumstances is so well developed that major life events have no lasting impact on happiness. How can two completely opposing myths exist simultaneously? One simple reason is that different people may hold different ideas about happiness, both of which may be wrong. Some people might believe that life circumstances are extremely important, whereas others may believe that there is nothing you can do to change happiness. A second reason relates to a phenomenon called the "hindsight bias." Sometimes when you hear something, it makes perfect sense to you, and you believe that you would have "known it all along." This can be true

Great Myths of Personality, First Edition. M. Brent Donnellan and Richard E. Lucas.
© 2021 John Wiley & Sons, Inc. Published 2021 by John Wiley & Sons, Inc.

even if you would have found an opposing fact equally compelling had you heard it first. Finally, sometimes the existence of opposing myths results from shifting views about empirical evidence. In the history of research on subjective well-being, it seems that early researchers expected to find that situations mattered, but when strong evidence for this view failed to emerge, they swung too far in the opposite direction, positing theories that downplayed or even ignored the impact that life circumstances have on people's lives (Diener, Lucas, & Oishi, 2018).

As we have written several times in this book, many of the myths that we cover have a kernel of truth. In fact, many myths can be directly traced to specific research findings that have grabbed the attention of both journalists and of interested nonscientists who keep up with scientific news. Some of the studies on which these myths are based have been published in highly prestigious, peer-reviewed scientific journals. And often, these studies themselves are of high quality. So how does a myth develop out of such solid bases? In general, as we have seen throughout this book, this can happen in one of three ways. First, no single research study is perfect, and the conclusions drawn from the original finding may turn out to be incorrect as additional studies accumulate. Second, a valid finding may not generalize beyond the laboratory in which it was initially found. Finally, as we have repeatedly emphasized in this book, when one pays attention to effect sizes, dramatically different interpretations may result than if one just focuses on statistical significance.[1] Even if a result turns out to be statistically significant, the actual effect size might be trivial. As we shall see, all three of these factors have played a role in this myth about life events.

The belief that happiness is unaffected by life circumstances is based on the findings discussed in the previous chapter. This idea that people can adapt to just about anything has had a broad influence both on debates about theories of well-being and on debates about the use of well-being measures for policy purposes. For instance, in an early paper, Brickman and Campbell (1971) used evidence from adaptation studies to argue

---

[1] We have not spent much time on statistical significance in this book given that many personality researchers focus on effect sizes. Statistical significance is a technical term that boils down to whether there is statistical evidence to assume that a correlation is different from zero (i.e., no linear relation) or whether a difference between groups is different from zero (i.e., absolutely no group difference). Extremely small correlations and trivial mean differences can be statistically significant if the sample size is large. Likewise, respectably sized correlations and mean differences can fail to attain statistical significance with small samples. A general formula is that statistical significance is the product of the effect size and sample size found in a study. Given this formula, we think it is usually more sensible to focus on effect sizes directly.

that subjective well-being is not based on objective judgments about a person's quality of life. Instead, Brickman and Campbell argued, subjective well-being is a relative phenomenon. According to this perspective, when judging whether life is going well, people do not just consider whether things are good at an absolute level, they also compare their current circumstances to the past, to relevant others, and even to future expectations. The idea is that if something great happens to someone, this extremely positive event won't actually lead to greater happiness (at least not for long) because people will adjust their expectations and want something even better. Habituation occurs for most things. (Just consider how you felt about an exciting birthday gift a few weeks after you received it.)

One of the most heated debates within the literature on subjective well-being concerns the question of whether subjective well-being increases as the wealth of a society increases. Intuition (and the logic behind some public policies) suggests that increasing wealth will benefit society as a whole. In turn, this rising wealth should increase happiness. However, in 1974, Richard Easterlin published a paper (Easterlin, 1974; also see Easterlin, 1995) suggesting that even when income increases dramatically over time within a nation, average subjective well-being of that nation remains stable (though see Stevenson & Wolfers, 2008, and Veenhoven & Hagerty, 2006, for an alternative perspective). Consistent with the ideas of Brickman and Campbell (1971), Easterlin suggested that people base their happiness on how they compare to others around them, and if everyone else's life circumstances improved at the same rate, then a single individual will experience no net change in happiness. This so-called *Easterlin paradox* reflects this idea that improving conditions for all does not lead to a corresponding increase in happiness. This possibility has had a very real impact on the debate about whether well-being measures can guide policy decision, and whether it is even possible to improve well-being at all.

In addition, researchers who study adaptation note that there are strong theoretical reasons to expect that people will adapt to most life circumstances. The process of adaptation may itself be beneficial to humans (Frederick & Loewenstein, 1999). It may be good for people to be especially sensitive to things that change in the environment and to pay less and less attention to those things that remain the same. If there is something in the environment that has not yet proved lethal, then chances are that it will not prove lethal in the future, and therefore, it can be more or less ignored. Thus, the reasoning goes, people adapt to things that stay the same so they can focus more attention on the potentially more important things that do change.

If this idea is correct, then it is the novel features of the environment that play the strongest role in determining subjective well-being; people eventually adapt to those things that remain the same. A brand new car may not continue to produce good feelings forever. Likewise, a major life-altering injury may not continue to produce negative feelings forever. As we noted in the previous chapter, some of the most salient evidence in support of this idea came from the striking findings from Brickman, Coates, and Janoff-Bulman (1978), who compared lottery winners and patients with spinal-cord injuries to a group of controls. Remember, the conclusions from this study were that the differences were not as large as one might expect.

The second version of the belief that life events and other situational factors do not matter for subjective well-being amounts to a criticism of the techniques used to measure happiness. According to this view, happiness is actually affected by life circumstances, but, for a variety of reasons, the measures themselves are not sensitive to these changes (Kahneman, 1999; Schwarz & Strack, 1999). In other words, people may not be able to recognize or quantify the true effects that life circumstances have on their well-being, and thus, they may fall back on a response to life satisfaction questions that is based on how they compare with others. This view has led to the search for alternative ways of assessing well-being that might be more valid (Kahneman, 1999). The concern with existing measures is that simply asking people how they feel about their life as whole is too crude of an approach to measuring an important psychological attribute.

Although the idea that situational factors have little lasting effect on well-being was initially motivated by empirical findings, our view is that these empirical findings do not justify such extreme beliefs about the role of life events in happiness. For instance, consider the famous study by Brickman et al. (1978). Although this study is one of the most frequently cited studies in the scientific literature on subjective well-being, it is actually quite limited from the vantage point of current research. As we noted in the prior chapter, the sample size was very small, which means that happiness levels for the various groups was not estimated with a great deal of precision. Furthermore, the participants in the spinal-cord-injury and lottery-winner groups knew that they were being asked to participate precisely because of the event that occurred to them. Smith, Schwarz, Roberts, and Ubel (2006) have shown that people change their responses to well-being questions depending on who they think is conducting the survey. Specifically, Smith et al. found that people who have a specific health condition report lower levels of life satisfaction than they otherwise would if they think that they were selected for the survey precisely because of this health condition. More importantly, however, the conclusion was not that there were no differences between these groups. Instead, the conclusion that Brickman et al. (1978) reached was that the differences among these groups was not as large as one might expect. Although the patients with spinal cord injuries were lower than the lottery winners and the comparison group, these patients did not report well-being scores that were toward the bottom of the scale, which was surprising to the authors.

So, what does the research that has been conducted since the Brickman et al. (1978) study say about the association between disability status and subjective well-being? In contrast to the common interpretation of the Brickman et al. (1978) finding, this newer research consistently shows that disability—and especially severe disability—is associated with considerably lowered levels of subjective well-being. For instance, Lucas (2007) reviewed a number of studies that examined this question, including a meta-analysis by Dijkers (1997), and this research consistently showed that in cross-sectional studies, people with disabilities report lower levels of satisfaction. These differences are consistently in the range that psychologists describe as medium to large effect sizes. Furthermore, Dijkers (1999) examined individuals with different severity of disability, and he showed that those with the most severe disabilities reported considerably lower levels of life satisfaction than those with less severe disabilities. For instance, after dividing individuals into different levels of mobility, Dijkers found that those with the lowest levels of mobility (a group comprising approximately 20% of the sample) reported life satisfaction scores that were much lower than those who had full mobility (but still had some form of disability). These differences are striking in the context of most psychological research and would typically be considered as a large effect size.

The cross-sectional results are consistent with those of Lucas (2007), who used longitudinal data from two nationally representative panel studies to examine whether individuals who acquire a new disability experience lasting changes in their life satisfaction. Cross-sectional data alone cannot tell researchers whether people's life satisfaction actually changed after the onset of the disability—it's possible that people have characteristics that predispose them to acquire a disability, and these same characteristics may be associated with life satisfaction. Thus, it's possible that people with disabilities might, on average, be less happy than those who never become disabled even before any disability occurs. Only longitudinal data can rule out this possibility, and the studies by

Lucas confirmed that life satisfaction does indeed change after onset. Specifically, in two nationally representative panel studies (one from Germany and one from the United Kingdom), he showed that people who would later acquire a disability were no different from average before the onset. However, once people acquired the disability, their satisfaction levels declined and remained at that reduced level. Importantly, the effect size was similar to those estimated from the cross-sectional designs, and again, those with the most severe disabilities declined the most. Thus, this research suggests (at least to us) that some life circumstances can matter, as long as researchers pay careful attention to effect sizes.

As a final example, we will consider the oft-cited "weak" correlation between income and life satisfaction. Considerable research has been conducted on this topic, and it is clear that within relatively wealthy Western nations, the correlation typically falls near to but lower than a correlation of .20. Given the theoretical importance of money, this effect has been described as surprisingly small, and many are surprised that money doesn't "buy" more happiness. However, as we have argued elsewhere (Lucas & Schimmack, 2009), people must be particularly careful in interpreting this specific effect size because of the distribution of variables being compared. (As a word of warning, we are about to dive into some technical discussion about correlations and statistics; if this is not something that you find interesting, feel free to skim over the next several paragraphs. The gist is that we believe people need to interpret correlations and behavioral genetic findings with some degree of caution. Our view is that both situations and personality factors are relevant when considering happiness such that any extreme view is misguided.)

Before we discuss more about the interpretation of a correlation, we need to say something about a descriptive statistic called the "standard deviation." The standard deviation measures the typical or average amount of variability in a sample. When researchers note that a score is one standard deviation higher or lower than the average score, they usually mean that the score is fairly high or low. In most cases, the interpretation of correlations is straightforward. If there is a correlation of .50 between two variables, then this can be interpreted as follows. If one moves up one standard deviation in one variable (and we can assume a causal association just for the sake of this example), then that person should move up .50 standard deviations in the other variable. This metric is meaningful because much of the variability in a distribution of scores falls between one standard deviation above and below the mean, and therefore, the correlation metric is helpful in describing how big a realistic change would be.

However, if people are interested in the effects of changes that go beyond a one-standard-deviation difference, then this correlation might be misleading. This might be true when the range of scores that is possible far exceeds the standard deviation, as is true with income. Because of income inequality, there is a small number of people who have incomes that are many standard deviations above the mean. Income in the United States does not have a clean symmetrical bell-shaped distribution typical of many other attributes. Income has a skewed distribution where there are a fair number of extremely large incomes that are substantially higher than the mean. For instance, in the United States, the median household income around 2010 (when these studies were conducted) was somewhere around $50,000, with a standard deviation of about $50,000. So if we ask whether people who are rich are happier than those who are poor, we are not asking whether someone who makes $75,000 a year is happier than someone who makes $25,000 a year (a one standard deviation difference), we are often thinking about whether someone who makes $1,000,000 a year is happier than someone who makes an average income of $50,000 a year. This difference reflects approximately 20 standard deviations in income! This means that even a small correlation can translate into very large differences between the very rich and the very poor, a suggestion that is supported by empirical evidence (Lucas & Schimmack, 2009).

So it is clear that when interpreting the evidence for the associations between life circumstances and subjective well-being, it is important to carefully consider the size of the effects from the studies. Our view is that many of these have been misinterpreted, which leads to the underestimation of the importance of life circumstances in subjective well-being. But remember that we are also skeptical of the view that life events are the biggest factor in happiness. We tend to take a middle-ground reading of the literature.

Issues regarding the interpretation of effect sizes are not the only factor influencing the myth that life circumstances don't matter. In addition, it is important to revisit the behavioral genetic studies we discussed in Chapter 18. Recall that studies show that twins who were separated at birth have remarkably similar levels of subjective well-being. This is sometimes interpreted to mean that the substantial variance that these twins share is directly influenced by inborn biological processes that are impossible to change. The reality is, however, that separated twins are usually similar in many ways, including the life circumstance variables that one might think influences subjective well-being. This raises the possibility that some of the similarity between twins is due to the effect of their similar genetic makeup on the life circumstances in which the twins find themselves, and that the true causal agent responsible for this similarity is these environments that the twins selected themselves into. Of course, we suspect that the connections between genes and life outcomes are extremely complex, and that there is no single path (either through choice of situations or through direct physiological processes) that explains how genetic factors are connected to happiness. Some of the effects may very well be difficult to modify through intentional behaviors. Our point is that high heritability does not rule out situational influence— this evidence simply constrains the range of possibilities to those that might themselves be affected by the genes that twins share.

In addition to the caution that must be used when interpreting behavioral genetic research, it is also important to be careful when interpreting evidence showing direct links between personality traits and subjective well-being. It is certainly true that personality traits exhibit some of the strongest associations with well-being of any predictors that have been tested. For instance, Steel, Schmidt, and Shultz (2008) conducted a comprehensive meta-analysis examining the associations between established trait measures and subjective well-being constructs, and they showed that many correlations, such as the associations between extraversion and aggregated positive affect or between neuroticism and aggregated negative affect, were close to .50. These correlations are much larger than those that are typically found with objective circumstances. However, one important difference is that personality traits are often measured using the same method as the subjective well-being outcomes to which they are compared. In other words, personality and subjective well-being are often both assessed using self-report questionnaires, whereas life circumstances can be assessed using more objective, non-self-report techniques. This shared method variance between measures of personality and well-being can inflate correlations, and it is not yet known how big of an effect this has. Lucas and Fujita (2000) conducted a meta-analysis of studies on extraversion and positive affect, and they found that the correlation dropped from an average of .37 when the same method was used for both the personality and well-being variables to .25 when different methods were used. This latter correlation is closer to some of the correlations for objective life circumstances. So it is likely that the correlation between personality traits and subjective well-being is inflated to some extent by shared method variance.

Psychologists and other social scientists are drawn to counterintuitive findings. The idea that situational factors have no lasting impact on subjective well-being has likely taken hold in part because of its counterintuitive nature. In fact, some have even praised the idea that there is a relatively weak influence of situational factors on well-being and a relatively strong influence of personality factors as the only example of an important, counterintuitive finding that has emerged from the entire field of personality psychology (Gilovich & Eibach, 2001). We, of course, disagree; but we also believe that some have accepted this finding precisely because it is counterintuitive rather than because it is based in solid empirical findings.

At the very least, it is important to acknowledge that when longitudinal studies are conducted, the long-term (i.e., 10–15-year) stability typically reaches a maximum of around .30, which means that many individual changes have occurred. Similarly, although the similarity across twins who grew up in different homes is remarkable, the research that has documented this impressive similarity still suggests that less than half of the variance in well-being can be accounted for by genes. In addition to this basic and indisputable response to the idea that situations and life circumstances do not matter for well-being are the ideas presented in this chapter. We have shown that if one carefully considers the interpretation of the effect sizes that have been used to support the idea that life circumstances do not matter, we see that a very different conclusion can be drawn. Life events matter, but they just might not be everything. Thus, this myth and its responses illustrate the need to think carefully about effect sizes and what they mean when drawing conclusions about them.

It is useful to think about the messages of Chapters 18 and 19 together as perhaps two sides of the same coin. The coin here is the idea that the determinants of happiness are complicated and multifaceted. There is no magic bullet or single major cause of happiness. Subjective well-being depends on a wide range of things—some dispositional and some experiential. The trick for researchers is to figure out all of the pieces of this puzzle. The myths in these two chapters are simply exaggerations of the truth that happiness is a complicated phenomenon with many influences.

References

Brickman, P., & Campbell, D. (1971). Hedonic relativism and planning the good society. In M. Appley (Ed.), *Adaptation-level theory: A symposium* (pp. 287–305). New York, NY: Academic Press.

Brickman, P., Coates, D., & Janoff-Bulman, R. (1978). Lottery winners and accident victims: Is happiness relative? *Journal of Personality and Social Psychology, 36*(8), 917–927.

Diener, E., Lucas, R. E., & Oishi, S. (2018). Advances and open questions in the science of subjective well-being. *Collabra: Psychology, 4*(1). doi:10.1525/collabra.115

Dijkers, M. (1997). Quality of life after spinal cord injury: A meta analysis of the effects of disablement components. *Spinal Cord, 35*(12), 829–840.

Dijkers, M. P. (1999). Correlates of life satisfaction among persons with spinal cord injury. *Archives of Physical Medicine and Rehabilitation, 80*(8), 867–876.

Easterlin, R. A. (1974). Does economic growth improve the human lot? Some empirical evidence. In P. A. David & M. W. Reder (Eds.), *Nations and households in economic growth: Essays in honour of Moses Abramovitz* (pp. 89–125). New York, NY: Academic Press.

Easterlin, R. A. (1995). Will raising the incomes of all increase the happiness of all? *Journal of Economic Behavior & Organization, 27*(1), 35–47.

Frederick, S., & Loewenstein, G. (1999). Hedonic adaptation. In D. Kahneman, E. Diener, & N. Schwarz (Eds.), *Well-being: The foundations of hedonic psychology* (pp. 302–329). New York, NY: Russell Sage Foundation.

Gilovich, T., & Eibach, R. (2001). The fundamental attribution error where it really counts. *Psychological Inquiry, 12*(1), 23–26.

Kahneman, D. (1999). Objective happiness. In D. Kahneman, E. Diener, & N. Schwarz (Eds.), *Well-being: The foundations of hedonic psychology* (pp. 3–25). New York, NY: Russell Sage Foundation.

Lucas, R. E. (2007). Long-term disability is associated with lasting changes in subjective well-being: Evidence from two nationally representative longitudinal studies. *Journal of Personality and Social Psychology, 92*(4), 717–730. doi:10.1037/0022-3514.92.4.717

Lucas, R. E., & Fujita, F. (2000). Factors influencing the relation between extraversion and pleasant affect. *Journal of Personality and Social Psychology, 79*(6), 1039–1056.

Lucas, R. E., & Schimmack, U. (2009). Income and well-being: How big is the gap between the rich and the poor? *Journal of Research in Personality, 43*(1), 75–78.

Schwarz, N., & Strack, F. (1999). Reports of subjective well-being: Judgmental processes and their methodological implications. In D. Kahneman, E. Diener, & N. Schwarz (Eds.), *Well-being: The foundations of hedonic psychology* (pp. 61–84). New York, NY: Russell Sage Foundation.

Smith, D. M., Schwarz, N., Roberts, T. R., & Ubel, P. A. (2006). Why are you calling me? How study introductions change response patterns. *Quality of Life Research, 15*(4), 621–630.

Steel, P., Schmidt, J., & Shultz, J. (2008). Refining the relationship between personality and subjective well-being. *Psychological Bulletin*, *134*(1), 138–161.

Stevenson, B., & Wolfers, J. (2008). Economic growth and happiness: Reassessing the Easterlin paradox. *Brookings Papers on Economic Activity*, *39*, 1–102.

Veenhoven, R., & Hagerty, M. (2006). Rising happiness in nations 1946–2004: A reply to Easterlin. *Social Indicators Research*, *79*(3), 421–436.

20 HAPPINESS RESULTS PRIMARILY FROM PERSON– ENVIRONMENT FIT

The last two chapters (Chapters 18 and 19)—the first focusing on the myth that situations completely determine our levels of happiness and the second focusing on the opposing myth that we can adapt to all situations— may give you the feeling of déjà vu. Indeed, the debates about the relative role of dispositional and situational influences on happiness mirror similar debates in the broader field of personality psychology (see Chapters 1 and 12). Remember, in the 1960s and 1970s, social psychologists proposed that broad dispositions play only a minor role in guiding behavior, at least in comparison to the size and importance of situational effects. This claim, and the ensuing research that was used to support it, led to the lasting and heated "person–situation debate" regarding the extent to which behavior is determined by the person or by the situation. Somewhat interestingly, within the domain of subjective well-being, the debate has played out in reverse of what happened within the broader field of personality psychology. For instance, the situationists of the 1960s and 1970s argued that people intuitively believe that traits cause behavior when in fact (at least according to those aligned with this school of thought) situational factors play a more important role. Within the domain of subjective well-being, however, intuition typically suggests that situations matter most, and the empirical evidence suggests otherwise (with all the caveats and qualifications discussed in our previous chapters).

Great Myths of Personality, First Edition. M. Brent Donnellan and Richard E. Lucas.
© 2021 John Wiley & Sons, Inc. Published 2021 by John Wiley & Sons, Inc.

These kinds of discussions about whether intrinsic or extrinsic factors are the more important determinants of the course of human lives are largely reflections of a much older debate about the role of nature versus nurture. These issues have vexed philosophers for millennia, and therefore, it is no surprise that they repeatedly emerge when psychologists study and discuss the causes of thoughts, feelings, and behavior. Perhaps more importantly, the fact that variations of this debate have raged for so long suggests that something beyond just empirical evidence is likely influencing people's beliefs and opinions on these issues. As Stephen Pinker pointed out in his book on the nature/nurture debate (Pinker, 2003), people's opinions about the role of nature and nurture are often wrapped up with their views on morality and their expectations (and hopes) about the way the world should work.

For instance, Pinker notes that the idea that the quality of people's lives might be due to inborn dispositions is, to some, a pessimistic perspective on the world (Pinker, 2003). The idea that the nature perspective is a pessimistic worldview often stems from the belief that anything that is linked to inborn traits must be unchangeable and predetermined. Many people have the sense that this perspective takes away free will or may even justify the maintenance of social inequalities. Pinker points out that linking nature and nurture perspectives with such broader values is not as straightforward as people often believe, and that both the nature and nurture perspectives may have some desirable and undesirable implications. More importantly, however, Pinker notes that scientists should seek the truth about these influences regardless of their implications, and people should be wary of the ways that their own beliefs about how things should work influence their evaluation of the empirical evidence (for a discussion of precisely how this plays out in the person–situation debate, see Lucas & Donnellan, 2009).

In any case, the nature/nurture debate seems to play an important role in the questions that are asked and the answers that people find to be convincing in psychological science. In addition, the types of arguments that emerge and the attempts to resolve these disagreements often proceeded in a similar way. Specifically, one class of explanation (situational or dispositional) is first emphasized and then questioned. Then evidence against this perspective accumulates, and the pendulum swings in the opposite direction. Finally, once people realize that extreme statements in support of either view cannot be supported by empirical evidence, the field adopts a more moderate view that incorporates both perspectives (at least in the ideal situation).

Often, this more moderate view takes the form of *interactionism*. According to interactionists, it is not only the case that both the person and the situation matter. Instead, in addition to the so-called main effects of these two influences, it is also important to understand how these factors *interact* with one another. For instance, in the context of the original person–situation debate, it may not just be that conscientious people work harder than less conscientious people (a *main effect* of the person, in statistical jargon) or that people work harder when they are paid than when they are not (another main effect, but this time due to the situation) or even an additive combination of these two effects (i.e., the net effect of these two factors that occurs by adding them together). Instead, it may be the case that the effect of the situation actually depends on one's personality (or that the effect of one's personality depends on the situation). For example, it may be that highly conscientious people work hard regardless of the rewards they receive, whereas low conscientious people only work hard when they are paid handsomely. Or alternatively, it may be that neither high nor low conscientious people work hard when there are no rewards, and only the highly conscientious respond to financial rewards. If either of these two interactionist patterns were true, one would need to know something more precisely about how the person and the situation combined to maximize the prediction of behavior.

In the domain of subjective well-being, this type of interactionist perspective typically focuses on person–environment fit. This is a natural and intuitive way to resolve the debates about whether dispositional or situational factors matter more. According to this perspective, different people can thrive in different environments, and so we need to find the correct combination that predicts happiness for different people. Extraverts might like loud and exciting environments, which may lead them to be happiest if they have jobs and lifestyles that promote such environments. In contrast, introverts may like quiet and sedate environments and may thrive emotionally when they create a lifestyle that allows for such experiences. The idea here is that happiness flows from the match between the person and the situation. So what does the empirical evidence say about this interactionist perspective?

Before we go any further discussing this idea, we note that this is somewhat of an unusual myth for this book. We will not say that the belief that person–situation fit matters is definitely wrong. Instead, we want to highlight the fact that there are some known obstacles to finding evidence for such effects, and therefore we need to be very careful in our expectations for studies that investigate them. This chapter is really about skepticism about whether certain scientific claims have a sufficient evidentiary basis.

Let's begin with some clear cases where interactions between person and environment would be expected; we will then move to a broader discussion of the issues that are involved in testing these interactions. This might be one of those sections of the book where we get technical, but we promise not to go too far down a rabbit hole.

One area where there's been much research on person–environment fit is in the context of research on extraversion and its links with subjective well-being. As noted in Chapter 18, extraversion is one of the strongest correlates of subjective well-being of the Big Five traits (Steel, Schmidt, & Shultz, 2008). Specifically, extraverts tend to experience more positive affect than do introverts (as we noted in Chapter 5, we are using extraverts and introverts as a shorthand for saying a person high in this dimension of personality and a person low on this dimension). A considerable amount of research has been conducted to explain this effect, and much of this work has looked at interactions and person–environment fit.

For instance, one possibility is that society may require both extraverts and introverts to participate in a variety of social situations and activities. Extraverts—by definition—enjoy these situations to a much greater degree than introverts. Therefore, if person–environment fit is important for high levels of subjective well-being, we should find evidence that extraverts are happier than introverts when in social situations, but the reverse should be true (introverts should be happier than extraverts) when people are alone.

A number of studies have now tested this hypothesis in a variety of ways. For instance, in one of the earliest studies, Diener, Sandvik, Pavot, and Fujita (1992) used a national probability sample to compare the happiness of extraverts and introverts and to link these differences to characteristics of their lifestyles. If the person–environment-fit hypothesis is true, then extraverts in environments that allow for a great deal of social contact should experience greater happiness than those who have less opportunity for such contact. In contrast to this idea, however, Diener et al. found that extraverts were happier than introverts regardless of whether they worked in social or nonsocial occupations and regardless of whether they lived alone or with others. Extraverts were just happier than introverts regardless (this is an example of a main effect of the person unqualified by a statistical interaction, in statistical lingo).

This study by Diener et al. (1992) is interesting because it uses a large national probability sample to examine broad features of one's life. However, it's not without problems. Most notably, it's not always clear whether the proxy variables they used to measure the situation—whether a person works in a job that typically allows for social contact or whether that person lives alone or with others—are really good indicators of a person's total amount (or quality) of social contact. It's possible that extraverts who live alone still make time to see others throughout the day, just as it's possible that extraverts who work in a traditionally non-social job can intentionally increase the social contact that they have or can replace social interaction at work with increased social activity out-side of work. Furthermore, it may be only certain types of social activities that extraverts enjoy. Therefore, it's important to conduct additional studies that track what people actually do on a day-to-day basis.

This is where studies that use the experience sampling method (ESM) come in. This approach is a way to get reports of emotional experience in a more naturalistic and immediate way. In these studies, people are sig-naled to report at random times of the day, often for many days. In the early days of ESM research, people wore watches programmed to sound an alarm multiple times per day, and then they completed paper-and-pen-cil inventories when they heard an alarm. More recent research uses handheld computers or smartphones to accomplish the same goals. Regardless of the specific methods, however, ESM studies allow research-ers to track what people are doing and how they're feeling over time by asking them questions in the moment. This strikes us as a strong method for testing hypotheses about person–environment fit.

Again, however, most studies that have looked at the links between extraversion and positive affect as a function of the situation find little evidence of the person-by-environment-fit interaction. For instance, Lucas, Le, and Dyrenforth (2008) conducted two studies that used ESM to test this possibility. Participants kept track of various types of social situations (e.g., leading, helping, social entertainment) and specific types of interaction partners (e.g., friends, family members, strangers). In addi-tion, they reported their mood at various times throughout the day. Although these situational factors did matter for people's happiness—they were happier with other people than when alone—these effects did not vary for extraverts or introverts. It appeared that people got a similar boost in positive affect regardless of their personality. Thus, even when detailed records of social activity were examined, no evidence for the person–environment fit explanation was found (see Srivastava, Angelo, & Vallereux, 2008, for a similar result).

Another way that person–environment fit could potentially lead to greater happiness is through the links between specific life domains (including social relationships, experiences at work, or the state of one's health) and their effects on overall evaluations of life as a whole. Consider how broad life satisfaction judgments might be made. If you were to rate on a scale from 1 to 10 how satisfied you are with your life as a whole, what information would you use to come up with this judgment? One intuitive model for how such judgments are made is that people think about various domains in their lives, consider how they are doing in each of these domains, weight each domain by their personal importance, and then aggregate across these weighted domains to get an overall evaluation. In other words, if you are someone for whom romantic relationships are important, then the domain of romantic relationships would get a high weight in your overall rating, whereas for someone for whom work was more important than romantic relationships, whether the person was doing well in his or her job might get a higher rating. Many measurement strategies for well-being and the related construct of quality of life use such a weighting scheme. These are based on the idea of person–environment fit, because they assume that some environments will play more of a role for some people, depending on their personalities and values.

Although the idea that domains should be weighted by personal importance is an intuitively appealing one, the evidence for its utility is mixed at best (e.g., Rohrer & Schmukle, 2018, or Marsh & Scalas, 2018, for a technical perspective). There are both substantive and methodological reasons for this. For instance, in a review of the evidence called "Why Are We Weighting?" Trauer and Mackinnon (2001) listed a number of reasons why weights often do not work. For one thing, when people conduct research on life domains, they usually select those domains that would reasonably be expected to be important for most people, like relationships and health. Thus, asking people about importance ratings tends not to provide that much more information because most people rate the given domains as important (in technical terms, there is not a great deal of variability in the importance ratings). Moreover, although individuals may have the intuition that people vary considerably in the things they find interesting or important, there is often a surprising degree of consensus. This consensus makes it difficult to find interactions. Many people rate relationships as being very important.

Take our previous example of extraverts and introverts in social and nonsocial situations. Although people may picture a prototypical introvert trying to enjoy himself or herself in a prototypical social environment (perhaps a loud party), the fact is that most individuals are not so extreme in either direction on the dimension of extraversion, and most social situations do not reflect this prototypical party. Instead, most social interactions—spending time with friends, working in small groups, making small talk with coworkers you see on a day-to-day basis—are neutral to moderately pleasant for most people who experience them. Thus, although the authors of this book believe that there are clear and important individual differences (this is, after all, a book on personality), people may have the tendency to forget how similar people can be to one another in terms of their basic human nature. Humans are social creatures and need to feel a sense of belonging to a larger collective.

Trauer and Mackinnon (2001) also note that when researchers ask people about their satisfaction with a domain and the importance of that domain, the two are often correlated. In short, people do not usually provide extreme ratings for domains that are unimportant to them, and thus, when people rate their satisfaction with a domain as being especially high or especially low, then this usually means that they consider the domain to be important.

A third reason why importance weighting does not usually lead to interesting and theoretically meaningful results—and this is a somewhat esoteric methodological reason—is that there are psychometric problems once researchers start multiplying satisfaction scores with importance ratings to arrive at an overall score. As we talked about in the measurement chapters, assessing internal psychological attributes is a challenging task. The kinds of intuitions and expectations some researchers have about how something should be measured do not fit with psychometric studies showing how measures actually work. Oftentimes, intuitively appealing transformations of relatively simple responses (such as when researchers subtract one rating from another or multiply two things together to get a single response) lead to problems with the resulting numbers. Just because a researcher can compute something from given data does not mean this is a good idea. Although the psychometric problems that can occur are beyond the scope of this book, Trauer and Mackinnon (2001) point out that measures constructed from such interactions are poorly understood in theoretical terms and often have poor psychometric characteristics. Think about it this way—if all measures have error so that scores are imprecise, what might happen if two sets of scores are multiplied? Can researchers truly trust the product of two poorly measured constructs? And what precisely does that product mean in psychological terms? The same concerns apply when applying other kinds of mathematical operations to two sets of scores.

So, although intuitions related to ideas about person–environment fit might suggest that importance weighting should improve results, researchers like Russell, Hubley, Palepu, and Zumbo (2006) have concluded that such attempts have "produced uniformly negative results" (p. 143). In general, simply averaging across different domain ratings provides a better sense of how a person is doing overall than applying a complicated weighting scheme that might suffer from deeper problems. This is consistent with the broader principle that simpler is better in data analysis (Cohen, 1990) and that across a wide range of analytic questions, most weighting by importance schemes often fare worse than simple averages (also see Marsh, 1986).

What are the general lessons that one should take from this chapter? Are we saying that person–environment fit will never help explain the happiness that people experience? Of course, the answer is "no." We believe that such interactions might be a fruitful area of study. Our point in this chapter is that there are known challenges that make identifying interactions difficult. For a variety of substantive and methodological reasons, interactions are hard to find and to replicate, and thus, researchers should be cautious when beginning research programs that hope to find such effects. Readers of such studies should be cautious when reading about and interpreting such findings, as they may reflect false positives that will not replicate. Right now, researchers might have to settle for a "main effects" understanding of happiness—both internal and external factors matter, but it is hard to say much about how the two things may combine to better understand the mystery of why some people are happier than others.

References

Cohen, J. (1990). Things I have learned (so far). *American Psychologist*, *45*(12), 1304.

Diener, E., Sandvik, E., Pavot, W., & Fujita, F. (1992). Extraversion and subjective well-being in a US national probability sample. *Journal of Research in Personality*, *26*(3), 205–215.

Lucas, R. E., & Donnellan, M. B. (2009). If the person–situation debate is really over, why does it still generate so much negative affect? *Journal of Research in Personality*, *43*(2), 146–149.

Lucas, R. E., Le, K., & Dyrenforth, P. (2008). Explaining the extraversion/positive affect relation: Sociability cannot account for extraverts' greater happiness. *Journal of Personality*, *76*(3), 385–414.

Marsh, H. W. (1986). Global self-esteem: Its relation to specific facets of self-concept and their importance. *Journal of Personality and Social Psychology*, *51*(6), 1224.

Marsh, H. W., & Scalas, L. F. (2018). Individually weighted-average models: Testing a taxonomic SEM approach across different multidimensional/global constructs because the weights "Don't make no nevermind.". *Structural Equation Modeling: A Multidisciplinary Journal, 25*(1), 137–159.

Pinker, S. (2003). *The blank slate: The modern denial of human nature.* New York, NY: Penguin.

Rohrer, J., & Schmukle, S. C. (2018). Individual importance weighting of domain satisfaction ratings does not increase validity. *Collabra: Psychology, 4*(1), 6. doi:10.1525/collabra.116

Russell, L. B., Hubley, A. M., Palepu, A., & Zumbo, B. D. (2006). Does weighting capture what's important? Revisiting subjective importance weighting with a quality of life measure. *Social Indicators Research, 75*(1), 141–167.

Srivastava, S., Angelo, K. M., & Vallereux, S. R. (2008). Extraversion and positive affect: A day reconstruction study of person–environment transactions. *Journal of Research in Personality, 42*(6), 1613–1618.

Steel, P., Schmidt, J., & Shultz, J. (2008). Refining the relationship between personality and subjective well-being. *Psychological Bulletin, 134*(1), 138–161.

Trauer, T., & Mackinnon, A. (2001). Why are we weighting? The role of importance ratings in quality of life measurement. *Quality of Life Research, 10*(7), 579–585.

21 THERE IS A 3-TO-1 POSITIVITY-TO-NEGATIVITY RATIO FOR FLOURISHING

My problem is that I have been persecuted by an integer. For seven years this number has followed me around, has intruded in my most private data, and has assaulted me from the pages of our most public journals. This number assumes a variety of disguises, being sometimes a little larger and sometimes a little smaller than usual, but never changing so much as to be unrecognizable. The persistence with which this number plagues me is far more than a random accident. There is, to quote a famous senator, a design behind it, some pattern governing its appearances. Either there really is something unusual about the number or else I am suffering from delusions of persecution.

(George Miller, 1956, p. 343)

A popular paperback book was released in 2009 with a catchy title *Positivity: Top-Notch Research Reveals the 3-to-1 Ratio That Will Change Your Life* (Fredrickson, 2009). This book featured strong endorsements from major figures in psychology such as Martin Seligman and Daniel Gilbert as well as the journalist Daniel Goleman (the author of another popular book about emotional intelligence). The *Positivity* book promised to give readers the tools to become "the best version of yourself" (see www.positivityratio.com) and emphasized the importance of obtaining a 3-to-1 balance between positive emotions (e.g., feelings of happiness, energy, gratitude, zest) and negative emotions (e.g., feelings of nastiness, contempt, and irritation) for promoting human growth and potential.

Great Myths of Personality, First Edition. M. Brent Donnellan and Richard E. Lucas.
© 2021 John Wiley & Sons, Inc. Published 2021 by John Wiley & Sons, Inc.

The idea of a specific 3-to-1 ratio of positivity to negativity was described in an earlier academic article by Fredrickson and Losada (2005) published in a prestigious journal. The central thesis of the academic article (like the popular book) was the existence of a specific ratio of positive emotions to negative emotions that one should experience to promote human flourishing. Flourishing was defined by Fredrickson and Losada (2005) as living "within an optimal range of human functioning, one that connotes goodness, generativity, growth, and resilience" (p. 678). The ratio was specified to a seemingly precise four digits: 2.9013 (p. 683) but rounded up to a 3-to-1 ratio for the popular book. Taken literally, a person is said to be flourishing if one experiences at least 3 positive mood states for each negative mood state (or 2.9013 positive mood states for every 1 negative state if one wants to be pedantic). Fredrickson and Losada also suggested that the positivity ratio applies beyond individuals to apply to business teams and close relationships like marriages.

An interesting extension of the positivity ratio was the idea of an upper limit to the positivity ratio—a point at which the individual (or presumably teams or marriages) becomes imbalanced. According to Fredrickson and Losada (2005), there was such a thing as too much positivity, and they precisely quantified this upper limit. Using apparently sophisticated mathematical modeling, they determined that the upper limit for flourishing was a ratio of 11.6 to 1. In other words, individuals who experienced more than 11.6 positive states for every 1 negative state had reached a saturation point and were no longer flourishing. These individuals were in danger of experiencing too much of a good thing! Altogether, the article was noteworthy because it claimed that "a set of general mathematical principles may describe the relations between positive affect and human flourishing" (p. 678).

Discovering precise numbers that distinguish optimal human functioning from suboptimal functioning (if accurate) would represent an impressive scientific feat with clear practical benefits. For example, an individual's particular balance of positive to negative affect could serve as an index of psychological health on par with the kinds of measures available to quantify physical health like blood pressure, body mass index (BMI), and resting heart rate. This ratio could therefore assist mental health professionals in making important decisions about diagnosis and treatment of emotional problems. On a personal level, individuals whose emotional life falls below the 3-to-1 ratio (sometimes called the Losada line; see Fredrickson & Losada, 2005, p. 683) could consider making changes to improve their lives and promote optimal functioning. Likewise, individuals with ratios above 11.6 to 1 might need to worry about experiencing too much positivity and try to balance out their emotional lives with more negativity.

Specifying the positivity ratio and a "zone of optimality" between 2.9 and 11.6 would also suggest that psychological scientists have a sophisticated enough understanding of the dynamics of emotional life to specify exact numbers much like engineers can specify the kinds of car speeds that will maximize fuel economy while also minimizing the time it takes to travel from point A to point B. Precision is the hallmark of mature sciences and something that is often viewed as a critical goal of psychological research. The critical problem is that this level of precision associated with the positivity ratio is a myth.

The somewhat embarrassing truth is that the 2.9013 number was the output of a complex equation that would have produced different values had Fredrickson and Losada (2005) simply selected different (but nonetheless arbitrary) constants to provide a "convenient" solution to the complex equation (Brown, Sokal, & Friedman, 2013). In short, the mathematical basis for the positivity ratio was critically flawed. It was not based on top-notch research but rather on a set of arbitrary assumptions.

As it stands, there are very few areas of psychology that have produced the kind of precision associated with the 2.9013 positivity ratio that stand the test of replication and critical scrutiny. Even Fredrickson and Losada admitted that their ratio seemed "absurdly precise," but they nonetheless suggested that it was consistent with empirical studies. A number in psychology that seems to come closest to the positivity ratio is the so-called magic number 7 proposed by George Miller to characterize the number of "chunks" of information that humans can hold in their working memory (Miller, 1956). On the other hand, even Miller's magical number 7 is accompanied by imprecision with the caveat that it is bounded by plus or minus 2 chunks. One immediate red flag, therefore, is the degree of precision embodied in the positivity ratio (Zwaan, 2013). Psychological science is rarely this precise!

The mathematical underpinnings behind the positivity ratio were debunked by Brown et al. (2013) in an important corrective article. The bottom line is that the positivity ratios identified by Fredrickson and Losada should not to be taken literally as anything that has strong psychological relevance to everyday life. Accordingly, a correction concerning the original Fredrickson and Losada (2005) article appeared in the scientific literature in 2013. The correction read, in part, that the "the modeling element of this article is formally withdrawn as invalid and, along with it, the model-based predictions about the positivity ratios of 2.9 and 11.6." This is a clear-cut case of myth busting in the scientific literature. The bottom line is devastating—there is nothing magical about a 3-to-1 ratio, and there is no bright red line that clearly delineates flourishing from languishing (see our discussion of types in Chapter 5).

Lessons can be learned from this debacle. The precision of the positivity ratio itself should have probably raised concerns when it was first introduced in the literature (see Brown et al., 2013). This is related to two facts about psychological science. The first is the reality of individual variation (as you should know by now, this is also a major theme of personality psychology in the first place). People are often different from one another in fairly dramatic ways. It would be unusual to find a precise positivity ratio that could characterize flourishing in all people everywhere. The second fact is that all psychological constructs are measured with error, and thus a certain degree of imprecision must accompany any scientific estimate (recall all of that somewhat technical and potentially boring stuff we covered back in the measurement sections of this book). Affective states are internal psychological experiences that are measured indirectly and using arbitrary metrics. This fact about measurement adds additional imprecision to psychological research that makes the idea of specific ratio without qualification all the more unlikely. Consider political polls that assess the intention of voters on relatively clear-cut issues such as a willingness to vote for a candidate. Those polls are almost always issued with a note about the margin of error. Likewise, some methodologically oriented psychologists believe the margin of error and precision of estimates is a critically important element of research that should be routinely reported in scientific papers (Cumming, 2012). The fact that the positivity ratio was described without attention to imprecision is problematic.

The debunking of the Fredrickson and Losada (2005) mathematical modeling was something of an embarrassment to the field of positive psychology (the branch of psychology that focuses on happiness and other "positive" attributes). The academic paper was cited with some regularity by other researchers in the field, and the idea of a 3-to-1 positivity ratio was marketed to the public. Concerns were raised that academic researchers were not skeptical enough of the original target article (Brown et al., 2013), and these concerns strike us as having merit. Thus, the myth busting of the positivity ratio raises tough questions for psychological science.

To be fair, it's hard to evaluate whether researchers are too gullible. Once something is shown to be false, it can be deceptively easy to believe that others should have known it all along (something called a *hindsight bias*). One of the major functions of scientific research is to continually evaluate evidence for particular claims. Thus, the positivity ratio episode may simply serve as a vivid example of how science works. Accordingly, the immediate lesson we drew from this event was the importance of healthy skepticism (this is also the overarching theme of this entire book!). Indeed, we hope that a better understanding of this myth encourages readers to exercise caution when reading about exact numbers (with no margins of error) attached to very complex psychological phenomenon. Skepticism is critical when it comes to consuming pop psychology books and watching recorded talks on the Internet. Even books written by professors with advanced degrees can be based on dubious scientific claims.

Although the specific 3-to-1 positivity ratio turns out to be a myth, we believe some potentially important research findings behind the specific ratio should not be discarded. Remember the cliché about throwing out babies with bathwater and that many myths we have discussed reflect a kernel of truth. The first important research idea is the suggestion that well-adjusted individuals tend to experience more positive than negative emotional states. All other things being equal, positive mood states are probably more pleasant than negative mood states, and the chronic experience of negative mood may indicate the presence of psychopathology. It is also important to point out that there is well-established literature that points to a possible (emphasis here on possible) causal connection between positive emotions and important life outcomes (e.g., Lyubomirsky, King, & Diener, 2005). The second interesting idea is the possibility that extremely high levels of energy and positivity uncoupled from reality might characterize certain kinds of psychopathologies rather than optimal adjustment (see, e.g., Fredrickson, 2013). Mania is one such example whereby too much energy, zest, and positivity might have negative ramifications for the individual and his or her loved ones.

In short, we want readers to be skeptical of the 2.9013 ratio and not so much the idea that positive emotions are important or valuable. We also think this myth illustrates the importance of ongoing scientific review of research findings. A published paper is not the last word on a given topic. Likewise, there is no reason to trust a book or well-produced talk just because the author or speaker has an advanced degree (the same suggestion holds for this book). The episode of the positivity ratio shows that flawed findings can easily find themselves published in top-tier journals. Healthy skepticism is useful, and it is valuable to search for converging lines of evidence about a particular phenomenon.

References

Brown, N. J. L., Sokal, A. D., & Friedman, H. L. (2013). The complex dynamics of wishful thinking: The critical positivity ratio. *American Psychologist, 68,* 801–813.

Cumming, G. (2012). *Understanding the new statistics: Effect sizes, confidence intervals, and meta-analysis.* New York, NY: Routledge.

Fredrickson, B. L. (2009). *Positivity: Groundbreaking research reveals how to embrace the hidden strength of positive emotions, overcome negativity, and thrive.* New York, NY: Crown. Published in paperback as *Positivity: Top-notch research reveals the 3-to-1 ratio that will change your life*

Fredrickson, B. L. (2013). Updated thinking on positivity ratios. *American Psychologist, 68,* 814–822.

Fredrickson, B. L., & Losada, M. F. (2005). Positive affect and the complex dynamics of human flourishing. *American Psychologist, 60,* 678–686. doi:10.1037/0003-066X.60.7.678

Lyubomirsky, S., King, L., & Diener, E. (2005). The benefits of frequent positive affect: Does happiness lead to success? *Psychological Bulletin, 131,* 803–855. doi:10.1037/0033-2909.131.6.803

Miller, G. A. (1956). The magical number seven, plus or minus two: Some limits on our capacity for processing information. *Psychological Review, 63,* 81–97.

R Zwaan. (2013). The fanciful number 2.9013, plus or minus nothing [Web log post]. Retrieved from https://rolfzwaan.blogspot.com/2013/07/the-fanciful-number-29013-plus-or-minus.html

22 PERSONALITY TRAIT SIMILARITY MATTERS FOR ROMANTIC RELATIONSHIPS

Online dating is a billion-dollar industry that has changed how many people find their romantic partners (Cacioppo, Cacioppo, Gonzaga, Ogburn, & VanderWeele, 2013; Finkel, Eastwick, Karney, Reis, & Sprecher, 2012). Online dating companies assemble a large pool of individuals who are also interested in romantic relationship and often promise to match people based on their personalities.[1] Some of the services offered by online dating services are predicated on the idea that personality similarity matters for relationships. Unfortunately, the relevant research literature does not provide convincing evidence that personality trait similarity itself is meaningful to relationship outcomes such as marital satisfaction and stability. To be clear, people do seem to be attracted to people who they think are similar to them in terms of attributes like attitudes, according to classic research (Byrne, 1961). But that is a different issue than whether personality itself matters for relationship outcomes. As it stands, there is a gulf between the research evidence about personality similarity and relationships and the popular idea that compatible partners are those who are actually the most similar. In fact, we believe the idea

---

[1] Feel free to Google any of the popular sites. We are hesitant to provide links for two reasons. One, we do not want to get in a lawsuit given the content of this chapter. Second, we are both married, and we are worried that our search histories might raise alarms with our partners.

Great Myths of Personality, First Edition. M. Brent Donnellan and Richard E. Lucas.
© 2021 John Wiley & Sons, Inc. Published 2021 by John Wiley & Sons, Inc.

that personality trait similarity matters for relationships is largely a myth (see Finkel et al., 2012, pp. 45–48, for a more technical discussion of this material; Montoya, Horton, & Kirchner, 2008).

It's important to clarify what we mean by personality traits when describing this myth. Here we are focusing on individual differences in the core personality dispositions captured by contemporary trait models such as the Big Five traits (extraversion, agreeableness, conscientiousness, neuroticism, and openness) or the Big Three traits (positive emotionality, negative emotionality, and constraint). We are not talking about values or demographic attributes such as age, religion, or educational attainment. There is evidence, for example, linking religious similarity with relationship outcomes (see Finkel et al., 2012). In this chapter, we consider these kinds of questions: If you are high on neuroticism, would your relationship be happier, more satisfying, and more stable if you also partnered with someone high on neuroticism? Are extraverts who pair up with introverts less happy, presumably due to a mismatch in the types of activities that they want to pursue?

Before we answer these questions, we have to answer what we mean by the term "similar" when evaluating the importance of personality for relationships. Common language usage indicates that similar means alike. Next, we have to find an operational definition of similarity to conduct research on this topic. An operational definition is a precise statement about how something is measured (or manipulated in an experiment). In this context, an operational definition refers to the precise way that researchers will measure personality trait similarity in couples. This turns out to be quite a thorny issue!

As a starting point, it is straightforward to measure the Big Five traits of spouses: We can operationally define each person's traits as his or her scores on self-report personality questionnaires. The trickier question is how to quantify personality similarity to use as a statistical predictor of relationship outcome variables like relationship satisfaction (perhaps measured with a questionnaire) or likelihood of divorce (which can be measured more objectively). Similarity is a property of the connection between the two people's personalities, but how should researchers use those personality scores to define similarity?

A number of approaches exist for quantifying personality similarity, and these different methods could, in principle, provide different answers to the basic question about whether personality similarity is a factor in relationship longevity or satisfaction. One simple and straightforward way to quantify similarity is to take the absolute value of the difference between the personality scores for each partner. This is known as the *difference score approach.* For example, if Sue scores a 4.25 on a measure of neuroticism and Pat scores a 3.5 on that same measure, the difference score is .75 (i.e., the absolute value of the difference between 4.25 and 3.50). If we had differences like this from many couples, we could use the difference score as a statistical predictor of relationship variables.

The statistical task when using the difference score is to determine whether that couple-level attribute matters above and beyond the individual personality attributes that factored into the calculation of that difference score. In Chapter 20, we discussed the idea of statistical main effects and interactions. Here the main effects are the personality scores of both partners, and researchers need to know if similarity as operationalized as the difference score is important above and beyond these main effects. This is actually a fairly demanding task given how the difference score is computed. The only way to get a large difference between two people's scores on some personality measure is if one partner scores high on that dimension and the other partner scores low (i.e., similarity is minimized when one partner has the maximum possible score and the other partner has the minimum possible score). If this dimension was, say, neuroticism (a personality trait that tends to be associated with a wide variety of negative outcomes), that means that there is one person in the relationship who is very high on this trait. It would be critical to rule out the possibility that couples who are different in neuroticism have worse outcomes simply because a highly neurotic person in a relationship might contribute to high levels of relationship dissatisfaction and instability (e.g., Dyrenforth, Kashy, Donnellan, & Lucas, 2010; Karney & Bradbury, 1995, Malouff, Thorsteinsson, Schutte, Bhullar, & Rooke, 2010, Robins, Caspi, & Moffitt, 2000). This is why careful researchers control for each partner's personality traits when using the difference score to statistically predict relationship satisfaction. Using this strategy, it is quite difficult to find evidence that the personality difference score between trait scores has much to do with relationship outcomes (see e.g., Dyrenforth et al., 2010; Luo et al., 2008).

The difference score approach can be extended across a number of different attributes to capture whether couples have similar overall levels of multiple personality traits. This is simply a matter of summing (or averaging) the difference scores for the different attributes (e.g., extraversion, agreeableness, conscientiousness, openness) to create an overall personality difference composite score. The important statistical issue is to still control for all of the different traits that factored into that overall composite score. Once this is done, there is little evidence that this kind of composite predicts relationship variables above and beyond the constituent traits (see Dyrenforth et al., 2010).

Other approaches for computing similarity are even more complicated than the difference scores we have described (see, e.g., Furr, 2008). Going too far into these technical details will bore most readers, so we can just summarize the issues (see Humbad, Donnellan, Iacono, McGue, & Burt, 2013, for a detailed treatment). First, it is rarely clear what complicated similarity variables mean in psychological terms. Recall our discussions of validity, especially in Chapter 20 when we talked about measures of personality and environment fit. This lack of clarity makes it hard to defend the similarity variable. Second, there are many ways to compute similarity measures, so it is possible to use many different ones in different statistical analyses. This means that researchers can unwittingly capitalize on chance and identify fluke similarity findings that will not replicate. This is worrisome to us. Third, in most cases, researchers still need to address the main effects of the personality traits of both partners when considering whether the complicated similarity measures add predictive power. Many researchers skip this step, perhaps because they are unaware of this issue when dealing with complicated measures of personality similarity. As it stands, there is mixed evidence that complicated measures of similarity predict relationship outcomes when controlling for the main effects of the individual traits involved in computing similarity measures (see, e.g., Dyrenforth et al., 2010; Humbad et al., 2013).

Across studies, the individual personality attributes of each partner seem relatively more important than personality similarity (or dissimilarity). Put differently, personality traits themselves seem to matter for relationships more so than personality similarity itself. Indeed, certain individual personality attributes like neuroticism have what is known as both *actor* and *partner effects* when statistically predicting relationship outcomes. Actor effects occur when an individual's own personality attribute is associated with her or his relationship outcome, like marital satisfaction. Individuals who are high in neuroticism tend to view their relationships more negatively than individuals low in neuroticism. Partner effects occur when an individual's own relationship outcome can be predicted from her/his partner's personality. Individuals high in neuroticism have partners who are less satisfied with the relationship. Thus, the "action" with respect to personality traits and relationship outcomes seems to occur at the level of the individual instead of at the level of the couple. When actor, partner, and similarity effects are compared, personality similarity is not nearly as important as the actual traits of the two people involved in the relationship (e.g., Dyrenforth et al., 2010).

In sum, the idea that personality similarity is critical for relationships is largely a myth. Instead, the personality traits of each partner seem to be one factor (among many) related to relationship satisfaction and stability. Thus, when it comes to the importance of personality for relationships, we don't think there is much to be gained by considering personality similarity. This conclusion could change as researchers continue to find new ways to define and test similarity effects. But strong statements about the importance of personality trait similarity are not supported by the evidence (see also Finkel et al., 2012). Rather than worry about personality similarity, worry about the personality attributes of your potential partners! Online dating services are a useful service probably because they assemble a pool of potential partners interested in relationships. They may even screen out potential members from the pool with especially problematic personality attributes. We are just not convinced that fancy algorithms for matching people based on personality similarity are especially valuable. Make sure you know why you are paying for access to those online dating sites.

We should add that the research evidence we have cited is correlational, and thus proving causal links between personality attributes and relationships is quite difficult. This is a place where experiments are hard to conduct because we cannot randomly assign people to long-term romantic relationships. Thus, correlational research is the most widely used approach for addressing this issue. One piece of evidence that helps to constrain causal inferences is that personality traits measured in, say, late adolescence seem to predict later relationship experiences (Donnellan, Larsen-Rife, & Conger, 2005). Thus, personality traits seem to precede relationship experiences. Indeed, there is even some provocative evidence that temperamental qualities of young children predict differences in their adult relationships (Newman, Caspi, Moffitt, & Silva, 1997). It's also the case that involvement in an unsatisfying and distressing relationship might alter personality attributes (e.g., Robins, Caspi, & Moffitt, 2002), so the so-called causal arrows might flow in both directions such that personality traits influence relationships and experiences in relationships may influence relationships. But there's very little reason to think that personality trait similarity itself is a critical ingredient for a happy and stable romantic union. We briefly consider the possibility in the next chapter as to whether couples become more similar to each other over time.

Our last caveat is to remind readers that we addressed the topic of personality trait similarity. It might be the case that similarity with respect to values, political orientation, and interests is important for relationship processes. Having different life goals than a romantic partner might generate disagreements and distress. So please do not overgeneralize our conclusions! We reviewed the evidence for personality trait similarity. We also add that the issues about the operational definition of similarity for these other variables is relevant. Remember our caveat—just because a researcher can offer a way to quantify similarity does not mean that the approach is a sensible one. Look for replicable effects when thinking about similarity for all psychological variables!

References

Byrne, D. (1961). Interpersonal attraction and attitude similarity. *Journal of Abnormal and Social Psychology, 62*(3), 713–715.

Cacioppo, J. T., Cacioppo, S., Gonzaga, G. C., Ogburn, E. L., & VanderWeele, T. J. (2013). Marital satisfaction and break-ups differ across on-line and off-line meeting venues. *Proceedings of the National Academy of Sciences of the United States of America, 110*, 10135–10140.

Donnellan, M. B., Larsen-Rife, D., & Conger, R. D. (2005). Personality, family history, and competence in early adult romantic relationships. *Journal of Personality and Social Psychology, 88*, 562–576.

Dyrenforth, P. S., Kashy, D. A., Donnellan, M. B., & Lucas, R. E. (2010). Predicting relationship and life satisfaction in nationally representative samples from three countries: The relative importance of actor, partner, and similarity effects for personality traits. *Journal of Personality and Social Psychology, 99*, 690–702.

Finkel, E. J., Eastwick, P. W., Karney, B. R., Reis, H. T., & Sprecher, S. (2012). Online dating: A critical analysis from the perspective of psychological science. *Psychological Science in the Public Interest, 13*, 3–66. doi:10.1177/1529100612436522

Furr, R. M. (2008). A framework for profile similarity: Integrating similarity, normativeness, and distinctiveness. *Journal of Personality, 76*, 1267–1316.

Humbad, M. N., Donnellan, M. B., Iacono, W. G., McGue, M., & Burt, S. A. (2013). Quantifying the association between personality similarity and marital adjustment using profile correlations: A cautionary tale. *Journal of Research in Personality, 47*, 97–106.

Karney, B. R., & Bradbury, T. N. (1995). The longitudinal course of marital quality and stability: A review of theory, methods, and research. *Psychological Bulletin, 118*, 3–34.

Luo, S., Chen, H., Yue, G., Zhang, G., Zhaoyang, R., & Xu, D. (2008). Predicting marital satisfaction from self, partner, and couple characteristics: Is it me, you, or us? *Journal of Personality, 76*, 1231–1265.

Malouff, J. M., Thorsteinsson, E. B., Schutte, N. S., Bhullar, N., & Rooke, S. E. (2010). The Five-Factor model of personality and relationship satisfaction of intimate partners: A meta-analysis. *Journal of Research in Personality, 44*, 124–127.

Montoya, R. M., Horton, R. S., & Kirchner, J. (2008). Is actual similarity necessary for attraction? A meta-analysis of actual and perceived similarity. *Journal of Social and Personal Relationships, 25*, 889–922.

Newman, D. L., Caspi, A., Moffitt, T. E., & Silva, P. (1997). Antecedents of adult interpersonal functioning: Effects of individual differences in age 3 temperament. *Developmental Psychology, 33*, 206–217.

Robins, R. W., Caspi, A., & Moffitt, T. E. (2000). Two personalities, one relationship: Both partners' personality traits shape the quality of their relationship. *Journal of Personality and Social Psychology, 79*, 251–259.

Robins, R. W., Caspi, A., & Moffitt, T. E. (2002). It's not just who you're with, it's who you are: Personality and relationship experiences across multiple relationships. *Journal of Personality, 70*, 925–964.

23

SPOUSES ARE ESPECIALLY SIMILAR IN TERMS OF PERSONALITY TRAITS OR SPOUSES HAVE COMPLEMENTARY PERSONALITY TRAITS

Birds of a feather flock together.
Opposites attract.

(Two common clichés about couples)

Do people with similar personalities fall in love and marry more often than dissimilar people? Or, are people attracted to their opposites when it comes to personality attributes? These are two possible scenarios for the seemingly mysterious process of attraction and initial coupling. Whereas in Chapter 22 we discussed whether couple similarity predicts outcomes (are similar couples happier couples?), this chapter is about a more fundamental issue—just how similar are couples when it comes to their personality traits. Fortunately, spousal similarity (otherwise known as *assortative mating*) is a topic of active research in personality psychology (e.g., Humbad, Donnellan, Iacono, McGue, & Burt, 2010;

Great Myths of Personality, First Edition. M. Brent Donnellan and Richard E. Lucas.
© 2020 John Wiley & Sons, Inc. Published 2020 by John Wiley & Sons, Inc.

McCrae et al., 2008; Watson, Beer, & McDade-Montez, 2014). Thus, we are in a good position to address this myth with data.

Both opening clichés are myths when it comes to spouses and basic personality traits: There's little evidence for either strong spousal similarity or strong spousal complementarity (i.e., when someone high in neuroticism is attracted to someone low in neuroticism and vice versa) for core personality traits. Instead, the current evidence indicates there is only a small correlation (at best) between partners when considering their basic personality traits. This seemingly dry statistical finding actually suggests a somewhat surprising conclusion about mate choices in cultures that marry on the basis of love—there seems to be a degree of randomness to coupling when it comes to personality attributes. People don't seem to gravitate too strongly to people who are similar or to people who are wildly different from them. This surprising possibility motivated the psychologists David Lykken and Auke Tellegen to label mate choice as an *adventitious* process (Lykken & Tellegen, 1993). This is just a fancy way of saying that mate choice involves some degree of chance and serendipity. Apparently, there's no special formula when it comes to attraction and personality. Indeed, Gattis, Berns, Simpson, and Christensen (2004) noted there was "significant randomness in the initial pairing or mutual development of partner personalities" (p. 572). We suspect this reality might make poets and songwriters smile!

The Evidence

We talked about the issues related to operationally defining couple similarity in Chapter 22. In the context of describing similarity, researchers typically rely on the statistical workhorse of personality psychology—the correlation coefficient. This descriptive statistic is computed across a sample of couples where personality data are available from both partners. The number itself reflects the strength of the linear association between one partner's extraversion (for instance) and the other partner's level of this same trait. In more concrete terms, researchers obtain estimates of spousal similarity by collecting data from a large sample of couples and then computing the correlation between the attributes of one partner and the attributes of the other partner.[1] As we described in earlier chapters, this

---

[1] There are a few statistical complexities involved in this calculation, especially when it is entirely random as to who is designated as partner 1 versus partner 2 within a dyad. However, these details do not impact the current discussion, and readers interested in learning about the complexities of dyadic analyses should consult Kenny, Kashy, and Cook (2006) as one (more or less) accessible introduction to the topic.

process generates a descriptive statistic called the correlation coefficient. A correlation coefficient close to 0 indicates no linear association between partners, whereas values that approach either 1.0 or –1.0 indicate a relatively high systematic association within couples. A positive correlation indicates some degree of spousal similarity and a negative correlation indicates some degree of spousal complementarity.

When viewing the actual evidence from studies with large samples of couples, it's often surprising how low these partner similarity correlations appear to be for personality traits. Lykken and Tellegen (1993) reported an average correlation of .08 across 10 personality trait scales for more than 1,185 pairs of adult spouses. Humbad et al. (2010) found an average correlation of .15 for 11 personality trait scales administered to more than 1,200 couples. Watson et al. (2004) used statistical procedures to adjust for measurement error (measurement error can lead to underestimates of correlations) and found correlations for the Big Five trait domains that ranged from –.06 to .32 (average = .14). Specifically, these were –.06, .23, –.02, .21, and .32 for extraversion, agreeableness, conscientiousness, neuroticism, and openness, respectively. Similarly, McCrae et al. (2008) used four large samples and found only modest correlations between husbands and wives for more than 1,986 spouses. They reported that 67% of the 420 correlations they tested were below .20. At the level of the Big Five trait domains, they found correlations of .11, .11, .12, .13, and .21 for extraversion, agreeableness, conscientiousness, neuroticism, and openness, respectively (average = .14). Across all of these studies, there seems to be a consistent overall average correlation somewhere between .10 and .15.

Importantly, McCrae et al. (2008) found a similar pattern of correlations across spouses for the Big Five domains when they split their sample into younger (average = .14) and older participants (average = .13). This means that there were no indications that couples grow more similar over time. If that process was happening, researchers would expect the correlations for personality trait similarity to be higher for older spouses than younger spouses, given that older spouses would be together longer (on average) than younger spouses. Humbad et al. (2010) drew a similar conclusion by testing whether the length of the relationship itself was associated with the correlation between wives' and husbands' personality traits. The available evidence seems to indicate that couples do not generally become more similar over time in their personalities. Personality psychologists typically believe that any similarity appears to be largely an outcome of the initial coupling process rather than a matter of personality convergence over the course of the relationship.

In short, personality similarity between spouses tends to be fairly modest. Moreover, a consideration of attributes beyond core personality traits provides interesting points of comparison. For example, there is some evidence that attractive people seem to partner with other attractive people (but even these correlations are not large, as typically defined in psychological research). One recent study reported a correlation of .24 using observers to separately code the attractiveness of spouses from a still frame taken with 1 min of videotaped interaction (McNulty, Neff, & Karney, 2008). Higher values have also been reported, such as a .38 correlation using photographs for 98 couples (Murstein, 1972).[2]

Higher levels of similarity are often found for attributes like political orientation, religious values, and education (e.g., Vandenberg, 1972). For example, Watson et al. (2004) found a correlation of .75 for a measure of religiousness and .63 for political conservativism using a sample of more than 275 married couples. This fact might explain one of the interesting patterns observed for the Big Five traits with respect to openness. This is the one trait domain that seems to blend into values (more or less depending on the specific measure), and this is the Big Five trait domain that seems to have the highest level of similarity in couples. Similarity is also relatively high for education level (between .45 and .55; see, e.g., Lykken & Tellegen, 1993; Maes et al., 1998; Watson et al., 2004). So the story seems to be that birds of a feather really do flock together when the feathers are education, religion, and political values.[3] There is also similarity when it comes to intelligence (i.e., $r = .33$; Bouchard & McGue, 1981), although similarity might differ depending on domain, with verbal abilities showing larger effects than speed and spatial abilities (see Watson et al., 2014). Viewed in this light, personality trait similarity is fairly low on the list of attributes that show some correspondence across spouses.

---

[2] Observers actually show a considerable degree of agreement on attractiveness ratings, thereby contradicting a different myth that beauty is in the eye of the beholder. A full discussion of this issue is outside the scope of this chapter, but readers can consult the method section for the cited papers to learn more about the degree of consensus that exists for observer ratings of attractiveness. The upshot is that raters seem to agree about attractiveness more than some people might expect.

[3] We should point out the correlations are not perfect, so it is entirely possible to find a number of mismatched couples on these variables. The overall correlations indicate general tendencies for aggregates of people, and they are not ironclad rules that apply to all couples without exception.

Putting It Together

Personality trait similarity appears to be lower than spousal similarity for attributes like education, verbal intelligence, religiousness, and political values (see also Watson et al., 2004). When viewed against other individual differences, it does not seem like personality trait similarity ends up being terribly strong or impressive. Nonetheless, the consideration of this myth points to something intriguing about the processes involved with mate selection and raises interesting directions for additional research. Attitudinal variables show spousal consistency to a stronger degree than basic personality traits. (Do you have any ideas why this might be the case?) Moreover, researchers know surprisingly little about how relationships are actually first formed, and there is something of a scientific "black box" when it comes to understanding how the initial sparks of attraction lead to the coupling of two individuals that must occur for a long-term relationship to be established. Understanding the processes that account for spousal similarity will help address this gap in the literature and prove to be quite interesting. Researchers still have many things to learn about how people find partners and fall in love.

References

Bouchard, T. J., & McGue, M. (1981). Familial studies of intelligence: A review. *Science, 212*(4498), 1055–1059.

Gattis, K. S., Berns, S., Simpson, L. E., & Christensen, A. (2004). Birds of a feather or strange birds? Ties among personality dimensions, similarity, and marital quality. *Journal of Family Psychology, 18*(4), 564–574.

Humbad, M. N., Donnellan, M. B., Iacono, W. G., McGue, M., & Burt, S. A. (2010). Is spousal similarity for personality a matter of convergence or selection? *Personality and Individual Differences, 49*(7), 827–830.

Kenny, D. A., Kashy, D. A., & Cook, W. L. (2006). *Dyadic data analysis.* New York, NY: Guilford Press.

Lykken, D. T., & Tellegen, A. (1993). Is human mating adventitious or the result of lawful choice? A twin study of mate selection. *Journal of Personality and Social Psychology, 65,* 56–68.

Maes, H. H., Neale, M. C., Kendler, K. S., Hewitt, J. K., Silberg, J. L., Foley, D. L., … Eaves, L. J. (1998). Assortative mating for major psychiatric diagnoses in two population-based samples. *Psychological Medicine, 28*(06), 1389–1401.

McCrae, R. R., Martin, T. A., Hrebickova, M., Urbánek, T., Boomsma, D. I., Willemsen, G., & Costa, P. T. (2008). Personality trait similarity between spouses in four cultures. *Journal of Personality, 76*(5), 1137–1164.

McNulty, J. K., Neff, L. A., & Karney, B. R. (2008). Beyond initial attraction: Physical attractiveness in newlywed marriage. *Journal of Family Psychology*, 22(1), 135–143.

Murstein, B. I. (1972). Physical attractiveness and marital choice. *Journal of Personality and Social Psychology*, 22(1), 8–12.

Vandenberg, S. G. (1972). Assortative mating, or who marries whom? *Behavior Genetics*, 2(2–3), 127–157.

Watson, D., Beer, A., & McDade-Montez, E. (2014). The role of active assortment in spousal similarity. *Journal of Personality*, 82(2), 116–129.

Watson, D., Klohnen, E. C., Casillas, A., Nus Simms, E., Haig, J., & Berry, D. S. (2004). Match makers and deal breakers: Analyses of assortative mating in newlywed couples. *Journal of Personality*, 72(5), 1029–1068.

24 HIGH SELF-ESTEEM AND NARCISSISM ARE THE SAME ATTRIBUTE

Can you be a confident and self-assured person without being a raging narcissist? Can you accept yourself without necessarily feeling you're better than others? Where's the distinction between feeling good about yourself versus feeling you are entitled to more than everyone else? In other words, what is difference between high self-esteem and narcissism? These questions form the backdrop for this myth.

The description of this myth is a bit unusual when compared with many of the other chapters in this book because it requires a somewhat lengthy digression about how narcissism and self-esteem are measured in contemporary research. Likewise, this myth might also be unusual because the myth itself is sometimes propagated by researchers. Some psychological researchers seem to equate high self-esteem with narcissism, especially when they express worries that efforts to enhance or support self-esteem run the risk of turning children and adolescents into narcissists (see, e.g., Baumeister, Campbell, Krueger, & Vohs, 2003; Baumeister, Smart, & Boden, 1996; Bushman & Baumeister, 1998). This worry about self-esteem enhancement and narcissism is overstated for two reasons. First, the empirical evidence does not support a strong association between self-esteem and narcissism. Although the most widely used measure of narcissism and measures of self-esteem are correlated (Rosenthal, Montoya, Ridings, Rieck, & Hooley, 2011), the level of association is far below the level researchers expect to find when correlating two measures of the same psychological variable. Second, narcissism

Great Myths of Personality, First Edition. M. Brent Donnellan and Richard E. Lucas.
© 2021 John Wiley & Sons, Inc. Published 2021 by John Wiley & Sons, Inc.

and self-esteem have different conceptual definitions in the literature (see Krizan & Herlache, 2018). This is an issue because narcissism is multifaceted, with elements that might reflect grandiosity (an inflated sense of one's importance), vulnerability (a deep-seated feeling of insecurity), and entitlement (a sense that one is more deserving of things than others for unjustifiable reasons) (see Krizan & Herlache, 2018). Connections between narcissism and self-esteem differ depending on which aspects of narcissism are being considered (e.g., Donnellan, Trzesniewski, & Robins, 2015). Thus, it is imprecise (at best) to equate high self-esteem and narcissism. Two approaches can be used to refute this myth. Let's start first with conceptual issues.

Conceptual Issues

Narcissism is a hot topic among researchers who study clinical, developmental, personality, and social psychology. It isn't much of a stretch to suggest that at least one new article concerning narcissism is published in a major mainstream psychological journal each month. Although narcissism is an extremely popular subject, it's also a controversial topic, and debates continue about how to best conceptualize and measure it (Brown, Budzek, & Tamborski, 2009; Pincus & Lukowitsky, 2010). Pincus and Lukowitsky summarize the somewhat troubling state of affairs in this way: "Simply put, there is no gold standard as to the meaning of the construct and thus whether it is clinically described or empirically measured, it can be difficult to synthesize among and across clinical observations and empirical findings" (p. 423). In simple language, this means that the literature surrounding narcissism can be somewhat confusing.

The concept of narcissism is rooted in Greek mythology in the well-known story of a character named Narcissus. The exact details of the story vary among sources, but there are common themes across the various accounts. Narcissus was portrayed as a beautiful and proud individual who went through life spurning romantic suitors. The mountain nymph Echo fell in love with Narcissus, but she was rejected like others before her. Echo became devastated by unrequited love and wasted away broken hearted. This motivated Nemesis, the goddess of revenge, to punish Narcissus for his indifference and arrogance. Narcissus was cursed to fall in love with his own reflection in a pool of water. Each time he reached out to touch his image in the pool, the image was disturbed. Transfixed and afraid of losing touch with the object of his affection, Narcissus stayed by the pool until he wasted away and died. In some stories, his body is eventually replaced by a flower.

A point of the story about Narcissus is to illustrate the dangers of hubris, self-absorption, and indifference to the suffering of others. Interestingly, this was not precisely how narcissism was first discussed in a psychological journal. Narcissism first appeared in a psychological journal in 1898 in an obscure paper by British sexologist Havelock Ellis. Ellis (1898; see also 1927) wrote about a condition in which sexual energy is pathologically invested inward toward the self in the form of autoerotic activities[1]—behaviors that were not viewed as especially healthy at the turn of the 20th century.

The connections between narcissism and autoerotic activity were largely limited to the writings of Ellis, but his idea of psychic energy being inappropriately invested in the self was a critical part of how Freud and other psychoanalytic writers subsequently described narcissism. Beyond this broad generalization, though, there was considerable disagreement about the origins and outward manifestation of narcissism. These disparate ideas provided the backdrop for how Narcissistic Personality Disorder was first described in the third edition of the diagnostic manual published by the American Psychiatric Association (the DSM-III). The DSM-III is a sort of catalogue of psychiatric illnesses and personality disorders. Narcissistic Personality Disorder, as the name suggests, is a clinical disorder with characteristics that overlap with the features that we typically associate with narcissism today. However, these characteristics are considered disordered when they become problematic in some way for the person who expresses them or those around that person. The organizers of the DSM-III tried to be inclusive in their description of narcissism and enumerated "consensus" characteristics (i.e., those that most researchers tended to agree about). These characteristics included (a) a grandiose sense of self-importance, (b) a preoccupation with fantasies of greatness, (c) a need for attention, (d) feelings of rage in response to criticism or defeat, (e) a sense of entitlement, (f) exploitativeness, (g) personal relationships that alternate between devaluation and overidealization, and (h) a lack of empathy (American Psychiatric Association, 1978).

The criteria for narcissistic personality disorder in the DSM-III influenced Robert Raskin and Calvin Hall's (1979) development of a measure for narcissism back in the late 1970s. They originally published a one-page description in which they described how they initially created 223 items to measure the DSM-III attributes. Raskin and Terry eventually reduced this 223-item pool into a 40-item version of their inventory, which they called

---

[1] We want to keep this chapter rated G, but this term refers to solo sexual activities. Use some caution if you decide to use a search engine to look up the term.

the Narcissistic Personality Inventory (NPI; Raskin & Terry, 1988). The NPI went on to become the most widely used measure of narcissism in social and personality psychology. A 2008 review paper concluded that the NPI was used in roughly 77% of all research in this subdiscipline of psychology (Cain, Pincus, & Ansell, 2008). One potential problem is that the NPI has been criticized because it has content that does not seem directly relevant to how narcissism and narcissistic personality disorder were traditionally defined in the literature (Brown et al., 2009; Rosenthal & Hooley, 2010). The NPI also seems to capture a mix of different attributes that might be best characterized as different psychological constructs. Some constructs measured by the NPI might even be psychologically adaptive, such as sense of confidence and a willingness to take leadership initiative in situations. Those elements of the NPI might be related to self-esteem more strongly than the other elements that are more closely aligned with how narcissism is conceptualized by those thinking about personality disorders. Researchers are currently working to develop alternatives to the NPI, but no single measure has risen to the top as we write this entry (Back et al., 2013; Pincus et al., 2009; see Donnellan, Ackerman, & Wright, in press).

In short, debates continue regarding the best conceptualization and measure of narcissism. The most widely used measure of narcissism might need to be revised or even replaced. Thus, when considering the empirical research on narcissism, it's important to consider how the construct is conceptualized and measured. Not all researchers who investigate narcissism are studying the same construct. This makes it somewhat difficult to summarize research conclusions about connections between self-esteem and narcissism without lots of caveats and qualifications. This is a perfectly normal part of evolving psychological science, but it means that it can be difficult to give simple take-home messages about whether narcissism is the same thing as high self-esteem. Narcissism seems to involve many things, and not all of them might be associated with self-esteem in the same ways as we discuss in the next section about empirical results.

In contrast to narcissism, self-esteem is a less controversial construct that seems to reflect a single psychological attribute. It is widely understood to refer to the subjective evaluation of a person's overall worth (see Donnellan et al., 2015; Rosenberg, 1989/1965; Tangney & Leary, 2003). If a person thinks poorly of herself, then she has low self-esteem regardless of whether she appears to be a competent and successful individual to outsiders. Likewise, if a person thinks highly of himself, then he has high self-esteem regardless of whether he lacks talent, friends, or social status. What matters is how people feel about themselves. Morris Rosenberg created the most widely used measure of global self-esteem, and he discussed the conceptual distinctions between self-esteem and attributes that are often associated with narcissism. Below is an important passage:

> When we speak of high self-esteem, then, we shall simply mean that the individual respects himself, considers himself worthy; he does not necessarily consider himself better than others, but he definitely does not consider himself worse; he does not feel that he is the ultimate in perfection but, on the contrary, recognizes his limitations and expects to grow and improve.

> (Rosenberg, 1989/1965, p. 31)

Thus, self-esteem is conceptually distinct from narcissism, and self-esteem researchers have typically taken pains to clarify the distinctions between the two constructs. Researchers who gloss over these controversies simplify these important distinctions and the research literature that exists about these constructs. The fact that both narcissists and those with high self-esteem often evaluate themselves positively suggests at least a modest empirical association between measures of narcissism and self-esteem. However, the specific association between self-esteem and narcissism may depend on the conceptualization or component of narcissism that is considered. Researchers are working to better understand these issues by paying close attention to specific dimensions of personality associated with narcissism such as entitlement, grandiosity, and feelings of vulnerability. This attention to narrower, and more specific constructs might end up providing an interesting psychological story. As it stands, the story will be much more complicated than simply asserting that high self-esteem and narcissism are the same thing. We now turn to the evidence about the actual associations between self-esteem and constructs related to narcissism.

Empirical Evidence

Although we started by reviewing conceptual issues, the clearest refutation of the myth that self-esteem and narcissism are the same is based on empirical research. Rosenthal et al. (2011) conducted a meta-analysis of the connections between narcissism, as measured by the NPI, and global self-esteem. Rosenthal and his colleagues combined the results of 43 studies that involved 36,092 participants and found an overall correlation of .30. This figure is above zero—so the two measures are related—but it is below the level of convergence that researchers expect to see when they correlate two measures of the same construct using the same method (recall the concept of convergent validity from our measurement discussions). Although a precise figure is hard to pin down, researchers typically expect a minimum correlation somewhere between .60 and .70 to have some confidence that two different instruments are measuring the same thing. Pace and Brannick (2010) offered the figure of .70 as an "aspirational" minimum (p. 674).

Why do we think a correlation somewhere above .60 is a good standard for convergent validity? One reason is that this level of convergence is observed for different measures of the Big Five personality trait domains that we have talked about so much in this book. Indeed, Pace and Brannick found that the overall convergent correlations were above .60 for extraversion (.62), agreeableness (.61), neuroticism (.68), and conscientiousness (.63). The lowest level of convergence occurred for measures of openness (.48), a trait domain that is the most controversial in the existing literature. Thus, the correlation between the NPI and self-esteem is lower than the convergence found among self-report measures of what are intended to be the same personality trait constructs. The .30 correlation between self-esteem and the NPI total score across studies undermines the idea that high self-esteem and narcissism are the same construct.

Moreover, the correlations between self-esteem and narcissism can even be negative depending on the measure of narcissism that is used. Pincus et al. (2009) created an inventory designed to measure pathological narcissism. This inventory included aspects of narcissism associated with a sense of vulnerability along with elements of grandiosity and entitlement. Using a sample of 812 college students, Pincus et al. found that scores on their measure of narcissism and self-esteem had a negative correlation (a correlation of –.37, to be exact). In other words, those who were highest in what they considered pathological narcissism were actually lower in self-esteem. Maxwell, Donnellan, Hopwood, and Ackerman (2011) replicated this result almost perfectly by finding a correlation of –.34 using a sample of 587 college students from a different university. These findings also undercut this myth that self-esteem and narcissism are the same thing.

In a different strand of research attempting to make distinctions about constructs associated with narcissism, Brown et al. (2009) emphasized a sense of entitlement and a sense of grandiosity as two separable elements. Entitlement captures interpersonal aspects of narcissism, as it relates to promoting the self at the expense of others (see Ackerman & Donnellan, 2013); grandiosity captures more intrapersonal (or internal) aspects of narcissism that relate to self-enhancement and feeling self-important. Brown et al. found a very small correlation between self-esteem and entitlement ($r = .05$), whereas the association between self-esteem and grandiosity was larger but still below levels of convergent validity expected for measures of the same construct ($r = .29$). These results further show how the connections between self-esteem and narcissism depend on the precise element of narcissism that is being considered. Entitlement, the more interpersonally toxic element of narcissism, has a lower correlation with self-esteem than grandiosity.

In sum, there are important distinctions between high self-esteem and narcissism. And researchers are working to actually clarify the nature of the construct of narcissism itself. The nature of self-esteem seems far less contentious. The correlation between the most common measure of narcissism in social/personality, the NPI, and self-esteem is around .30. This is below the level of convergence expected for measures of the same construct. Moreover, measures of pathological narcissism that emphasize vulnerability are often negatively correlated with self-esteem, which suggests that people with low self-esteem may tend to exhibit some forms of narcissism. When researchers make distinctions between grandiosity and entitlement, feelings of grandiosity are modestly associated with self-esteem but not necessarily feelings of entitlement. Collectively, these diverse and often complicated empirical results undermine the claim that narcissism and high self-esteem are the same attribute.

References

Ackerman, R. A., & Donnellan, M. B. (2013). Assessing narcissistic entitlement: Further evidence for the utility of the entitlement/exploitativeness subscale from the narcissistic personality inventory. *Journal of Psychopathology and Behavioral Assessment, 35*, 460–474.

American Psychiatric Association. (1978). *Diagnostic and statistical manual of mental disorders: DSM-III draft/prepared by the task force on nomenclature and statistics of the American Psychiatric Association.* Washington, DC: Author.

Back, M. D., Küfner, A. C., Dufner, M., Gerlach, T. M., Rauthmann, J. F., & Denissen, J. J. (2013). Narcissistic admiration and rivalry: Disentangling the bright and dark sides of narcissism. *Journal of Personality and Social Psychology, 105*, 1013–1037.

Baumeister, R. F., Campbell, J. D., Krueger, J. I., & Vohs, K. D. (2003). Does high self-esteem cause better performance, interpersonal success, happiness, or healthier lifestyles? *Psychological Science in the Public Interest, 4*(1), 1–44.

Baumeister, R. F., Smart, L., & Boden, J. M. (1996). Relation of threatened egotism to violence and aggression: The dark side of high self-esteem. *Psychological Review, 103*(1), 5–33.

Brown, R. P., Budzek, K., & Tamborski, M. (2009). On the meaning and measure of narcissism. *Personality and Social Psychology Bulletin, 35*(7), 951–964.

Bushman, B. J., & Baumeister, R. F. (1998). Threatened egotism, narcissism, self-esteem, and direct and displaced aggression: Does self-love or self-hate lead to violence? *Journal of Personality and Social Psychology, 75*(1), 219–229.

Cain, N. M., Pincus, A. L., & Ansell, E. B. (2008). Narcissism at the crossroads: Phenotypic description of pathological narcissism across clinical theory, social/personality psychology, and psychiatric diagnosis. *Clinical Psychology Review*, *28*(4), 638–656.

Donnellan, M. B., Trzesniewski, K. H., & Robins, R. W. (2015). Measures of self-esteem. In G. J. Boyle, D. H. Saklofske, & G. Matthews (Eds.), *Measures of personality and social psychological constructs* (pp. 131–157). San Diego, CA: Academic Press.

Donnellan, M. B., Ackerman, R. A., & Wright, A. G. C. (in press). Narcissism in contemporary personality psychology. In O. John & R. W. Robins (Eds.), *Handbook of personality: Theory and research* (4th ed.). New York: Guilford Press.

Ellis, H. (1898). Auto-eroticism. *Alienist and Neurologist*, *19*, 260–299.

Ellis, H. (1927). The conception of narcissism. *Psychoanalytic Review*, *14*, 129–153.

Krizan, Z., & Herlache, A. D. (2018). The narcissism spectrum model: A synthetic view of narcissistic personality. *Personality and Social Psychology Review*, *22*, 3–31.

Maxwell, K., Donnellan, M. B., Hopwood, C. J., & Ackerman, R. A. (2011). The two faces of Narcissus? An empirical comparison of the narcissistic personality inventory and the pathological narcissism inventory. *Personality and Individual Differences*, *50*, 577–582.

Pace, V. L., & Brannick, M. T. (2010). How similar are personality scales of the "same" construct? A meta-analytic investigation. *Personality and Individual Differences*, *49*(7), 669–676.

Pincus, A. L., Ansell, E. B., Pimentel, C. A., Cain, N. M., Wright, A. G., & Levy, K. N. (2009). Initial construction and validation of the pathological narcissism inventory. *Psychological Assessment*, *21*, 365–379.

Pincus, A. L., & Lukowitsky, M. R. (2010). Pathological narcissism and narcissistic personality disorder. *Annual Review of Clinical Psychology*, *6*, 421–446.

Raskin, R., & Terry, H. (1988). A principal-components analysis of the Narcissistic Personality Inventory and further evidence of its construct validity. *Journal of Personality and Social Psychology*, *54*(5), 890–902.

Raskin, R. N., & Hall, C. S. (1979). A narcissistic personality inventory. *Psychological Reports*, *45*(2), 590–590.

Rosenberg, M. (1989/1965). *Society and the adolescent self-image* (rev. ed). Middletown, CT: Wesleyan University Press.

Rosenthal, S. A., & Hooley, J. M. (2010). Narcissism assessment in social–personality research: Does the association between narcissism and psychological health result from a confound with self-esteem? *Journal of Research in Personality*, *44*(4), 453–465.

Rosenthal, S. A., Montoya, R. M., Ridings, L. E., Rieck, S. M., & Hooley, J. M. (2011). Further evidence of the narcissistic personality inventory's validity problems: A meta-analytic investigation—Response to Miller, Maples, and Campbell (this issue). *Journal of Research in Personality*, *45*(5), 408–416.

Tangney, J. P., & Leary, M. R. (2003). The next generation of self research. In M. R. Leary & J. P. Tangney (Eds.), *Handbook of self and identity* (pp. 667–674). New York, NY: Wiley.

25 PERCEPTIONS OF NATIONAL CHARACTER REFLECT "REAL" GROUP DIFFERENCES

When thinking about personality characteristics, people might not limit themselves to considering the personalities of individuals. Instead, people may consider broader groups and wonder whether, on average, these groups differ in terms of their collective "personality." For instance, it might seem reasonable that people who do certain jobs may differ in their typical personality from people who do other types of jobs. There may exist the stereotype that librarians, as a group, are introverted and conscientious, whereas salespeople are outgoing and assertive. Importantly, there is likely to be a kernel of truth to these stereotypes about group-level characteristics. Because people tend to self-select into certain types of positions, certain personalities might simply be a better fit for certain types of jobs. Thus, when personality psychologists study the personalities of employees in different occupations, they often find group-based personality differences.

However, some stereotypes are completely unfounded, and questions can be raised about the extent to which any specific stereotype one might have about a particular group's typical personality is based on true underlying differences between groups. One particularly interesting group-based stereotype concerns perceptions of national character or national personality. Anyone who has traveled to a different country may have come away from that experience thinking that the people in that country differed

Great Myths of Personality, First Edition. M. Brent Donnellan and Richard E. Lucas.
© 2021 John Wiley & Sons, Inc. Published 2021 by John Wiley & Sons, Inc.

dramatically from those in their home country, not just in culture and traditions but also in the very personality characteristics that the people in the new country exhibit. For instance, there are stereotypes that the French are rude, the English are reserved, and Canadians are friendly. However, social psychologists know that a variety of factors contribute to such perceptions and stereotypes, and it is important to consider whether such observations are based in truth. Do these stereotypes have a kernel of truth? If so, how big are the differences? Or, put differently: "Are perceptions of national character accurate?" As you can probably guess from our decision to discuss this idea in this book, we believe that the evidence indicates that perceptions of differences in national character are mostly exaggerations.

As you may imagine, answering questions about national character are actually quite difficult and potentially controversial. The existence of stereotypes is often considered to be negative. Although travelers in a foreign land may believe that the people they meet are quite different from those in their home country, testing the validity of this belief can be challenging. For one thing, it is necessary to know what people in different countries are actually like. Researchers would need personality ratings from large samples of participants from many different countries throughout the world to answer this question. Although a great deal of cross-cultural research has been conducted, this type of systematic, large-scale, multi-nation investigation is rare. In addition to obtaining ratings of personality, researchers would need some procedure for quantifying the national character of countries themselves.[1]

Fortunately, at least one major study has attempted to do just this. In a large study involving many different researchers from around the world, Terracciano et al. (2005) attempted to assess the validity of perceptions of national character. To address the challenges noted above, they asked researchers in different countries to conduct surveys with college students in their home country. The researchers asked these students to complete a survey about what the typical person in their country is like. If any one person's perception of the typical person was unusual or idiosyncratic, this wouldn't be a major problem, because the researchers were able to average over many raters' perceptions. Once they had the data, the researchers could compare these national-character ratings to the aggregate ratings of actual people in different countries.

---

[1] An even thornier issue is making sure that the personality measures have the same psychometric properties across all of the different countries in a study. It is important that an observed score of 42, for example, reflects the same standing on the underlying latent trait for people from all of the different countries (see Chen, 2008).

What did the authors find? Consistent with the idea that perceptions of national character are not based on real differences between populations, Terracciano et al. (2005) found that national differences in self-reported personality did not correspond at all to perceptions of national character. For instance, consistent with one of the stereotypes mentioned earlier, Canadians tended to believe that the typical Canadian is especially high on agreeableness, whereas their actual self-reported scores were almost exactly average for the sample of nations studied. Similarly, participants from the United States said that the typical American was extremely low on agreeableness, when in reality, they too were close to the average. Although we won't go into too much detail about the specifics of their analytic technique, Terracciano et al. (2005) used a variety of statistical procedures to determine whether there is any truth to perceptions of national character, and with each different method they used, very little evidence for accuracy was found. Thus, this large study provided relatively compelling evidence that perceptions of national character are not very accurate.

As is true of all research, however, the study by Terracciano et al. (2005) was not without limitations, and many psychologists have criticized their conclusions. For instance, the strength of these conclusions rests on the validity of both the measures of national stereotypes and the measures of actual national character. Concerns can be raised about both. In regard to the latter measures, Heine, Buchtel, and Norenzayan (2008) suggested that when people rate their own personality or the personality of someone they know well, these ratings are inherently comparative. In other words, it is quite difficult to rate how extraverted a person is in an absolute sense. Because of this, people usually make relative ratings. This means that high scores only mean that someone scores high relative to a typical person. So, when people say that someone is "extraverted," they might really mean that he or she is more sociable and outgoing than the typical person.

But if ratings of any specific person are based on how that person compares to the "typical" person, what happens if that typical person differs across countries? That would mean that the same individuals could receive different personality scores depending on the reference person to which they are compared. To use the example of agreeable Canadians again, a moderately agreeable person may only receive a score of 5 on a 1 to 7 scale if compared to the typical Canadian, whereas that same person might receive a 7 on agreeableness if the comparison standard is the typical (stereotypically rude) French person. So, if the reference person against which people are compared differs across countries, then the average personality scores across countries could be very difficult—if not impossible—to interpret.

More recently, McCrae et al. (2013) acknowledged this concern but argued that other results support the idea that the measures of national character have an acceptable degree of validity. For instance, if each nation chose its own unique "typical person" with which to compare, then this would eliminate all cross-national differences in personality. To explain why, consider the following: Imagine that when rating your own personality traits, you compared yourself to the typical member of your culture. Let's say that you were rating your extraversion on a scale that ranged from 1 to 7, and you chose a score of 5 if you were a little more extraverted than the typical person in your culture, whereas you chose a score of 3 if you were a little less extraverted than the typical person in your culture. If everyone used this same strategy, then that would mean that on average, people would score a "4"—the score for the "typical person" in your culture. If people from all different countries used this strategy, then all nations should have a mean of around 4, and only within-nation differences in personality would be meaningful. However, as McCrae et al. noted (and as we discuss in a bit more detail in the next chapter), nations do differ in average levels of personality.

Furthermore, these differences appear to be meaningful. Remember in the chapters on measurement (especially Chapter 11), we noted that to evaluate the validity of a measure, researchers need to have a theory of how the measure should behave and then test whether scores on that measure actually behave in line with expectations. The aggregated measures of personality traits can be considered measures of national character that can be subject to tests of validity. McCrae et al. (2013) argued that existing empirical evidence appears to support the validity of such measures. For instance, countries that are geographically close, have close contact, and share various cultural features outside of personality tend to have similar national characters. The United States and Canada are similar, as are Denmark and Norway. In addition, McCrae et al. noted that there is evidence of *convergent validity*, with different measures of national character providing similar pictures of how nations differ. Thus, there appears to be evidence that the measures of national character really do capture some of the differences in personality that exist across cultures.

Critical readers might also raise concerns about the measures of stereotypes or perceptions of national character. How can researchers tell whether these measures really do reflect such perceptions? Again, it is possible to turn to standard techniques for evaluating psychometric properties to see whether the measures are doing their job well. For instance, one question that comes up is whether robust perceptions of national character even exist. However, McCrae et al. (2013) argued that people within a country actually agree pretty well about what the typical person in their country is like. As you might remember from the measurement chapters, this is actually a question about reliability. Remember, we noted that reliability is about consistency or repeatability. In this case, we're asking whether perceptions of national character are consistent across many raters: Terracciano et al. (2005) and others found that they were.

An additional concern about the Terracciano et al. (2005) results (and one that we think is a relatively serious one) concerns the samples of participants. If the samples are not representative of the population, then we cannot draw firm conclusions about the population from that sample. Think about this in terms of public polling prior to national elections. In the United States and elsewhere, many pollsters spend quite a bit of money trying to predict who will win major national elections. Professional pollsters do this by conducting surveys of likely voters. However, they do not just ask the first people they can find who they will vote for or ask classes of psychology students. Instead, they use accepted practices for identifying people who are representative of the population as a whole. If, on the other hand, they used what are called *convenience samples* (people who, as the name suggests, are recruited just on the basis of whether it is convenient to contact them), then the sample may be biased. For instance, if pollsters only asked college students whom they were going to vote for, this strategy would probably not provide an accurate prediction of the ultimate results because college students might differ from the entire U.S. population in any number of ways (e.g., age is one clear example).

This sampling bias issue could also be a problem for studies of national character. For one thing, the ratings of the stereotypes or perceptions were completed almost entirely by college students (this was certainly true for the original study, but even in the more recent follow-up described above, most participants were in their 20s). Thus, the national stereotypes that were assessed actually reflect young people's stereotypes, and not even a representative sample of young people. In addition, although the self-report ratings of personality come from a broader sample, they too were not from representative samples, and thus, they may not provide a true measure of national character.

A final issue that is important to remember when evaluating these results is that in most studies that examine this topic, ratings of the stereotypes only came from those living within the nation being rated rather than from residents of other nations. In other words, only Germans rated the national stereotype of Germans, and only the English rated the national stereotypes of the English. It is possible that people from within a particular "in-group" cannot recognize their unique and distinguishing characteristics, which would make these ratings suspect. McCrae and Terracciano (2006) noted that at least one early study asked both in-group and out-group (i.e., members of other countries) to rate national characteristics, and the in-group and out-group ratings tended to agree. However, there is much less evidence from studies that use these procedures.

Of course, conducting a study that assesses stereotypes from a broad range of cultural groups would be difficult because few people know the national characters of many different nations. Thus, even when using out-groups, valid perceptions may be difficult to obtain. To address this issue, Rogers and Wood (2010) tackled a slightly more manageable but related question. They tested whether respondents from within the United States had accurate stereotypes about people living in different parts of the United States. They reasoned that people within the United States may have more exposure to the differences that exist across regions. In addition, they may be able to infer certain things about regional personality from other known characteristics, such as whether the region was rural or urban, whether it was wealthy or poor, and whether it had certain types of industries (e.g., entertainment industry versus technology versus manufacturing). In support of the idea that this type of analysis would lead to greater accuracy in regional stereotypes, Rogers and Wood found that people's ratings of the typical person from a region did correlate with average trait scores of people from that region. Thus, although studies of national stereotypes have found little evidence of accuracy, it is possible that a different method might lead to different results.

Although questions certainly remain, it appears that stereotypes of national character are mostly unrelated to the personality traits that members of different nations actually report. This finding is interesting because it might contradict the perceptions that those who travel to many different countries might hold. Why is it that people's personalities seem so different when we visit other countries, when the empirical evidence suggests that at least in terms of personality traits, our perceptions of precisely how they differ are not accurate? This is an interesting question that psychologists still strive to answer; the important lesson for you is to pay careful attention to the perceptions that you have of people from other countries, focusing specifically on ways that they may be inaccurate. By attending to the cultural cues that could lead to perceptions of specific personality traits, you may be able to come up with ideas about how and why these perceptions emerge. It is also useful to remember a well-known bias identified by social psychologists called the *out-group homogeneity bias* (e.g., Park & Rothbart, 1982). The gist of this bias is that people tend to see out-groups (i.e., groups to which a person him- or herself does not belong) as being more similar than in-groups. The idea is that people might have a tendency to see strangers and casual acquaintances from a foreign country as more monolithic and similar to each other than they really are. In other words, people seem better able to pick up on diversity within their own group as opposed to seeing it within an outside group. Thus, the next time you hear something along the lines that "People from Country X are all really [insert attribute]," you might ask yourself if this is really true or whether this is just a classic example of an out-group homogeneity bias.

References

Chen, F. F. (2008). What happens if we compare chopsticks with forks? The impact of making inappropriate comparisons in cross-cultural research. *Journal of Personality and Social Psychology, 95*(5), 1005–1018.

Heine, S. J., Buchtel, E. E., & Norenzayan, A. (2008). What do cross-national comparisons of personality traits tell us? The case of conscientiousness. *Psychological Science, 19*(4), 309–313.

McCrae, R. R., Chan, W., Jussim, L., De Fruyt, F., Löckenhoff, C. E., De Bolle, M., ... Avdeyeva, T. V. (2013). The inaccuracy of national character stereotypes. *Journal of Research in Personality, 47*(6), 831–842.

McCrae, R. R., & Terracciano, A. (2006). National character and personality. *Current Directions in Psychological Science, 15*(4), 156–161.

Park, B., & Rothbart, M. (1982). Perception of out-group homogeneity and levels of social categorization: Memory for the subordinate attributes of in-group and out-group members. *Journal of Personality and Social Psychology, 42*(6), 1051–1068.

Rogers, K. H., & Wood, D. (2010). Accuracy of United States regional personality stereotypes. *Journal of Research in Personality, 44*(6), 704–713.

Terracciano, A., Abdel-Khalek, A., Adam, N., Adamovova, L., Ahn, C.-k., Ahn, H.-n., ... McCrae, R. R. (2005). National character does not reflect mean personality trait levels in 49 cultures. *Science, 310*(5745), 96–100.

26 PERSONALITY IS RADICALLY DIFFERENT FROM CULTURE TO CULTURE

In Chapter 25, we addressed questions about the accuracy of stereotypes about national character. Although this is a difficult question to answer definitively, most of the evidence that exists suggests that such stereotypes only represent a kernel of truth at best. Some might even argue that these stereotypes have no empirical support. People from around the world may agree that the French are especially rude and that Canadians are especially agreeable, but these beliefs are not borne out in the average personality trait levels that people from these countries exhibit, at least when these traits are assessed using standard personality questionnaires. However, this finding leads to an even more basic question about cultural differences in personality. Specifically, do the same personality traits emerge in the same way across cultures, or does the very structure of personality shift in important ways from culture to culture? In other words, are trait structures like the Big Five something of a cultural universal, or are they specific to only a handful of cultures? As we will describe, one factor contributing to the unfounded belief in national stereotypes may be that people tend to overestimate the differences that exist across cultures. Thus, in this chapter, we address the myth that personality is radically different from culture to culture.

Before we get to the evidence, it's necessary to clarify two things. First, when examining cross-cultural differences in personality traits, it's important to separate personality characteristics themselves from behaviors that more directly reflect cultural practices. For instance, certain customs

Great Myths of Personality, First Edition. M. Brent Donnellan and Richard E. Lucas.
© 2021 John Wiley & Sons, Inc. Published 2021 by John Wiley & Sons, Inc.

and traditions clearly vary across cultures. People wear different clothes, eat different foods, and even have different ideas about what behaviors are socially acceptable. For example, people from some cultures frown upon eating beef or pork, whereas those from other cultures find these practices to be perfectly fine. In general, social scientists consider these expressions and practices to be essential features of culture, rather than manifestations of people's personality. This distinction can be particularly difficult to recognize, however, when some of the specific cultural differences may also reflect personality characteristics when looking within a specific culture. For instance, in the United States, where people rarely eat insects on purpose, it may only be those who are especially high in openness to experience or high in sensation seeking (an aspect of personality related to the desire for intense experiences and a willingness to take risk to have such exciting experiences) who are likely to try such a novel food. However, in some cultures, eating insects may be more normative, which means that more people do it. This does not mean that that such a culture is inherently more open to experiences or more sensation seeking than the United States.

Likewise, in countries where eating beef is taboo, eating steak might reflect tendencies toward deviancy, whereas in countries that regularly consume beef, such a practice may reflect conformity to social norms. Both of these food-related examples point to the fact that there are somewhat arbitrary customs regarding what is an acceptable source of food. Thus, behaviors that signal individual differences in personality traits within one culture may not reflect cultural differences in personality when examined at a cross-cultural level. When evaluating cross-cultural differences in personality, it is important to isolate and think carefully about the meaning of observed behaviors and how those might connect to underlying dispositions.

Admittedly, this is not always easy to do. For instance, as we will describe, one claim about the differences between East Asian countries like China and Japan versus Western nations like the United States and Canada is that the former are more *collectivistic* or *interdependent* than the latter, whereas the latter are more *individualistic* or *independent* than the former (Markus & Kitayama, 1991). In collectivist cultures (compared with individualist cultures), the social group is strongly emphasized, and people often exhibit behaviors that reflect the importance of maintaining ties with that group. People in collectivist cultures are less likely to do things that make them stand out as individuals than are people in individualist cultures. Again, within any particular culture, individual differences in behaviors related to "standing out" versus "fitting in" may indicate personality traits and facets like extraversion, assertiveness, or agreeableness. So, if differences in related behaviors emerge across cultures, does this mean that the cultures differ in their average personality, or is this a cultural difference that does not reflect personality (like eating insects in our previous example)? Unfortunately, there is no simple answer to this question, and therefore careful research must be carried out to try to clarify what these differences represent.

The second issue that must be addressed concerns exactly what is meant when researchers ask whether personalities vary across cultures. For instance, the first thing that may come to mind when you consider whether personality varies across cultures is whether the average levels of a personality trait vary. Are people from some countries more extraverted or more neurotic than others? This is a question of cultural differences in mean levels. However, there are subtler questions that can be asked when examining cross-cultural differences, questions you may never have considered before. For instance, it is possible that levels of traits vary from country to country and that the specific traits that are emphasized may vary. Some traits may simply not matter in some cultures. In other words, the Big Five trait domains may not be evident in all cultures or countries. Is it possible to find a culture where differences in extraversion (for example) are evident? Therefore, one goal for cross-cultural personality research has been to test whether the same personality traits emerge in the same ways across a wide variety of cultures or whether the way that personality manifests is culture specific.

Finally, some people have suggested that the entire concept of personality may be more or less relevant across cultures. Again, think back to the idea of collectivist versus individualist cultures. If in collectivist cultures, the group really is more important than the individual, then perhaps personality plays less of a role or may not even exist in collectivist cultures (see Markus & Kitayama, 1991, for a discussion of related ideas). In other words, the entire field of personality might be an invention of researchers from Western cultures who mistake their own culture-biased view of the importance of the individual as a cultural universal. Given these different meanings, it is important to keep straight the various ways that personality may vary across cultures.

Because the idea that personality may not exist in some cultures is the most extreme version of the cultural-differences hypothesis, we address it first.[1] Remember, the idea is that in collectivist cultures, the group is more important than the individual. Importantly, researchers who study these cultural differences do not just suggest that the group has more influence

---

[1] This extreme view is one that few researchers espouse, but it helps clarify the subtler versions of this suggestion.

than the individual, but that an individual's entire way of viewing the world may be more group focused than it would be in an individualist culture. Thus, it might be possible that people in collectivist cultures only think of themselves as being intertwined with others and may not even conceive of themselves as separate individuals. Although this may seem like a difficult idea to grasp if you are from a more individualistic culture, it is a possibility that personality researchers must take seriously.

What is the evidence for this view that personality may not exist in all cultures? We do not have space to review it all (and again, we refer you to the influential paper by Markus & Kitayama, 1991, for more detailed information), but the effects of culture are thought to be far reaching enough that they affect even the most basic features of cognition. For instance, Markus and Kitayama reviewed evidence that when asked to come up with words or phrases to describe themselves or close acquaintances, people from individualistic cultures tend to use more decontextualized personality descriptors (I'm bold), whereas those from collectivist cultures are more likely to use phrases that incorporate contextual features of the situation, such as how a person behaves with his or her parents (I'm respectful when I'm with my parents). This type of evidence could suggest that people from collectivist cultures focus on the independent individual to a lesser extent, which could lead to personality characteristics playing less of a role in everyday life.

Note that the claim being made (at least the extreme version) is actually quite similar to the claim discussed in the very first chapter of this book that personality is overwhelmed by situational factors. In this cultural version, however, the power of the situation is believed to be greatest in collectivist cultures. Not surprisingly, the same types of evidence discussed in Chapter 1 can be used to address the extreme claim in this chapter. Remember, the strongest responses to the situationist critique involve showing that (a) people agree about other people's personality, (b) measures of personality are stable across situations and over time, and (c) measures of personality predict consequential outcomes. As far as we know, using these criteria, there is very little evidence that personality functions differently in different cultures. For instance, as long as good translations of existing scales are carefully developed (e.g., by carefully evaluating the language using bilingual translators), personality measures often have equally strong psychometric properties across a wide range of cultures. This wouldn't be possible if the thing that these scales was measuring—personality itself—did not exist. Thus, although there are clear differences in culture across individualist and collectivist nations, the strong claim that personality plays less of a role in collectivist cultures is not especially well supported by existing data.

The second way that personality might vary across cultures concerns the precise traits that exist and are important in different places. One of the major achievements of personality psychology in the past century has been to arrive at some consensus about the structure of human personality traits in terms of the number of basic trait dimensions and their qualities. One approach to accomplishing this goal has been to examine the words and phrases that people use to describe personality to see whether the large number of adjectives that people use to describe others can be boiled down to a smaller set of traits that reflect some fundamental dimensions for describing personality. Personality psychologists hope that these fundamental dimensions might be able to be linked to a small set of psychological or biological systems that can further explain individual differences in those dimensions. As we have noted elsewhere in this book, many personality psychologists focus on the Big Five trait domains of extraversion, neuroticism, conscientiousness, agreeableness, and openness to experience. However, even where there is disagreement (such as whether the precise number of fundamental traits is three or five, or six, or seven), there is considerable overlap and agreement regarding the specific traits that are relevant for everyday life.

The question that cross-cultural personality psychologists must answer is whether or not the same traits emerge in different cultures. It is possible that certain cultural features make certain personality traits more salient or even more important. For instance, if a culture was very strongly hierarchical (where those with lower status were very deferential to those high in status), perhaps assertiveness would be less important because everyone would know their place in the hierarchy, and it would be crystal clear who was going to lead and who was going to follow. Thus, differences in assertiveness would be irrelevant. Alternatively, if there were important, culturally unique tasks that people had to achieve, there may be salient individual differences in the tendency to accomplish behaviors related to these tasks that only emerge in certain cultures. Regardless, testing whether the same personality traits emerge has been a critical goal for cross-cultural researchers.

As with many of the "big questions" in personality psychology, testing whether the structure of personality is the same in different cultures is challenging. The initial effort at identifying personality trait structure took decades, and most of this research took place just within Western cultures. Expanding this work to incorporate diverse cultures from around the world could be extremely time consuming. However, the initial effort that personality psychologists have made provides a starting point that can speed research along. For instance, two researchers, Paul

Costa and Robert McCrae, developed one of the most widely used measures of the Big Five, along with a theory that helps explain its existence (McCrae & Costa, 2003). In an influential paper, McCrae and Costa (1997) asked whether their measure behaved similarly in a variety of diverse nations around the world. Specifically, McCrae and Costa used a statistical technique called *factor analysis* to see whether the questionnaire items clustered together in the same way across all of these different nations. If the items did in fact cluster together, it would suggest that the same personality structure exists around the world. In general, the evidence supported the conclusion that the structure of personality was consistent across the cultures assessed, at least as measured by Costa and McCrae's questionnaire.

This type of approach, where researchers take an existing questionnaire and test whether it behaves similarly in different cultures, builds upon existing research from Western cultures to speed the process of investigating whether that structure is similar in other cultures. However, it is not without problems or limitations. One glaring limitation is that if there is a trait that is important in these additional cultures, but not important in the culture where the original questionnaire was developed, then it cannot be recovered when that questionnaire is translated and administered in different cultural groups. There would be no trait-relevant items on the inventory to translate in the first place! One cannot find something one is not looking for. An alternative procedure is to start the process of identifying the structure of personality from scratch within each additional culture that is investigated. Remember, one approach to doing this in Western cultures was to start with the dictionary and reduce the number of words through iterative procedures. Other approaches have been to ask research participants to nominate the most important characteristics and then work with those descriptors to investigate personality structure.

As even McCrae and Costa (1997) acknowledge, these efforts have led to somewhat more mixed evidence regarding the fundamental personality characteristics that exist. For one thing, when different languages are used, it is not always the case that the same five factors emerge (De Raad et al., 2010). Although at least three of the factors appear to be universal (traits that seem to resemble extraversion, agreeableness, and conscientiousness), traits beyond these three emerge in slightly different ways across cultures. However, for reasons that we do not have the space to go into, the requirement that all personality descriptors cluster together in the exact same way across different languages is a relatively strong one, and it may not be the best way to judge whether the structure of personality is the same. For instance, the factors beyond the initial three may be highly similar across cultures but not perfectly identical, which would still lend some support to the universality of personality structure.

Additional research has focused less on the technical details of personality structure and more on the narrow question of whether additional traits exist that are not found in Western cultures. For instance, at least one group of researchers who attempted to develop a culture-specific model of Chinese personality has emphasized a trait that they labeled "Chinese Traditions" and that emphasizes harmony with others and one's relationship orientation. It is possible that this is either a construct that does not exist in other cultures or one that is deemphasized to such a degree within Western cultures that it does not emerge as one of the fundamental traits. However, it is also possible that this is a variant of one of the other traits that is included in the Big Five domains (such as an element of agreeableness) and that has subtly different connotations in different cultural contexts. Regardless, even if some additional traits have been identified in different cultures, there are not a lot of these culture-specific traits with a strong evidentiary base, and those that have been suggested are not likely to be wildly unfamiliar to citizens of more individualistic nations. That is, people from individualistic cultures can still recognize that dimension of individuality.

The final way that personality may vary across cultures, and again, the most intuitive way, is that average levels of the same personality traits vary across groups. The question here is whether people from some cultures score, on average, higher or lower on certain personality traits than do people from other cultures. As we noted in the previous chapter, if these differences do exist, they do not correspond closely to national stereotypes, but this does not mean that differences are nonexistent. What does cross-cultural research suggest? Well, as the studies described in the chapter on national stereotypes made clear, not only do people have incorrect beliefs about the national character of people from different countries, they also exaggerate how different people are. In other words, the mean levels of personality traits vary less across nations than many people believe.

Despite this fact, however, there are some differences. For instance, McCrae and Terracciano (2005) used methods similar to those described in the previous chapter to create aggregate personality profiles for people from 51 different cultures. They noted that Europeans and Americans generally scored higher in extraversion than did Asians and Africans. However, cross-national differences for all traits tended to be relatively small, at least relative to the variability in personalities that exist within countries. In other words, although people vary pretty dramatically in terms of what their personalities are like within a culture, the average personalities of groups of people living in diverse areas around the world tend to be quite similar. In other words, within-group variability was large (within a country, people differ widely on an attribute) whereas between-group variability was small (across countries, the averages tended to be fairly similar).

So why do people seem to think that personalities are so different among the different groups they encounter? Part of the reason is that people may experience individuals from different cultures in settings that might be somewhat unusual. For instance, a person may interact with these people from a different group when traveling and in unfamiliar situations; or alternatively, people may interact with those from outside groups when those individuals are themselves traveling. In either case, individuals are likely exposed to just a small portion of the other person's characteristic behaviors, which can generate limited and perhaps biased perceptions. Thus, given the research reviewed here, it is worth remembering to be cautious in the interpretations made of other people's behaviors and to think carefully about whether perceptions about a person truly reflect his or her personality. Doing this can help prevent the inaccurate stereotypes that could in turn lead to misunderstandings or other negative outcomes. It is also good to remind yourself of another concept we introduced in Chapter 25—the out-group homogeneity bias. When people first learn about people from a different group, there might be a tendency to overlook the presence of within-group variability. That does not mean it does not exist or that personality differences are unimportant for that group.

References

De Raad, B., Barelds, D. P., Levert, E., Ostendorf, F., Mlačić, B., Blas, L. D., ... Katigbak, M. S. (2010). Only three factors of personality description are fully replicable across languages: A comparison of 14 trait taxonomies. *Journal of Personality and Social Psychology*, 98(1), 160–173.

Markus, H. R., & Kitayama, S. (1991). Culture and the self: Implications for cognition, emotion, and motivation. *Psychological Review*, 98(2), 224–253.

McCrae, R. R., & Costa, P. T., Jr. (1997). Personality trait structure as a human universal. *American Psychologist*, 52(5), 509–516.

McCrae, R. R., & Costa, P. T., Jr. (2003). Personality in adulthood, a five-factor theory perspective (2nd ed.). New York, NY: Guilford Press.

McCrae, R. R., & Terracciano, A. (2005). Personality profiles of cultures: Aggregate personality traits. *Journal of Personality and Social Psychology*, *89*(3), 407–425.

27 MEN ARE FROM MARS, WOMEN ARE FROM VENUS (MEN AND WOMEN HAVE DRAMATICALLY DIFFERENT PERSONALITIES)

In this chapter, we tackle one additional set of stereotypes that is the target of much speculation and discussion, that is, the difference in personalities between men and women. You may often hear that "men are from Mars and women are from Venus" (there was even a popular book with this title), suggesting that not only do the two sexes differ but that they are so different that they might as well be from different planets.[1] But beyond the obvious physical differences, is this idea that men and women are completely different borne out in the empirical data? Do men and women see the world and behave in dramatically different ways? Do men and women score dramatically differently on measures of core

---

[1] Researchers often draw distinctions between "sex" and "gender." Sex is often used to refer to biological differences between males and females (including, but not limited to, chromosomes and reproductive anatomy) whereas gender is often used to refer to the identities and norms that might be associated with sex. Much of the research that we review in this chapter either does not distinguish between these concepts or purports to focus on sex differences even though the studies often do not clearly distinguish between sex and gender. This is a limitation of this work that is important to keep in mind.

Great Myths of Personality, First Edition. M. Brent Donnellan and Richard E. Lucas.
© 2021 John Wiley & Sons, Inc. Published 2021 by John Wiley & Sons, Inc.

personality traits? Fortunately, there is a considerable amount of evidence addressing this possibility, and as you will see, the idea that men's and women's personalities are wildly different on most basic personality traits is certainly a myth.

In most of the myths discussed in the book, intuitions about the way people think, feel, and behave are pitted against empirical data from psychological research studies. Although intuitions can be correct, there are also many times where they are way off. For instance, we noted that people often have stereotypes about individuals from different countries, and these stereotypes often have relatively little basis in fact. Intuitions sometimes reflect considerable exaggerations of kernels of truth.

As is often true in psychological research, the best way to answer simple descriptive questions like this one about the differences between women and men is not with a single study, but rather by looking at patterns that consistently emerge across studies. Although you may hear news reports describing results from a recently published study as if this study has revealed some universal truth, it is often the case that this single study is limited in some important way. The sample size might have been small, the population from which the sample was drawn might be unusual, or some idiosyncratic feature of the procedures may lead to results that do not generalize. Thus, rather than relying on single studies, when possible, scientists often focus on meta-analyses, which (as you should know well by now) aggregate results from different studies to see whether there is a consistent pattern in the results. Meta-analyses are not perfect, but they can provide useful information about questions that have been investigated repeatedly.

Meta-analyses concerning differences between women and men have been conducted for the major personality traits that we have been discussing in this book. In 1994, Feingold (1994) went back to the manuals that are published when new personality inventories are introduced. During the process of scale development, the people who develop the inventories usually test their new measure on large samples of participants from populations who are similar to those who might ultimately take the questionnaire (see Chapter 11, where we described this process). These initial tests help show that the measure has an acceptable degree of reliability and validity. Test creators often report basic information about how people typically score (these are called "norms") that can be used as comparison when researchers use the measures in their own studies. These initial norms are often presented separately for men and women. The existence of these published norms allowed Feingold to examine the size of these sex differences in relatively large samples of participants selected to be relatively representative of the broad population.

As we have noted repeatedly, when interpreting results, it is important to consider not only the direction of the effect (e.g., are men statistically more assertive than women?) but also the size of that effect (e.g., how big is the difference between women and men?). Small group differences can attain statistical significance in very large sample sizes even if the effects themselves are not especially important. It may be that the directions of sex differences that exist are consistent with intuition, but that the size of these could be quite small. One type of effect size that is frequently used when comparing women and men is the standardized mean difference (technically the differences between the means of the two groups divided by the pooled standard deviation). A standardized effect size of zero means there is no group difference (a zero mean difference divided by a pooled standard deviation is still zero). A standardized effect size of 1.0 means that the average score of one group is one standard deviation higher the average of the second group (a standard deviation is the amount of average variability in the sample). This is a way of expressing the size of the differences between two groups in a way that allows researchers to compare across studies that might use measures with different response scales. One commonly cited set of criteria for evaluating the size of standardized mean differences is that a difference of .20 is small, a difference of .50 is medium, and a difference of .80 or larger is large. These guidelines are not without their problems, but they provide a reasonable starting point for the interpretation of the differences between men and women. Under this rubric, a standardized mean difference of, say, .05 would be smaller than small or close enough to zero to call it a day.

Feingold (1994) noted that each of the Big Five traits can be broken down into narrower facets, and he considered some of the more important facets rather than reporting mean differences for the full scales. The precise facets he examined were determined partly by McCrae and Costa's (2003) popular model of the narrower facets of each Big Five domain and partly by the data that were available for other measures. For instance, although McCrae and Costa's model of neuroticism contains six different facets, Feingold focused on two: anxiety and impulsivity.

There are some good reasons to expect that women may score higher on trait levels of anxiety than men. When evaluating diagnoses of psychological disorders, many more women are diagnosed with depression than men (Hyde, 2014). In addition, neuroticism is a risk factor for depression, and some of the defining characteristics of neuroticism include the tendency to experience some of the negative emotions that are associated with depression. So, do women score much higher on this emotional component of neuroticism? According to Feingold's (1994) meta-analysis, there is a difference, but it is not as large as you might expect. Specifically, the standardized mean difference for the anxiety variable was .28, which is just a bit larger than the criterion for a "small" effect. Thus, although women do score higher than men on measures of anxiety, the differences are not especially large.

Another way to think about effect sizes is by visualizing two partially overlapping normal distributions. Many personality traits have a bell-shaped distribution with a bunch of scores in the middle ranges and relatively few extremely high or low scores. Within a sample of women, you will find a few women with extremely high scores, a few women with extremely low scores, and a whole bunch with middle-range scores. The same is true for men. The standardized mean difference tells you the difference between the two peaks of the distributions. As the standardized mean difference gets bigger, the two distributions start to spread apart and become more and more distinct. If one makes a few statistical assumptions, it is possible to calculate the percentage of overlap in the two distributions if one knows the standardized mean difference. For an effect size of .28, the percentage overlap between the distributions is 89%. The figure gets smaller as the standardized effect size gets bigger. An effect size of 1.0 (a large effect) yields 62% overlap and an effect size of 2.0 (a really large effect) yields 32%. A nifty online calculator is available to help you visualize standardized effect sizes (http://rpsychologist.com/d3/cohend). A good thing about this way of thinking about effect sizes is that it emphasizes the fact that there is variability within groups. Some men are highly anxious and others are very low in anxiety. The same is true for women.

More recently, the authors of this book have been looking at age and sex differences in the Big Five personality traits using large (larger than those in the studies analyzed by Feingold), nationally representative samples of participants (Donnellan & Lucas, 2008; Lucas & Donnellan, 2009). Although we noted above that meta-analyses are often better than single studies for addressing questions like the size of sex differences, our studies were distinctive in their large size and the quality of their samples. Notably, our results for the broad trait of neuroticism (the measures we used did not allow us to separate the score into distinct components) were consistent with those reported by Feingold (1994). In two of the studies (from Germany and the United Kingdom) there were small- to medium-sized effects, such that women scored higher than men. In the third study (from Australia), women scored higher than men in young adulthood, but the difference (which was never large to begin with in this study) reversed among older adults. This result from Australia might be a fluke or might be driven by the fact that the measures in our study were short. We accepted a trade-off between large sample sizes and a brief measure of personality. Our point is that we have observed a difference between women and men emerge for neuroticism in multiple samples. And we think it is important to see if those differences are consistent across all age groups and countries.

Returning now to a big picture issue, how can researchers resolve the discrepancies between the findings for depression diagnoses and those for a personality trait that is related to and predicts future occurrences of depression? Hyde (2014) points out that sometimes, when sex differences do emerge, they only occur at the extreme ends of a distribution. In other words, although the average woman may not be much more anxious or depressed than the average man, women may have a tendency to reach the especially high level of depression that would lead to a diagnosis of major depressive disorder. Such a pattern might suggest that different factors affect typical levels and the more extreme levels that are characteristic of diagnosable disorders. This also appears to be the case with traits like aggression, where differences in average levels are not large between men and women, even though men commit the vast majority of truly aggressive acts that lead to violent crimes (Hyde, 2014).

The second component of neuroticism that Feingold (1994) examined concerned impulsiveness. The differences between women and men were even smaller than for anxiety. Although some may expect males to be more impulsive than females, the standardized mean difference was just .06 (with males scoring higher)—a very small difference. So, men and women are almost identical in the mean levels of impulsiveness that they exhibit. Here again, this difference might be restricted to the measure of impulsiveness that was investigated because it emphasized an inability to control bodily impulses related to cravings and emotions. Even so, Feingold found that in many other traits he examined, sex differences were quite small. For instance, women had just slightly higher levels of conscientiousness (with a standardized mean difference of .13), and men had just slightly higher levels of openness to new experiences (here the difference was even smaller, just .03). Similarly, for two components of extraversion, gregariousness (the tendency to want to be with and interact with groups of people) and activity level (the tendency to be energetic and active), differences were quite small, just .15 for gregariousness (with women scoring higher) and .09 for activity level (with men scoring higher). These results are also broadly consistent with those from our own studies using nationally representative data (Donnellan & Lucas, 2008; Lucas & Donnellan, 2009). We found that sex differences in conscientiousness, openness, and extraversion were quite small.

Are there any differences that are large and consistent with widely held stereotypes? It turns out that although most sex differences are small, there are a couple that are medium to large in size. The largest differences that Feingold (1994) found were in one component of extraversion and one component of agreeableness (especially one component called "tender-mindedness"). Specifically, for the trait of assertiveness, Feingold found a mean difference of .50, with men scoring higher than women. This is a medium-sized difference, and it does fit with stereotypes that men are more likely to take charge or be bossy.

The second difference—that for the tender-mindedness component of agreeableness—was actually the largest effect that Feingold (1994) found, with standardized mean differences of almost a full point. That's even larger than the .80 guideline for a "large" effect (and even here there is 69% overlap in the two distributions). The trait of tender-mindedness is one that captures a variety of characteristics related to empathy or nurturance of others. Again, the fact that women score higher than men fits with general stereotypes about men's and women's behaviors. Studies that look just at the broad trait of agreeableness tend to find smaller differences, perhaps because agreeableness includes other components with smaller sex differences. For instance, Lucas and Donnellan (2009) and Donnellan and Lucas (2008) found small-to-medium effect sizes (with women scoring higher) when examining a broader agreeableness measure. In addition, it is important to note that the large effect size in Feingold's meta-analysis appears to be driven by one particular measure of tender-mindedness, and when other measures of the same construct are examined, smaller sex differences emerge. Costa, Terracciano, and McCrae (2001) found differences that were roughly the same size as for the broad trait of agreeableness, effects in the range of .30. In short, women reliably score higher on this characteristic, but the precise size of the difference varies depending on the specific measure that is used.

It is also possible to consider whether there are factors that affect the size of the difference between men and women. For instance, one possible explanation of the effects that do exist is that they are driven by culture: There may be societal pressures for men to act one way and women to act another. If so, we may expect those pressures to differ by culture, which would lead to variation in the size of the sex differences that are found. Costa et al. (2001) examined this possibility by surveying tens of thousands of respondents from 26 cultures around the world. Indeed, Costa et al. found that although the direction of the differences was consistent across cultures, the size of these effects varied, with the largest differences emerging in Western cultures. You might ask yourself why this might be the case.

One theory is that when men and women have more freedom and opportunity to express their preferences (as might be true in fairly wealthy and more individualistic cultures), researchers tend to see larger differences.

Age might be another factor that minimizes or maximizes differences between women and men. In our own studies, we tested whether the sex differences we found varied by age (Donnellan & Lucas, 2008; Lucas & Donnellan, 2009). It did appear that for some traits, the small differences that emerged changed over the course of the life span. Specifically, for extraversion and conscientiousness in both the German and British samples, there were some small initial differences (with women scoring higher than men) among young adults that declined in size with increasing age. However, for the traits with the largest differences (neuroticism and agreeableness), the differences were relatively consistent across the age groups studied. So as was true when culture was examined as a moderator, the direction of sex differences appears to be consistent across different age groups, but the size of the difference varies somewhat.

We have organized our discussion around the Big Five personality traits because they serve as a useful organizing framework and because most important personality characteristics tend to be included somewhere within these Big Five traits. However, it is possible that there are important gender differences in other traits. Just as tender-mindedness may show larger gender differences than the broad trait of agreeableness to which it belongs, there may be additional narrow traits that we did not address that may show larger differences. One specific trait that people may wonder about concerns aggression, as stereotypes suggest that men are more aggressive than women. Indeed, meta-analytic evidence shows that men tend to be more aggressive than women, and this result emerges regardless of the way aggression is measured (Archer, 2004). Like some of the other personality traits we discussed, there are differences in the size of the effect across ages and cultures, but in general, men are more aggressive than women, with medium-size effects.

What does this research mean for the idea that men are from Mars and women from Venus? It should be clear from the research that we reviewed (most of which consisted of meta-analyses or very large studies using broad samples of national populations) that although some gender differences in personality do exist, they are usually not large, and for many traits examined, there are hardly any differences at all. The task for researchers then becomes to identify the causes of these differences. Are they due to inherent biological differences or to the roles that men and women fill within society? Regardless of the causes, however, the empirical research suggests that men and women are more similar to one another than they are different, at least when it comes to personality traits. Indeed, a reasonably popular idea in psychology is known as the *gender similarity hypothesis* (see Hyde, 2014). This one is pretty easy to remember—it is the idea that women and men are similar on "most, but not all, psychological variables" (Hyde, 2014, p. 375).

References

Archer, J. (2004). Sex differences in aggression in real-world settings: A meta-analytic review. *Review of General Psychology, 8*(4), 291–322.

Costa, P., Jr., Terracciano, A., & McCrae, R. R. (2001). Gender differences in personality traits across cultures: Robust and surprising findings. *Journal of Personality and Social Psychology, 81*(2), 322–331.

Donnellan, M. B., & Lucas, R. E. (2008). Age differences in the big five across the life span: Evidence from two national samples. *Psychology and Aging, 23*(3), 558–566.

Feingold, A. (1994). Gender differences in personality: A meta-analysis. *Psychological Bulletin, 116*(3), 429–456.

Hyde, J. S. (2014). Gender similarities and differences. *Annual Review of Psychology, 65*(1), 373–398. doi:10.1146/annurev-psych-010213-115057

Lucas, R. E., & Donnellan, M. B. (2009). Age differences in personality: Evidence from a nationally representative Australian sample. *Developmental Psychology, 45*(5), 1353–1363.

McCrae, R. R., & Costa, P. T., Jr. (2003). *Personality in adulthood, a five-factor theory perspective* (2nd ed.). New York, NY: Guilford Press.

28 CLINICIANS CAN'T TREAT PERSONALITY DISORDERS

In this book, we've focused on personality as the stable patterns of thoughts, feelings, and behaviors that distinguish people from one another. This definition is broad enough to capture all the various ways that people differ, from the broad traits (the Big Five), to narrower goals and values, to the narratives and life stories that people tell about themselves. If each of these characteristics is relatively stable over time and situations and distinguishes people from one another, then it is fair game as a topic of study for personality psychologists.

Across all of these topics, it has generally been assumed (by us in these chapters and by most of the researchers who have conducted the research studies that we described) that most of these characteristics reflect "normal" variations in personality. In other words, the differences in patterns of thoughts, feelings, and behaviors are typically thought to reflect unproblematic variations of normal personality. These are the characteristics that we see in people every day.

Yet it is not hard to imagine that for any characteristic that exists, a person's standing on that dimension might be so extreme as to cause problems for himself or herself. A person could be so high on neuroticism that his or her feelings of anxiety become unbearable, preventing the person from leaving the house or getting any work done. Even seemingly positive traits like conscientiousness could have negative consequences in the extreme: Extremely high scores on this trait might take the form of an unhealthy obsession with perfection. When traits deviate from the norm in this problematic way, they start to move into the territory of what are called *personality disorders*.

Great Myths of Personality, First Edition. M. Brent Donnellan and Richard E. Lucas.
© 2021 John Wiley & Sons, Inc. Published 2021 by John Wiley & Sons, Inc.

The topic of personality disorders raises interesting questions about the nature of psychological functioning and our ability to change. On the one hand, we often think of disorders somewhat like illnesses, or at least like problematic habits: We think of them as patterns of thought and behavior that, with the help of a trained clinician, might be able to be changed to something more positive. Yet if these are personality disorders, and our personalities are central (and stable) features of who we are as people, then what does that mean for our ability to change?

Perhaps because of this issue of stability, there is sometimes a belief that personality disorders are something of "a life sentence" (Hengartner, Zimmermann, & Wright, 2018). Their stability across the life span implies to some that any personality disorder would also be difficult, if not impossible, to treat. However, we believe this is myth. And we think that considering this myth and the theorizing and evidence around personality disorders is a useful way to revisit and expand on several themes in this book.

We begin by briefly refuting the myth that personality disorders are a life sentence but then turn to an extended discussion about the definition of personality disorders and evidence about treatment. In a nutshell, the empirical evidence about the actual stability of personality disorders and pathology does not support strong claims of immutability (e.g., Clark, 2007; Morey & Hopwood, 2013), and the treatment literature is far less conclusive than is portrayed by this myth. The reality is that the literature is not well developed enough to make definitive statements (Bateman, Gunderson, & Mulder, 2015; Berg et al., 2013; Cristea et al., 2017), and there are hints that some psychotherapies and drug treatments for particular symptoms of personality disorders might even be effective (Cristea et al., 2017; Duggan, Huband, Smailagic, Ferriter, & Adams, 2007; Lieb, Völlm, Rücker, Timmer, & Stoffers, 2010). Further, other evidence supports the idea that psychological interventions can change negative traits (Roberts et al., 2017). Thus, we believe it is a myth—and a pessimistic and potentially problematic one—that pathological personality characteristics are a life sentence because they are set in stone or unresponsive to treatment. Nonetheless, we acknowledge that treating personality disorders can be difficult (Critchfield & Benjamin, 2006).

Imagine trying to help someone who both needs to change maladaptive patterns of behavior but is also extremely sensitive to feeling unsupported and rejected. A therapist would need to walk a fine line when dealing with such an individual. Moreover, definitive statements about individual prognoses (statements about the likely course of a malady or ailment) based on group-level trends are fraught. In this chapter, we discuss this myth in more detail by acknowledging the challenges of conceptualizing and measuring personality disorders and then summarizing the results of some recent reviews of treatment studies. Much of what is known about the treatment of personality disorders is based on research focused on borderline personality disorder (BPD) (e.g., Bateman et al., 2015), so we also spend some time describing that personality pathology in the next section.

What are personality disorders?

Personality disorders are defined and cataloged in manuals used by clinical psychologists and psychiatrists such as the *Diagnostic and Statistical Manual of Mental Disorders* (e.g., DSM-5; American Psychiatric Association [APA], 2013). Personality disorders are sets of traits that generate interpersonal distress or otherwise impair the ability of the individual to succeed at the major tasks of life (as defined by cultural expectations) such as holding a job, having meaningful close relationships, participating in social/community life, and following rules and norms. Disorders reflect behavior patterns considered to be inflexible and consistent across contexts and situations. Beyond providing a general definition of personality disorder, sources like the DSM-5 list several specific constellations of personality attributes that create distress and impairment. Table 3 lists the 10 specific personality disorders described in the DSM-5 along with a brief description arranged by their so-called cluster or common features.

Borderline personality disorder (or BPD) is the most well-studied personality disorder and is an active subject of treatment studies (Cristea et al., 2017). Thus, it is useful to have a good understanding of the attributes associated with this pathology. The typical way BPD is diagnosed is by determining if a person has five or more of the attributes listed in Table 4.

As seen in Table 4, emotional instability and self-destructive tendencies are the hallmark attributes of BPD. The self-harm associated with BPD is a common motivator for treatment, and high rates of suicidal behavior have been reported for those suffering from BPD. Indeed, considering the elements of personality associated with BPD should hopefully make it obvious how distressing this condition would to the individual and to society. Considerable amounts of suffering and discord are associated with BPD.

Table 3 Personality disorders described in the DSM-5

Disorder	Chief characteristics
Cluster A: disorders related to oddity, social aversion, and pathological eccentricity	
Paranoid	Irrational distrust of others and persistent fears of having rights violated by ill-intentioned others
Schizotypal	Disturbed patterns of thinking similar to schizophrenia; odd beliefs and magical thinking; retreat from relationships out of fear of others
Schizoid	Indifference to social relationships and norms; aloofness; attention directed inward to one's own mental life rather than to relationships or engagement with the social world; restricted emotional expression
Cluster B: disorders related to problems with emotion regulation, behavioral inhibition, and an off-putting interpersonal style	
Antisocial	Persistent impulsive and often criminal behavior characterized by a disregard for the rights of others; extreme callousness
Borderline	Profound instability in emotion regulation and self-image; tendencies toward self-harm; impulsivity
Histrionic	Craving of attention; pathological need for attention and approval from others; excessive emotionality
Narcissistic	Excessive feelings of entitlement and grandiosity; inflated sense of importance achieved at the expense of others; willingness to exploit others to promote the self
Cluster C: disorders related to anxiety and fear especially in the context of relationships	
Avoidant	Extreme anxiety in relationships due to fears of rejection and embarrassment
Dependent	Excessive need to be cared for by others often at the expense of one's self-worth, freedom, and dignity
Obsessive–compulsive	Perfectionistic tendencies that undermine productivity; preoccupation with order to provide a sense of control; rigid and unrealistic expectations of others

Note. Descriptions modified from the DSM-5 (APA, 2013, pp. 645–682).

Table 4 Attributes associated with borderline personality disorder described in the DSM-5

1.	Intense ("frantic") efforts to prevent abandonment or the perception of abandonment.
2.	Highly sensitive to rejection
3.	Unstable relationships that vacillate from the extremes of either love or hate. These feelings are often misaligned with the actual nature of the relationship
4.	Unstable sense of self or identity
5.	Impulsivity and involvement in damaging behaviors such as excessive spending, substance use, binge eating, gambling, or reckless driving
6.	Self-mutilation (e.g., cutting) and suicidal behaviors or ideation
7.	Extreme emotional liability (extreme fluctuations in mood)
8.	Sense of emptiness or profound dissatisfaction with life
9.	Difficulty managing anger often prompted by perceptions of abandonment and rejection in close relationships
10.	Temporary feelings of paranoia or dissociation, often in response to perceptions of abandonment and rejection in close relationships

Note. Descriptions modified from the DSM-5 (APA, 2013, pp. 663–664).

Thinking dimensionally about personality disorders

Although widely used in clinical practice, the conceptualization of personality disorders in manuals like the DSM-5 is controversial (e.g., Clark, 2007; Hopwood et al., 2018). The standard psychiatric approach behind the DSM-5 assumes that each personality disorder is a discrete entity. Concerns about this assumption relate to our discussions of personality types mentioned in Chapter 5. Disorders in this traditional model are categorical variables (present or absent) and are seen as natural kinds by proponents of the medical model (i.e., real diseases). A person either has a disorder or they do not, and each disorder might require a special treatment because they are distinct entities with different etiologies and treatments. As a simple example, medical professionals know that strep throat is something categorically different than influenza. These maladies have different causes, and different treatments are prescribed.

A critical consideration of Table 4 may help illustrate some of the concerns over the typical psychiatric or "medical model" approach to personality disorders. Consider the idea that disorders are categorical, and one needs five or more of the attributes in Table 4 to receive a diagnosis of BPD. Why five attributes and not four or six or even two or eight? What is so significant about five? There seems to be a degree of arbitrariness to this cutoff and thus the entire diagnosis of BPD. Is a person with four of those elements in Table 4 unlikely to experience distress and dysfunction in life, whereas there is a dramatic shift in adaptation with five elements? Such a bright line seems somewhat implausible as any one of the elements might prove problematic in terms of either distress or functional impairment depending on its severity.

Another problem is that many of the symptoms listed in Table 4 seem like matters of degree rather than either/or propositions. People might vary on each of those dimensions especially if patterns of thinking, feeling, and behaving are framed in more general terms. Some people might have excessively high levels of emotional instability, whereas others are not as severe in this attribute (i.e., people differ in terms of neuroticism). People might differ in terms of the stability of their self-image from someone who has a rock solid and unwavering sense of self to someone who vacillates in identity almost from moment to moment. Likewise, concerns about abandonment are not uncommon given the social nature of our species and the human need to feel accepted as part of our groups (e.g., Baumeister & Leary, 1995). Where does a clinician draw the line as to when a patient actually has a specific sign of BPD? What if a person gambles a bit too much and seems a bit too preoccupied with abandonment, should that count as meeting two symptoms or none?

Further reflection about the psychological portrait associated with BPD might make one question the assumptions behind the medical model. BPD as described in Table 4 may not seem like a natural kind. In fact, attempts to find statistical evidence that personality disorders like BPD make up taxa (a technical term for natural kinds) are typically unsuccessful (Haslam, Holland, & Kuppens, 2012). Thus, the all-or-none nature of personality disorder diagnoses in the medical model seems highly problematic because it does not seem to match the reality that personality attributes are matters of degree and not kind. People do not fall into discrete categories. Again, this perspective should remind you of the myth we discussed in Chapter 5.

Furthermore, the boundaries between the different disorders in Table 3 may seem a bit fuzzy once given critical scrutiny. For example, histrionic and narcissistic personality disorders seem to share common features. Many people with personality pathologies seem to exhibit elements of two or more personality disorders. The technical term for this issue is that comorbidity is high for personality disorders (see Clark, 2007). In other words, people might be diagnosed with two or more personality disorders rather than just one. Another issue is that the 10 disorders in Table 3 might not adequately capture the wide range of problematic or pathological expressions of personality. It is fairly easy to imagine a constellation of personality attributes that are impairing and distressing but are not precisely like the disorders in that table.

In light of these and other concerns, researchers and theorists have criticized the nature and description of the 10 distinct disorders in Table 3 (see e.g., Clark, 2007, or Hengartner et al., 2018). The evidence that they are legitimately different kinds of diseases seems tenuous. Comorbidity is high. It is challenging to conclusively assign a patient to just one of the 10 specific disorders. Given these (and other) concerns, some researchers suggest replacing the 10 personality disorders with an alternative approach rooted in dimensions rather than categories (see, e.g., the alternative model in the back of the DSM-5; APA, 2013, pp. 761–781).

The DSM-5 alternative model for personality disorders provides a set of pathological personality traits that look similar to at least four of the five Big Five domains we have so frequently talked about in this book: negative affectivity versus emotional stability (i.e., Big Five neuroticism), detachment versus extraversion (i.e., Big Five extraversion), antagonism versus agreeableness (i.e., Big Five agreeableness), disinhibition versus conscientiousness (i.e., Big Five conscientiousness), and psychoticism versus lucidity (this one seems somewhat different from Big Five openness, but it is possibly related). The approach of the alternative model is to conceptualize personality disorders as impairments in personality functioning in terms of the self (problems with identity or self-direction) and interpersonal relations (empathy and intimacy) in conjunction with extreme levels on one or more pathological trait domains. BPD, for example, seems to involve problems with the self and interpersonal relations that are related to specific elements of extreme negative affectivity, disinhibition, and antagonism.

Comorbidity is not a problem for this alternative approach because there is no strong claim about the existence of discrete disorders. The move from categories to dimensions prevents the arbitrariness inherent in trying to decide if someone is either completely healthy OR has a personality disorder. Gradations are possible. Having multiple trait dimensions broadens the scope of what is possibly considered a pathological personality beyond just 10 discrete disorders. Indeed, this alternative model has considerable flexibility. Altogether, the alternative dimensional approach might be more a valid way to understand personality problems than the categorical approach found in the main body of the DSM-5.

In the end, the idea of discrete personality disorder might itself be a misnomer. This is a simple reason why it is probably a myth to assert that a clinician can't treat personality disorders—the existence of discrete personality disorders is itself likely a myth. It might be more accurate to acknowledge that the lines between normal and abnormal personality attributes are hazy. It is probably more valid and useful to think about a distribution of general personality attributes that range from adaptive to pathological. A pathological trait is just an extremely high or low level of a regular old personality trait we have discussed at length in this book.

Once a dimensional perspective on personality pathology is adopted, a further way to evaluate claims about stability inherent in the myth described in this chapter is to recall two key ideas about personality trait stability and change discussed at length in Chapters 12 and 13. Namely, the ideas that (a) traits seem to change across the life span in terms of average levels toward the more adaptive (i.e., nonpathological) pole of common trait domains such as decreases in neuroticism and increases in conscientiousness; and (b) all personality traits (pathological or otherwise) are relatively stable rather than completely immutable (e.g., Morey & Hopwood, 2013). The data on general traits suggest that gradual personality changes occur, on average, over appreciable spans of time (e.g., years rather than days or weeks). Traits are not completely set in stone. Thus, the idea that personality disorders are a life sentence is a myth precisely because the idea that personality traits do not change is also a myth. Clark (2007) provided a vivid image that pathological traits might be set in clay rather than stone or plaster (recall the William James quotes from our earlier chapters) as she concluded that "change can occur, but gradually and with effort" (p. 242).

The move away from categorical diagnoses to dimensions seems like a positive step for moving forward in conceptualizing and studying personality problems. However, there is still more ground to cover in this chapter when thinking about the actual evidence for the treatment of personality disorders. Part of the myth is that treatment for disorders is ineffective. What do the actual studies suggest? Much of the treatment literature is oriented around specific disorders, especially BPD. Even so, these studies seem to point to the possibility of change for the better, thereby further contradicting this myth.

Evidence about treatments

In the introduction to the book, we talked about causal inference in personality science and observed that experiments are not especially common in the field given ethical and logistical considerations. This was a broad generalization with exceptions. The treatment of disorders is such an exception because it is possible to use randomization to assign people with personality problems to different kinds of treatment. It is sometimes possible to even create no-treatment control groups by placing people on waiting lists for treatment in the case of shortages and uncertainty regarding the effectiveness of existing approaches. These experimental approaches allow researchers to make inferences about the effectiveness of one treatment versus another or the effectiveness of one treatment over some control condition.

Two broad kinds of treatments are possible for personality pathologies—traditional psychotherapies usually involving interactions with a clinician (e.g., cognitive behavioral therapy, psychoanalytic therapy) and pharmacological (i.e., drugs). Both classes of treatments have been evaluated in more than one study, and meta-analytic reviews are available. Thus, we can offer a perspective based on multiple studies rather than just one or two.

The general sentiment one gleans from reading reviews of treatment studies is that the existing research base is limited (see, e.g., Cristea et al., 2017). Low statistical power is an issue in that not enough participants are typically involved in the research to be able to detect small treatment effects. One review pinned the average sample size for treatment and control conditions at about 28 participants in each (Duggan et al., 2007; see also Lieb et al., 2010). This provides less than a 50% chance of detecting a "medium"-sized effect and even less of a chance of detecting smaller effects. Low statistical power in conjunction with the tendency of journals to only publish statistically significant findings (also known as publication bias because there is a bias to publish significant findings) will often generate an inflated estimate of the effectiveness of treatments (see Button et al., 2013; Ioannidis, 2008). It is difficult to have excessive confidence in a given research literature when there is low power and publication bias.

In other words, the treatment literature might be too questionable to make definitive statements. This is an important recognition because it can temper any bold pronouncements for or against the effectiveness of treatments. Sometimes things are uncertain, and so any bold pronouncement is a myth. This is an observation we repeated multiple times in this book.

A recent paper summarized the impact of psychotherapies for BPD based on a meta-analysis of 33 trials with more than 2,250 participants (Cristea et al., 2017). These authors looked at various outcomes, and there seemed to be small positive effects for treatments for symptoms of BPD, self-harming behaviors, suicide, and psychological distress. Thus, the news is probably cautiously optimistic, but keep in mind the caveats about the treatment literature and read on.

Concerns about the treatment literature were described in the meta-analysis about the effectiveness of psychotherapies for BPD. Consider that the authors found hints that results that were not statistically significant might not be published at expected rates (e.g., they found indications of publication bias across the results of the various trials). As we noted, this practice can generate a more positive impression of the success of treatment because all successes are reported in the widely accessible published literature, whereas the failures are not published. Given this issue, Cristea et al. (2017) recommended formalizing an experimental registry to make information about unsuccessful trials more widely accessible. This way, reviewers of the literature and consumers of therapies have a better sense of the complete evidence base. Studies that did not show statistically significant effects would still be cataloged and available for future meta-analyses.

Other reviewers of the treatment literature reached similar conclusions. Bateman et al. (2015) noted that "psychosocial treatment gives ground for optimism especially for borderline personality disorder" (p. 740). Given that BPD is often considered one of the more severe personality pathologies, this seems like a clear statement to counter the myth discussed in this chapter—psychotherapies may be effective for some personality pathologies. Or at the very least, it is premature to conclude that psychotherapies are unsuccessful.

Pharmacology might also be effective for some aspects of personality pathology. This might strike some readers as shocking, but it is important to reemphasize a point we have made at various times in this book—biology matters when it comes to personality (see especially Chapter 3). Hengartner et al. (2018) make this point vividly: "ultimately, every behavior, cognition, and emotion has neurobiological correlates because the brain is the central organ that regulates all of these processes" (p. 14). In light of this reality, it is not a stretch to think that attempts to alter the functioning of the brain with drugs might help improve functioning.

Lieb et al. (2010) reviewed 37 drug trials designed to impact different aspects of BPD. Certain classes of drugs like mood stabilizers seemed to have positive effects for improving affective regulation. Again, the authors noted concerns with the quality of the evidence in terms of statistical power and the completeness of the reporting in the literature. Nonetheless, there seemed to be indications of positive effects on some outcomes. Altogether, findings about pharmacology and psychotherapy strike a more optimistic note to counter the myth that treatment for personality pathology is ineffective (see also Roberts et al., 2017).

Summary

Clinical lore holds that personality disorders are untreatable and immutable conditions that generate considerable discord (see Berg et al., 2013). If anything, treatments might make things worse (see e.g., Harris, Rice, & Cormier, 1994, for a report where it appeared that treating psychopaths created unintended negative effects). This perspective generates pessimism about personality pathology. We consider these ideas myths given the existing database. We started by talking about the controversial idea of discrete personality disorders and suggested that the idea of clear disorders might itself be a myth. We described the emerging perspective that what are labeled disorders might boil down to extreme standing on basic personality traits that contribute to distress and impairment. However, personality traits are not completely stable across the life span, so change is possible even if it is slow and gradual. Deliberate change likely requires considerable effort.

Reviews of studies that have explicitly tried to treat BPD with psychotherapies and drugs seem to show small positive effects. This is further grounds for optimism. However, these reviews highlight ways that the existing literature is flawed and in need of improvement, such as larger sample sizes and control over publication bias. There is a concern that studies that fail to support treatment effects might not be published, so the impression from the published literature might inflate success rates and effect sizes for treatment. Longer-term follow-ups are also needed (see Bateman et al., 2015; Cristea et al., 2017). Altogether, we acknowledge that personality pathology can have consequences in terms of suffering (personality is related to consequential life outcomes after all—see Chapter 2), but we are unwilling to endorse the idea that personality pathology itself is a life sentence without hope for improvement given the state of the evidence. Additional high-quality theorizing and research on the effectiveness of treatment is badly needed. Collectively, it seems too soon to be so pessimistic about personality pathology.

References

American Psychiatric Association. (2013). *Diagnostic and statistical manual of mental disorders (DSM-5)*. Washington, DC: Author.

Bateman, A. W., Gunderson, J., & Mulder, R. (2015). Treatment of personality disorder. *Lancet, 385*(9969), 735–743.

Baumeister, R. R., & Leary, M. R. (1995). The need to belong: Desire for interpersonal attachments as a fundamental human motivation. *Psychological Bulletin, 117*, 497–529.

Berg, J. M., Smith, S. F., Watts, A. L., Ammirati, R., Green, S. E., & Lilienfeld, S. O. (2013). Misconceptions regarding psychopathic personality: Implications for clinical practice and research. *Neuropsychiatry, 3*(1), 63–74.

Button, K. S., Ioannidis, J. P., Mokrysz, C., Nosek, B. A., Flint, J., Robinson, E. S., & Munafò, M. R. (2013). Power failure: Why small sample size undermines the reliability of neuroscience. *Nature Reviews Neuroscience, 14*(5), 365–376.

Clark, L. A. (2007). Assessment and diagnosis of personality disorder: Perennial issues and an emerging reconceptualization. *Annual Review of Psychology, 58*, 227–257.

Cristea, I. A., Gentili, C., Cotet, C. D., Palomba, D., Barbui, C., & Cuijpers, P. (2017). Efficacy of psychotherapies for borderline personality disorder: A systematic review and meta-analysis. *JAMA Psychiatry, 74*(4), 319–328.

Critchfield, K. L., & Benjamin, L. S. (2006). Principles for psychosocial treatment of personality disorder: Summary of the APA Division 12 Task Force/NASPR review. *Journal of Clinical Psychology, 62*(6), 661–674.

Duggan, C., Huband, N., Smailagic, N., Ferriter, M., & Adams, C. (2007). The use of psychological treatments for people with personality disorder: A systematic review of randomized controlled trials. *Personality and Mental Health, 1*(2), 95–125.

Harris, G., Rice, M., & Cormier, C. (1994). Psychopaths: Is the therapeutic community therapeutic? *Therapeutic Communities, 15*, 283–300.

Haslam, N., Holland, E., & Kuppens, P. (2012). Categories versus dimensions in personality and psychopathology: A quantitative review of taxometric research. *Psychological Medicine, 42*(5), 903–920.

Hengartner, M. P., Zimmermann, J., & Wright, A. G. C. (2018). Personality pathology. In V. Zeigler-Hill & T. K. Shackelford (Eds.), *The SAGE handbook of personality and individual differences: Vol. 3. Applications of personality and individual differences* (pp. 3–35). Thousand Oaks, CA: Sage.

Hopwood, C. J., Kotov, R., Krueger, R. F., Watson, D., Widiger, T. A., Althoff, R. R., ... Bornovalova, M. A. (2018). The time has come for dimensional personality disorder diagnosis. *Personality and Mental Health, 12*(1), 82–86.

Ioannidis, J. P. A. (2008). Why most discovered true associations are inflated. *Epidemiology, 19*, 640–648.

Lieb, K., Völlm, B., Rücker, G., Timmer, A., & Stoffers, J. M. (2010). Pharmacotherapy for borderline personality disorder: Cochrane systematic review of randomised trials. *British Journal of Psychiatry*, *196*(1), 4–12.

Morey, L. C., & Hopwood, C. J. (2013). Stability and change in personality disorders. *Annual Review of Clinical Psychology*, *9*, 499–528.

Roberts, B. W., Luo, J., Briley, D. A., Chow, P. I., Su, R., & Hill, P. L. (2017). A systematic review of personality trait change through intervention. *Psychological Bulletin*, *143*(2), 117.

INDEX

Great Myths of Personality, First Edition. M. Brent Donnellan and Richard E. Lucas.
© 2021 John Wiley & Sons, Inc. Published 2021 by John Wiley & Sons, Inc.

monozygotic (MZ) twins, 36, 150
mood stabilizers, for BPD, 252
moral justification, evolutionary
    psychology, 49
Morgeson, F. P., 70
multivariate analysis, 7
Myers-Briggs Type Indicator (MBTI)
  Big Five, 81–82
  continuous traits, 78–79
  correlations, 82
  dichotomous traits, 78–80
  empiricism, 81
  extraversion, 78, 79, 80
  feeling, 78
  introversion, 78, 79, 80
  intuitive, 78
  judging, 78, 80
  perceptive, 78
  personality types, 52, 77–82
  psychoanalysis, 81
  psychometric properties, 81
  reliability, 80
  sensing, 80
  test-retest, 80
  thinking, 78, 80
  unconscious, 77–78
MZ. *See* monozygotic twins

narcissism
  personality measurement,
    211–212
  self-esteem, 209–215
    convergent validity, 214–215
  sexuality, 211
narcissistic personality disorder,
    212, 246, 248–249
Narcissistic Personality Inventory
    (NPI), 212, 213
  self-esteem, 214
Narcissus, 210–211
national character personality
    stereotypes, 217–223

agreeableness, 219
extraversion, 220
in-groups, 222
psychometric properties, 218n1
reliability, 221
validity, 219, 220
natural selection, 44
nature/nurture debate, 180
negative emotionality
  Big Three, 10
  personality types, 56
  positive ratio, 193
neuroticism, 11
  birth order, 144
  consequential outcomes, 31
  costs and benefits, 47
  evolutionary psychology, 46, 47
  men and women personality
    differences, 237, 238, 239
  overcontrolled personality
    type, 55
  personality disorders, 248
  personality stability after age 30,
    122, 123
  personality types, 55
  resilient personality type, 5
  romantic relationship trait
    similarity, 197
  subjective well-being, 160
  variations, 51
Nisbett, R. E., 18–19
nonshared environmental effects,
    151–152
Norenzayan, A., 219
novelty seeking, genes, 39, 40
NPI. *See* Narcissistic Personality
    Inventory

obsessive-compulsive personality
    disorder, 246
On the Origin of Species
    (Darwin), 43